Incorporation

33 - 34 Pet : Ret

Criminal Corrections: Ideals and Realities

Edited by
Jameson W. Doig
Princeton University

LexingtonBooks
D.C. Heath and Company
Lexington, Massachusetts
Toronto

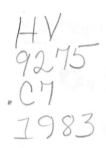
Library of Congress Cataloging in Publication Data

Main entry under title:

Criminal corrections.

   1. Corrections—United States—Addresses, essays, lectures. I. Doig,
Jameson W.
HV9275.C7 1982   365'.973   81–48633
ISBN 0–669–05467–4

Published simultaneously in Canada

Printed in the United States of America

International Standard Book Number: 0–669–05467–4

Library of Congress Catalog Card Number: 81–48633

Policy Studies Organization Series

General Approaches to Policy Studies

Policy Studies in America and Elsewhere
  edited by Stuart S. Nagel
Policy Studies and the Social Studies
  edited by Stuart S. Nagel
Methodology for Analyzing Public Policies
  edited by Frank P. Scioli, Jr., and Thomas J. Cook
Urban Problems and Public Policy
  edited by Robert L. Lineberry and Louis H. Masoti
Problems of Theory in Policy Analysis
  edited by Philip M. Gregg
Using Social Research for Public Policy-Making
  edited by Carol H. Weiss
Public Administration and Public Policy
  edited by H. George Frederickson and Charles Wise
Policy Analysis and Deductive Reasoning
  edited by Gordon Tullock and Richard Wagner
Legislative Reform
  edited by Leroy N. Rieselbach
Teaching Policy Studies
  edited by William D. Coplin
Paths to Political Reform
  edited by William J. Crotty
Determinants of Public Policy
  edited by Thomas Dye and Virginia Gray
Effective Policy Implementation
  edited by Daniel Mazmanian and Paul Sabatier
Taxing and Spending Policy
  edited by Warren J. Samuels and Larry L. Wade
The Politics of Urban Public Services
  edited by Richard C. Rich
Analyzing Urban-Service Distributions
  edited by Richard C. Rich
The Analysis of Policy Impact
  edited by John Grumm and Stephen Washby
Public Policies for Distressed Communities
  edited by F. Stevens Redburn and Terry F. Buss
Implementing Public Policy
  edited by Dennis J. Palumbo and Marvin A. Harder
Evaluating and Optimizing Public Policy
  edited by Dennis J. Palumbo, Stephen B. Fawcett, and Paula Wright
Representation and Redistricting Issues
  edited by Bernard Grofman, Arend Lijphart, Robert McKay, and Howard Scarrow
Strategies for Administrative Reform
  edited by Gerald E. Caiden and Heinrich Siedentopf
Values, Ethics, and the Practice of Policy Analysis
  edited by William N. Dunn

Specific Policy Problems

Analyzing Poverty Policy
  edited by Dorothy Buckton James
Crime and Criminal Justice
  edited by John A. Gardiner and Michael Mulkey
Civil Liberties
  edited by Stephen L. Wasby
Foreign Policy Analysis
  edited by Richard L. Merritt
Economic Regulatory Policies
  edited by James E. Anderson
Political Science and School Politics
  edited by Samuel K. Gove and Frederick M. Wirt
Science and Technology Policy
  edited by Joseph Haberer
Population Policy Analysis
  edited by Michael E. Kraft and Mark Schneider
The New Politics of Food
  edited by Don F. Hadwiger and William P. Browne
New Dimensions to Energy Policy
  edited by Robert Lawrence
Race, Sex, and Policy Problems
  edited by Marian Lief Palley and Michael Preston
American Security Policy and Policy-Making
  edited by Robert Harkavy and Edward Kolodziej
Current Issues in Transportation Policy
  edited by Alan Altshuler
Security Policies of Developing Countries
  edited by Edward Kolodziej and Robert Harkavy
Determinants of Law-Enforcement Policies
  edited by Fred A. Meyer, Jr., and Ralph Baker
Evaluating Alternative Law-Enforcement Policies
  edited by Ralph Baker and Fred A. Meyer, Jr.
International Energy Policy
  edited by Robert M. Lawrence and Martin O. Heisler
Employment and Labor-Relations Policy
  edited by Charles Bulmer and John L. Carmichael, Jr.
Housing Policy for the 1980s
  edited by Roger Montgomery and Dale Rogers Marshall
Environmental Policy Formation
  edited by Dean E. Mann
Environmental Policy Implementation
  edited by Dean E. Mann
The Analysis of Judicial Reform
  edited by Philip L. Dubois
The Politics of Judicial Reform
  edited by Philip L. Dubois
Critical Issues in Health Policy
  edited by Ralph Straetz, Marvin Lieberman, and Alice Sardell
Criminal Corrections: Ideals and Realities
  edited by Jameson W. Doig

Contents

Preface and Acknowledgments   ix

Chapter 1   The Uses of Government Power: Corrections as Both Typical and Extreme *Jameson W. Doig*   1

Part I   *Goals of Corrections Policy—and Results*   13

Chapter 2   The Ideology of Incarceration and the Cooptation of Correctional Reform *John Byrne* and *Donald Yanich*   15

Chapter 3   Problems of Theory-Based Corrections Policy *Albert C. Price* and *Kent E. Portney*   31

Chapter 4   Crime and Incarceration across American States *Jack H. Nagel*   43

Part II   *Innovations in Juvenile Corrections*   57

Chapter 5   Juvenile Justice in America *Bruce Bullington, Daniel Katkin,* and *Drew Hyman*   59

Chapter 6   A Statute Backfires: The Escalation of Youth Incarceration in England during the 1970s *Andrew Rutherford*   73

Part III   *Conditions in Prisons and Strategies for Change*   93

Chapter 7   American Jails: Still Cloacal after Ten Years *Karen A. Reixach* and *David L. Weimer*   95

Chapter 8   Should Prisoners Be Classified by Sex? *Judith Resnik*   109

Chapter 9   Designing Effective Transitions for New Correctional Leaders *Thomas N. Gilmore* and *Joseph E. McCann III*   125

Chapter 10   Conflict Resolution and Social Change in Corrections *John R. Hepburn*   139

Part IV   *The Role of the Courts*   153

Chapter 11   **Judicial Strategies in Prison Litigation**
                   Daryl R. Fair   155

Chapter 12   **Judicial Intervention and Jail Reform**
                   Thomas S. Ostrowski   167

Chapter 13   **Developing Legal Remedies for Unconstitutional
                   Incarceration**   *Candace McCoy*   179

Part V   *Further Perspectives on Reform*   193

Chapter 14   **Codifying Sentencing Experience**
                   Stuart S. Nagel   195

Chapter 15   **Restitution and Compensation: A Market
                   Model for Corrections**   *Charles M. Gray*   209

                   Index   219

                   About the Contributors   227

                   About the Editor   231

Preface and Acknowledgments

This book had its genesis in 1979, when Stuart Nagel of the Policy Studies Organization asked if I would organize a symposium on corrections policy. An announcement mailed to scholars and practitioners yielded more than three dozen proposals and subsequently more than two dozen draft papers; with the considerable assistance of outside reviewers, the essays were then winnowed to the fifteen now before you. All are original papers, not previously published. Almost all our authors are scholars and teachers engaged in ongoing research and consulting work in corrections, and the chapters draw on their field research and their personal experience.

We are particularly grateful to those who read and commented critically on draft papers during the past two years: Ronald Berkman of Brooklyn College; Robert Scott and Douglas Arnold of Princeton University; Ellen Comisso of the University of California, San Diego; Daryl Fair of Trenton State College; M. Kay Harris of the National Council on Crime and Delinquency; Richard Singer of the Rutgers Law School; Judith Resnik of the University of Southern California Law Center; and Michael Sherman of the Hudson Institute.

Draft chapters were also presented at meetings of the American Political Science Association and the Midwest Political Science Association, and we benefited from our colleagues' critical suggestions at these sessions.

Thanks go as well to June DeRose, Carol Dina, and Michael Fulop, whose administrative and typing skills kept the project moving forward against heavy odds; to Susan Lasser and Elizabeth Mott, our helpful editors at Lexington Books; and to Hope Michelsen, who prepared the index.

The Policy Studies Organization and the editor gratefully thank The Daniel and Florence Guggenheim Foundation and the Corrections Division of the National Institute of Justice for their financial aid to the symposium on which this book is based. However, no one other than the individual authors is responsible for the ideas presented here.

The book is dedicated by the editor to William Fauver and B.J. Urbaniak of the New Jersey Department of Corrections, career professionals who understand the pains and dangers of the labyrinth of steel, and who seek to achieve some measure of humanity as well as security for prisoners and their keepers.

1

The Uses of Government Power: Corrections as Both Typical and Extreme

Jameson W. Doig

In 1981, the daily total of Americans incarcerated in state and federal prisons, in local jails, and in juvenile facilities exceeded 500,000. When released, the vast majority of these men and women will have served more than a year behind bars, and for tens of thousands of inmates, this visit will be one of two, or five, or a dozen terms in prisons and local jails extending back through the 1970s and forward into the 1980s.[1]

During the past ten years, this slowly revolving door has brought a steady increase in the number of inmates incarcerated in state and federal institutions. The total number of state and federal prisoners (most of them serving actual terms of eighteen months or longer) rose from about 200,000 in 1970 to 300,000 in 1977 and to 329,000 in 1980. In 1981 the total reached a new high, at nearly 370,000. And with these increases have come severe overcrowding, sporadic efforts to renovate and expand existing prison and jail space, and growing financial burdens for the American taxpayer.[2]

Behind these trends lie others that have shaped public policy in the past decade—growing rates of reported crime and an increasing fear of violent crime; the desire of elected officials to respond to these apparent facts and fears, coupled with the willingness of the American public to elect and reelect those legislators, mayors, and governors who promise a "crackdown on crime" and who produce as evidence of their concern (and of their desire to be elected) laws calling for longer prison terms; and recurring public attacks on judges and parole board members who seem, in their sentencing and release decisions, too insensitive to the beneficent uses of prison.[3]

That the prison and the jail provide great benefits to a society has long been questioned by close observers, both liberal and conservative. In the 1960s, reviewing the history of such reforms as correctional institutions and mental hospitals, Kai Erikson concluded:

> It is by now a thoroughly familiar argument that many of the institutions designed to discourage deviant behavior actually operate in such a way as to perpetuate it. . . . [They] gather marginal people into tightly segregated groups, give them an opportunity to teach one another the skills and attitudes of a deviant career, and even provoke them into using these skills by reinforcing their sense of alienation from the rest of society.[4]

1

The 1970s and now the early 1980s have been punctuated with headlines and investigations that underscore this reality of the penal institution—to whose rigors we send men and women already marred by crime, from whose embrace they emerge, altered if not corrected. As the 1978 report on Tennessee's correctional facilities concludes, a combination of overcrowding, idleness, and violence have resulted in the "physical, psychological, and moral deterioration" of the state's prisoners. "State officials acknowledged," the report notes, that "prisoners frequently leave Tennessee's correction system in worse shape than when they enter it."[5]

The Nature and Burdens of Pervasive Power

The central concern of this book is this correctional system—in its harsh and at times self-defeating aspects, but also in its striving for reform: in the efforts of those within the system and without to attain reasonable standards of equity and social justice in a world of financial constraints, public skepticism, and legislative brickbats. Here we find the use of government power in a stark and extreme form, a form that at times exceeds civilized bounds—when prisoners are taped to bars and bed for days, or kicked by guards, or ravaged by other inmates.[6] And even when, as is often the case in this country, government acts with Constitutional constraint, we are in a domain of very extensive governmental intrusion indeed. Although we may view government action in such fields as welfare, schooling, and police as coercive, correctional policy weaves a web of control that is far wider and deeper: citizens reduced to subjects, their communication and clothing regulated, told when they shall eat and sleep and exercise—day and night for months and sometimes years on end. It is a field of policy, then, which deserves our close attention. Moreover, corrections policy increasingly demands our attention—as citizens and as students of policy choices— because of the burden of rapidly escalating costs and because of the impact that an effective correctional system—or an ineffective one—has on the freedom of movement, and freedom from fear, of the rest of us in an open society.

Contending Purposes in Criminal Justice

Almost all of the fifteen chapters in this book take the American correctional system as their central concern; indeed only one, Andrew Rutherford's analysis of juvenile justice in Britain, is explicitly directed toward experience outside the United States. Many of the chapters, however, explore issues that are central to understanding and reforming correctional policies in any society. For example, should prisoners be segregated by sex? How should top officials in corrections be trained? What strategies can be used to mediate conflict in prisons? These issues are discussed in the chapters by Judith Resnik, Thomas Gilmore and Joseph McCann, and John Hepburn.

Moreover, to understand correctional policies one must see their connections with the larger field of criminal justice; several essays examine corrections in the context of that wider terrain. The first two chapters examine tensions among the four major purposes that shape corrections and criminal justice in the United States and in most countries—the goals of retribution (or punishment), incapacitation, deterrence, and rehabilitation. In most civilized societies, criminal justice policies are also shaped by other values; thus equality, fairness, and the avoidance of "cruel and unusual punishment" have become important goals in corrections, especially in the past twenty years. In their chapters on the role of the courts, Daryl Fair, Thomas Ostrowski, and Candace McCoy explore the efforts of the judiciary to protect these values against the reluctance or active opposition of legislators and other officials. These essays and others also touch on a quite different goal—that of controlling costs—which is likely to become increasingly central in the 1980s.

In constructing or modifying a criminal-justice system, the question of how much weight should be given to the goals of punishment, rehabilitation, fairness, and "least cost" is far more than an academic exercise. The significance given to each of these (and other) goals shapes the types of correctional institutions provided for adults and juveniles, the ratio of security to other staff positions, and the role of prisoners in shaping their own institutional lives. In the continuing public debates over new policies and programs, the preferred mix of goals is sometimes examined explicitly, while at other times it remains implicit. But conflicts over specific legislation, court rulings, or administrative policies in corrections generally represent differences at a basic level regarding the question, "What should a correctional system be used for?" Stated more fully, the question is "How much weight should this correctional system and its structures and programs give to punishment, to fairness, and to other major goals?" The debate over how to answer this question is central to the evolution of juvenile-justice reform in Britain and America, recounted in part II of this book, to an understanding of the issues of jail reform and women prisoners discussed in part III, and, certainly, to the concerns of the opening chapters of part I.

Several of our authors range still further to note connections between the corrections system and broader aspects of the social system. Jack Nagel examines the relationships between crime rates and incarceration rates in the United States, raising questions as to the role of racism in incarceration patterns. John Byrne and Donald Yanich consider the causal relationships between exploitation and racism in society, on the one hand, and the patterns of crime and imprisonment on the other. Stuart Nagel, in seeking a solution to the problem of devising equitable criminal sentences, examines the role of legislative interests, public opinion, and other factors in obtaining a defensible and practical solution.[7]

Recurring Issues in Public Policy

This book is of intrinsic interest even for those whose interests are not mainly in corrections and crime-control policies. The fourteen chapters, although never quite innocent of criminal intent, treat issues and themes that recur in other parts of all complex societies:

1. *The Implementation Problem.* Students of public policy have often noted the divergence between policy ideals, as set forth in legislation or in announced program changes, and hard reality, as these reforms are shaped and shorn in the course of implementation and come to affect clients in quite different ways than the reformers intended.[8] This pattern is illustrated by a new community-based program approved by senior government officials; implementation depends on the cooperation of existing judicial and correctional institutions, but those bureaucracies are wary of or hostile to the new reform, and their actions undermine the effort. These implementation issues are discussed particularly in chapters 2, 5, and 6. Our authors also suggest strategies that might be useful in improving the implementation of reform; although their direct concerns are with correctional programs, some of the proposals apply more broadly.

2. *The Self-Fulfilling-Prophecy Syndrome.* In the field of highway construction, close observers have noted that new roads are soon filled with cars, generating the demand for still more highways, which are then built as part of a continuing cycle—a cycle that seemed never-ending in the 1950s and 1960s. The field of prison construction appears to be following the same pattern, and, while the causal dynamics are not entirely the same, there are clear similarities.[9] Some of these dynamics are described by John Byrne and Donald Yanich in chapter 2, and in Andrew Rutherford's exploration of the British debate on imprisoning young people in chapter 6.

3. *Strategies for Reform: The Role of Markets, Tighter Standards, Professionalism, and Other Ways to Reshape the Future.* The student of policy whose interests lie mainly in education, health care, or housing problems will be no stranger to the tools of reform discussed in the chapters that follow. In all these fields, judges and other officials have initiated a wide variety of changes during the past two decades.

In the United States, the judiciary has taken on a central role in altering policies and conditions affecting prisons, as it has in other fields. The importance of the courts is suggested by figures compiled early in 1982, which identified correctional facilities in thirty states—plus the District of Columbia and Puerto Rico—as currently being operated under judicial orders.[10]

The chapters on the role of the courts illustrate the range of problems that confront judicial activism in complex policy arenas, and they describe judicial strategies that are relevant to fields other than corrections. In chapters 11 and 12 Daryl Fair and Thomas Ostrowski explore the use of tightly drawn standards and continuous monitoring to bring about prison and jail reform, while in chapter 13 Candace McCoy turns to a contrasting strategy—greater court reliance on correctional professionalism, coupled with monetary damages when the efforts of elective and administrative officials are unsatisfactory.

The efforts of the courts touch on a broader subject—whether reform is better achieved through tighter bureaucratic standards or via greater reliance on the discretion of competent professionals. Several of the chapters are concerned with the long-standing debate between those who, in order to improve policy and bureaucratic performance, would extend control over agency activities through narrowly drawn laws and rules; and others, who would maintain only loose reins on public officials—in education, police, hospitals, corrections, and elsewhere—encouraging them to use their own initiative, combined with professional knowledge and judgement, to carry out complex programs. It is a debate well known to political scientists and lawyers, particularly through the writings of Carl Friedrich, Herman Finer, Kenneth Culp Davis, and Theodore Lowi.[11]

In addition to the chapters on judicial-monitoring strategies, several chapters address aspects of this complex issue. In chapter 7 Karen Reixach and David Weimer examine the attempts to use more exacting standards to improve conditions in local jails, and Stuart Nagel in chapter 14 considers ways to enhance equity, effectiveness, and efficiency through standards for criminal sentencing. In chapter 9 Thomas Gilmore and Joseph McCann turn their attention to top-level correctional administrators, whose efforts are likely to be crucial to any long-term improvement in prisons and jails; their chapter explores ways to use peer relationships and other strategies of professionalism in order to enhance the influence of new administrators on resistant bureaucracies.

Reorganization is another technique often considered useful in shaking up existing staff habits, providing leverage and additional resources for new leaders, forcing greater attention to neglected policy issues and program approaches, and encouraging improved coordination.[12] The reorganization approach is examined in chapter 2 by Byrne and Yanich, in chapters 5 and 6 on juvenile-system reforms, and in the discussions of regional jails (in chapter 7) and of integrating women's and men's prisons (chapter 8).

Two final strategies are examined in this book—a greater role for clients and greater reliance on marketplace mechanisms. The tendency of bureaucratic officials to treat clients as objects of control is found in schools, hospitals, and a wide range of other social-service agencies, as well as in correctional institutions. During the past fifteen years, however, the rights of students, patients, prisoners, and other organizational constituents have been expanded as a result of political, judicial, and administrative initiatives.[13] In his analysis of conflict resolution in correctional institutions, in chapter 10, John Hepburn describes the evolution of this campaign in prisons. He also questions whether newly introduced grievance mechanisms will have any significant impact on the actual distribution of power between prisoners and their keepers.

Most of the proposals for change (in prison policies and more generally) focus on the problem of power and on strategies for redistributing power—between clients and officials, between new administrative leaders and old-time staffs, or between prison administrators and outsiders (such as the courts or the general public). A quite different approach entails treating a policy field as a market, comprised of buyers and sellers, and then modifying aspects of that market to achieve greater efficiency and equity. For example, some critics of public education is the 1970s urged that greater influence be given to clients—students and their parents—in setting school policies and in deciding which teachers should be hired and fired. Others, however, argued that students should instead be provided with education vouchers, permitting them to select schools based on individual preference rather than geographic district. Similar arguments have developed in recent years in housing, with some urging a greater policy-making role for residents in public-housing projects while others place their emphasis on housing vouchers as the desirable way for government action. In pollution control as well, the market approach has challenged the tradition of detailed bureaucratically determined standards.[14]

In the final chapter, Charles Gray applies an economic perspective to the criminal-justice system. Gray argues that restitution might become the center-piece of a revised correctional policy for the United States—or possibly for any nation with the good sense to recognize that where a tight system of "command and control" has failed, perhaps the market should be tried.

Difficult Problems and Simple Solutions

In examining the complex problems of corrections and the range of imaginative reform strategies discussed in this book, we should be sensitive to a somber reality—that neither our knowledge nor our political and economic capacities seem equal to the challenge before us. It is a melancholy reality that we see in other fields as well: in determining how to improve the educational system, for example, or how to respond to the growing costs and other problems of health-care delivery.

In corrections, we lack the knowledge of how to rehabilitate those who are apprehended for committing robberies, burglaries, larcenies, or other kinds of street crime.[15] Finding that rehabilitation programs do not seem to work, we retreat to incapacitation and punishment as primary goals for the correctional system, carrying out these purposes in overcrowded institutions that seem destined to lead to results not unlike those described by two 19th century ob-servers: "Nowhere was this system of imprisonment crowned with the hoped-for success. In general it was ruinous to the public treasury; it never effected the reformation of the prisoners; every year the legislature of each state voted con-siderable funds towards the support of the penitentiaries, and the continued return of the same individuals into the prisons proved the inefficiency of the system to which they were submitted."[16]

Even if a correctional system oriented toward incapacitation and punish-ment could reduce (rather than increase) criminality, we probably lack the political and financial capabilities to pursue the implications of this strategy—at least in the United States of the 1980s. When the task force appointed by President Ronald Reagan's attorney general recommended that $2 billion in federal funds be made available over four years to aid the states in constructing new prisons, the president declined to support that proposal. Yet current trends —sending more people to prison and keeping them there longer—seem certain to require far larger sums, which financially strapped states will be very reluctant to provide.[17] The result, then, seems likely to be continued and intensified over-crowding, which liberals and conservatives alike agree is a sure way to increase tensions and interpersonal violence within prisons and to reduce further what meager prospects exist that prisoners will not leave in "worse shape than when they enter."

When we broaden the focus of inquiry beyond the specific domain of cor-rections, our ability to discern causes for street crime may be clearer, but our economic and political will, in the United States at least, seems even less ready for the challenge. On this wider search for causes, the view expressed by Presi-dent Reagan may be comforting: "It's obvious that deprivation and want don't necessarily increase crime. The truth is that today's criminals for the most part are not desperate people seeking bread for their families. Crime is the way they've chosen to live."[18] This perspective implies that offenders have simply made the conscious decision to engage in crime rather than working as honest members of the community. The solution, therefore, can be found largely within the criminal-justice system: harsh and more certain punishment, in order to in-capacitate offenders and deter those who are presently tempted by the "easy life of crime."

Although candidates for public office and elected officials frequently offer such explanations and solutions, among throughtful observers removed from the need for simplified campaign rhetoric this is a minority position indeed. Those who examine the problem carefully are likely to find the causes for street crime far more complex and the solutions more difficult. Academic observers, correc-tional administrators, judicial officials, and police officers all glimpse elements of a complex reality. For example, Amos E. Reed, president of the American Cor-rectional Association in 1982, argues that "as a nation we pay very dear, almost suicidal, prices for our inaction and unconcern." Reed continues: "We have hundreds of thousands of citizens whose childhood needs have been neglected or ignored and whose undisciplined—or overdisciplined—lives have been per-manently warped."[19] Based on his years of experience on the bench, Judge David L. Bazelon expresses a similar position regarding those prosecuted for violent street crime:

> They are invariably born into families struggling to survive, if they have families at all. They are raised in deteriorating, overcrowded housing. They lack nutrition and health care. They are subjected to prejudice and educated in unresponsive schools. They are denied the sense of

order, purpose, and self-esteem that makes law-abiding citizens. With nothing to preserve and nothing to lose, they turn to crime for economic survival, a sense of excitement and accomplishment, and an outlet for frustration, desperation, and rage.[20]

Finally, career police officer Anthony V. Bouza notes the close interrelationships among unemployment, drugs, and social frustration, creating a subculture of violence in urban areas. "We are manufacturing criminals" in the urban ghetto, Bouza argues. "We are very efficiently creating a very volatile and dangerous sub-element of our society. And we are doing it simply because we don't want to face the burdens and the problems and the responsibilities that their existence imposes on any society with conscience."[21]

If the perceptions of Bouza, Reed, and Bazelon are closer to reality in this world of deviant social behavior, it is a reality denied by governors and presidents, by national and state legislators, who otherwise would have to confront the need to devise more complex policies and to educate a skeptical public that, other things being equal, prefers bread and circuses of rhetoric. So our political will is weak. In time, we may be spared increasing rates of crime by demographic trends, as fewer men and women populate the crime-prone years.[22] Meanwhile, we seem destined to build and overcrowd more prisons, bemoaning the burdens on the public exchequer and watching those subjected to the disciplines of our corrections system as they return—tens of thousands every year—to the comfort of the streets that shaped them and to the patterns of crime for which we as well as they must take credit.

Notes

1. The figure cited in the text is an estimate, since accurate data for 1980 and 1981 are not yet available for all segments of the American corrections system. Subtotals (and dates of recent figures) are—state correctional institutions: 304,000 (12/31/80); federal correctional institutions: 24,000 (12/31/80); local jails: 160,000 (1978); and juvenile facilities: 43,000 (1979). See American Correctional Association, *Directory* (Washington, D.C., 1982), p. xxvii.

2. During the past decade, the number of sentenced prisoners climbed at a pace far exceeding the rise in U.S. population, setting new records (measured by the number of sentenced state and federal prisoners per 100,000 population) in the past five years. Each additional prisoner added roughly $20,000 in yearly correctional costs; each additional 1,000 prisoners therefore meant an increased tax burden of about $20 million annually. For useful detailed information on costs and crowding, see National Institute of Justice, *American Prisons and Jails* (Washington, D.C.: U.S. Department of Justice, October 1980), especially vol. 3.

3. As to crime rates and fears, the text summary does not, of course, capture the great variety of the data or the difficulty of obtaining accurate information on crime patterns. For further details, see for example publications of the Bureau of Justice Statistics, U.S. Department of Justice, especially its annual *Sourcebook of Criminal Justice Statistics* and its victimization surveys.

On the behavior of legislators and others, see the discussion in Michael Sherman and Gordon Hawkins, *Imprisonment in America: Choosing the Future* (Chicago: University of Chicago Press, 1981), chaps. 1 and 4. For the spirit of crime control in 1981–1982, a typical year for rhetorical flourishes, see Ronald Reagan, "Remarks of the President to the International Association of Chiefs of Police," 28 September 1981; Stuart Taylor, Jr., "Law-and-Order Is Easy to Say, Hard to Legislate," *New York Times,* 13 December 1981; "Governors against Crime," editorial, *New York Times,* 6 February 1982.

4. Kai Erikson, *The Wayward Puritans* (New York: Wiley, 1966), p. 14.

5. Memorandum of Chancellor Ben H. Cantrell, 23 August 1978, p. 48 (Trigg v. Blanton, Chancery Court, Davidson County, Tenn.). For other examples, see the report of the New York state commission on the September 1971 Attica riot (September 1972) and the report of New Mexico's attorney general on the February 1980 riot (September 1980).

6. These are among the recurrent patterns cited in investigative reports in the 1970s at some adult and juvenile institutions in Virginia, Indiana, Texas, Pennsylvania, and other states.

7. Because of constraints of space, we do not treat in this book the special issues of corrections that are presented by white-collar crime and organizational deviancy. On these issues, see Christopher Stone, *Where the Law Ends* (New York: Harper & Row, 1975); M. David Ermann and Robert J. Lundman, eds., *Corporate and Governmental Deviance,* 2d ed. (New York: Oxford University Press, 1982), Jameson W. Doig, Douglas E. Phillips, and Tycho Manson, "Deterring Illegal Behavior in Complex Organizations," manuscript, 1982. On corrections and its relationship to criminal justice generally, see Erik Olin Wright, *The Politics of Punishment* (New York: Harper & Row, 1973); Leon Radzinowicz and Marvin E. Wolfgang, eds., *Crime and Justice* (New York: Basic Books, 1971), 3 vols.

8. See, for example, Robert T. Nakamura and Frank Smallwood, *The Politics of Policy Implementation* (New York: St. Martin's Press, 1980).

9. On highway building, see Michael N. Danielson and Jameson W. Doig, *New York: The Politics of Urban Regional Development* (Berkeley, Calif.: University of California Press, 1982), chaps. 1 and 6. On prison building, with some interesting comparisons with the dynamics of constructing new military weapons, see Sherman and Hawkins, *Imprisonment in America,* chaps. 1 and 6.

10. These included one or more correctional institutions found in violation of constitutional standards (due to overcrowding and/or other conditions) in the

following states: Alabama (entire prison system), Arizona, Arkansas (entire), Colorado, Connecticut, Delaware, Florida (entire), Georgia, Illinois, Indiana, Iowa, Kentucky, Louisiana, Maryland, Michigan, Mississippi (entire), Missouri (entire), Nevada, New Hampshire, New Mexico, Ohio, Oklahoma, Oregon, Rhode Island (entire), Tennessee (entire), Texas (entire), Utah, Virginia, Washington, and Wyoming. Court suits were pending in at least seven other states. See the report of the National Prison Project of the American Civil Liberties Union, Washington, D.C., March 1982.

11. See Carl J. Friedrich, "Public Policy and the Nature of Administrative Responsibility" (1940) and Herman Finer, "Administrative Responsibility in Democratic Government" (1941), both reprinted in Francis E. Rourke, ed., *Bureaucratic Power in National Politics*, 2d ed. (Boston: Little, Brown, 1972), pp. 316–337; Kenneth Culp Davis, *Discretionary Justice* (Urbana, Ill.: University of Illinois Press, 1971), among other writings; Theodore J. Lowi, *The End of Liberalism*, 2d ed. (New York: Norton, 1979), chap. 11.

12. These and other promises of reorganization are explored with a critical eye in the essays by Philip Selznick, Harold Seidman, and Norman C. Thomas, in Alan A. Altshuler and Norman C. Thomas, eds., *The Politics of the Federal Bureaucracy* (New York: Harper & Row, 1977), pp. 276–301.

13. On traditional patterns of bureaucratic dominance and issues that such dominance raises, see Gideon Sjoberg et al., "Bureaucracy and the Lower Class" in Rourke, *Bureaucratic Power*, pp. 395–408, and Philip Selznick, *Law, Society, and Industrial Justice* (New York: Russell Sage, 1969); on the evolution of client rights in such fields as education, health care, welfare, and corrections, see National Clearinghouse for Legal Services (Chicago), *The Clearinghouse Review*, a monthly journal.

14. See for example Milton Friedman, *Capitalism and Freedom* (Chicago: University of Chicago Press, 1962), and Charles L. Schultze, *The Public Use of Private Interest* (Washington, D.C.: Brookings Institution, 1977). In the case of housing, the advocates referred to in the text are not generally focused on the same set of clients, and therefore the positions are not mutually exclusive.

15. For a recent review, see the report of the National Research Council's Panel on Research on Rehabilitative Techniques, and the panel's commissioned papers, collected in *The Rehabilitation of Criminal Offenders: Problems and Prospects* (Washington, D.C.: National Academy of Sciences, 1979). As to rehabilitation and deterrence, in the field of white-collar and organizational crime our knowledge may be slightly better; see the sources cited in 7.

16. G. de Beaumont and A. de Tocqueville, *On the Penitentiary System in the United States, and Its Application in France,* trans. F. Lieber (Philadelphia: Carey, Lea & Blanchard, 1833), pp. 3–4.

17. The proposal for federal funds is found in the Attorney General's Task Force on Violent Crime, *Final Report* (Washington, D.C., 17 August 1981), p. 75. For a critical analysis that concludes that the sums needed are far greater,

see Diana Gordon, "Doing Violence to the Crime Problem: A Response to the Attorney General's Task Force" (Hackensack, N.J.: National Council on Crime and Delinquency, 1981).

18. Ronald Reagan, "Remarks of the President to the International Association of Chiefs of Police," 28 September 1981.

19. Amos E. Reed, "Policy Challenges in the '80s," *Corrections Today,* 44 (February 1982): 6. Reed is a correctional official in the state of Washington.

20. David L. Bazelon, "The Crime Controversy: Avoiding Realities," 12 February 1982, pp. 5-6 (to be published in the *Vanderbilt Law Review*). Bazelon is senior circuit judge, U.S. Court of Appeals for the District of Columbia. Quote reprinted with permission of *Vanderbilt Law Review* and Judge Bazelon.

21. The quotations are from the *Philadelphia Inquirer,* 18 August 1978, quoted in Robert C. Tucker, *Politics as Leadership* (Columbia, Mo.: University of Missouri Press, 1981), pp. 83-84. Bouza was for several years commander of police forces in the Bronx; he is now chief of police in Minneapolis.

22. Burglaries, larcenies, robberies, and "street crime" generally are disproportionately found among those between the ages of 15 and 25. Present demographic trends for the United States indicate increases and decreases for the decade 1980-1990 in the number of citizens in various age groups as follows: under 15, 10-percent increase; 15-17, 20-percent decrease; 18-24, 15-percent decrease; 25-34, 14-percent increase; 35-44, 42-percent increase.

Part I
Goals of Corrections Policy—
and Results

2 The Ideology of Incarceration and the Cooptation of Correctional Reform

John Byrne and
Donald Yanich

The More Things Change, the More They Remain the Same

From the early era of American prison reform, which emphasized humanitarian concerns about prison conditions, to the recent period of judicial reform, which has stressed prisoner rights and rehabilitation, a pattern of failure emerges. David Rothman has characterized the history of prison reform in America thus:

> [E]ach generation, it seems, discovers anew the scandals of incarceration, each sets out to correct them, and each passes on a legacy of failure. The rallying cries of one period echo dismally into the next. Benevolent societies in the 1790s denounced prisons as "seminaries for vice," and their successors in the 1930s complained of "schools for crime" . . . We inherit, in essence, a two-hundred-year history of reform without change.[1]

This pattern has not gone unnoticed by political and correctional officialdom. The American prison system has been the subject of study of several national commissions including the 1931 National Commission on Law Observance and Enforcement (Wickersham Commission), the 1967 President's Commission on Law Enforcement and the Administration of Justice, and the 1973 National Advisory Commission on Criminal Justice Standards and Goals. In its report on the status of American corrections the 1973 Commission concluded: "The American correctional system . . . offers minimum protection for the public and maximum harm for the offender."[2] Equally condemnatory opinions have been voiced by wardens and prisoners alike. For example, Hans Mattick, former deputy warden of Cook County Jail and now director of the University of Illinois Center for Research in Criminal Justice, charges: "If men had deliberately set themselves the task of designing an institution that would systematically maladjust men, they would have invented the large, walled, maximum security prison."[3] The same analysis, with equal eloquence, is offered by Malcolm

The authors wish to thank Daniel Rich for his many and valuable criticisms. The authors also wish to acknowledge the support of the Center for the Study of Values and the College of Urban Affairs and Public Policy, University of Delaware, in the preparation of this chapter.

Braly, a former prisoner: "That single thing that grinds you down and finally begins to erode your confidence, your vitality, your most basic sense of yourself, is the moment-to-moment condemnation implicit in this situation."[4]

From these and numerous other voices have come demands for immediate and substantial change. However, the history of American corrections is filled with repeated attempts to achieve reform. The failure of past efforts, we think, has resulted from the inability of the reform movements to dislodge incarceration as the controlling image of corrections policy. The result has been a pattern of cooptation of reform by an organizational imperative that dictates that change must be accommodated to the requirements and limits of prison management.

Unfortunately, the future does not hold out significant hope for change in this pattern. Retrenchment is evident in corrections policy and in renewed intellectual and public support for retributive, incapacitative and deterrent rationales of incarceration. A serious challenge has been mounted by modern criminology against prison reform and the claims of rehabilitation. The basis for this attack rests on the paradox of reform—that reform concedes certain success to incarceration and accepts imminent failure for its own performance. In Robert Martinson's study, for example, reformist initiatives are taken at their word and evaluated as to whether they show some measurable change in recidivism or some other success variable relative to that achieved through warehousing alone.[5] The study catalogues the findings of 231 separate evaluations, which show the absence of any significant change. The author concludes that reform but not, interestingly, incarceration, has failed as a correctional policy. This study has been widely cited and is part of a growing literature that regards prison reform as a failed enterprise and advocates a return to incarceration.[6]

The legacy of prison reform without change and the recent turn toward a more conservative, less ambitious view of correctional policy will certainly shape the newest proposed strategy for reform—community-based corrections. Community-based corrections (CBC) is being advanced from various quarters as the answer to many of the problems of contemporary corrections. Emphasizing a small-scale approach focused on individual treatment and job training, CBC also implies a greater accessibility of family and friends, a less-pressured social environment, and an emphasis on program involvement.[7] It is our view, however, that this understanding of the purpose and limits of CBC has all but sealed its fate. Directly stated, we are convinced that CBC will follow its predecessors in being coopted by the demands of the primary incarceration system.

The Delaware experience with CBC is a case in point. Although political pressures and other factors influenced the situation in Delaware, the primary determinants were those that have shaped American corrections throughout its two-hundred-year history. Specifically, the general ideological environment surrounding corrections and the stable-state requirements of prisons are identified as the crucial elements affecting the fate of CBC. As long as CBC is implemented within a correctional system ideologically committed to incarceration, it will be absorbed by this system as an organizational device to relieve over-crowding, to further the illusion of rehabilitation, and, most importantly, to deflect demands for substantive reform.

If the fate projected for CBC is to be avoided, the focus of American corrections must be shifted from incarceration to decarceration, and principles of justice must replace those of organization as the basis for policy. Such a shift is needed if the failure of the current system is to be reversed and public accountability and control over it is to be restored.

The Delaware Case

Until recently, Delaware depended on an antiquated, gothic prison as its major correctional institution. The architecture reflected the correctional philosophy: crime required punishment and only punishment deterred crime.[8] Paralleling national trends, Delaware began modifying its punishment/deterrence posture in the 1960s toward rehabilitation. In 1971 Delaware opened a new campus-style prison with the professed aim of providing a setting more conducive to inmate rehabilitation. As demonstrated by the fact that 15 percent of the beds in the new institution were reserved for maximum security and 25 percent for medium, the state by no means abandoned its punishment/deterrence focus. Instead, the state integrated rehabilitation goals into an overarching incarceration philosophy.

This integration, however, was in jeopardy from the beginning. Within a year, the inmate population had exceeded the design capacity of the prison. As the population continued to climb, social areas, then program areas, then meal areas, and finally the hospital were pressed into service as bed areas to handle the overflow. The predictable result was that tensions inside the prison began to build. The situation was further exacerbated by the fact that the institution was located in a corn field 35 to 40 miles from the relatives and friends of most of the inmates.

This charged atmosphere provided the opportunity for the major political forces in the state to enter the correctional debate. The Delaware legislature, as was its custom in correctional matters, attempted to assert its authority over the prison administration. It went to war with the corrections commissioner who was trying to implement a policy of rehabilitation and, in the long term, to move Delaware corrections toward a wider use of community-based corrections. Appropriation requests were held in committee, legislators threatened to delete salaries of key personnel from future budgets, and severe restrictions were placed on administrators' discretionary authority to use rehabilitative and community-based programs. Further, while limiting the administration's ability to cope with the overcrowding, the legislature enacted a number of determinate-sentencing statutes that greatly aggravated the problem. Like his predecessors, the governor during this period (1972-1976) found it difficult to protect executive authority from such legislative intrusion and finally was forced to sacrifice his reformist corrections commissioner to free the corrections budget from legislative hostage.

The struggle for control between the legislative and executive branches and the attendant standstill in corrections administration assured that correctional policy would become a major concern in the upcoming (1976) gubernatorial campaign. The challenger (and eventual winner) in the gubernatorial race ran on a prison-reform plank calling for the expanded use of CBC programs—work release, furloughs, half-way houses, and so on. Interestingly, he linked support for these programs to the high level of state indebtedness, which had resulted in a decreased bond rating. Community-based programs, he argued, offered an alternative to costly prison expansion and the accompanying strain on the state's fiscal situation. Although corrections policy was not the only issue in the campaign, it was an important one, and the challenger's ability to tie prison reform to financial reform certainly contributed to his victory. Indeed, the endorsement of the challenger's candidacy by the state's major newspaper explicitly cited his prison-reform stance.

The new governor's position received immediate political support from the state criminal-justice-planning agency. The agency had completed its corrections Standards and Goals Project as mandated by the Law Enforcement Assistance Administration (LEAA) in January 1977. The object of this project was to determine current correctional conditions and practices and to recommend how these conditions and practices might be modified to comply with national standards. The standards and goals recommended by LEAA were of two types: one established CBC as the preferred focus of corrections policy and recommended the creation or expansion of furlough, work-release, half-way-house, and other decentralized correctional programs; the other set up criteria for upgrading conditions and programs in correctional systems still guided by incarceration philosophies. Thus, the evaluation of these standards necessarily included the examination of distinct policy modes for corrections.

The study findings delivered a strong if unexpected endorsement of community-based corrections.[9] With regard to the inmate-population growth in the state, the report indicated that increased lengths of sentences were a primary cause of this growth. Delaware had been among the earliest states to ratify minimum-mandatory and consecutive-sentencing legislation, and the study indicated that it was now paying the price for these statutes. This was an important finding from a CBC standpoint, because it showed that the overcrowding was a creature of policy rather than increasing crime rates, and it meant that the eligible population for CBC was substantial and could be expanded by changes in policy.[10] A further finding of the study favorable to CBC was that there appeared to be a significant reductive effect on recidivism flowing from the one rehabilitative program examined in the study. Although no inference could be made from this program to others, it was at least encouraging in that if a decline in recidivism could happen in such an inhospitable environment, it was even more likely to occur under the less restrictive conditions of CBC. But most important, the study found that CBC is a way to break the circle of escalating tensions into which the state correctional system had fallen. The central finding of the study was that the state was grossly underutilizing CBC programs and that a continuation of its present course would cost the state handsomely in budgetary terms and would require that it escalate the already existing tensions by having to introduce further totalitarian measures to keep the lid on the pressure cooker.

This predicament was the result of two largely ignored forces. The first was that the overcrowding at the new prison was causing it to change its security status. The institution was changing from a predominantly minimum-security prison to a medium- and maximum-security one: overcrowding had forced prison officials to take measures to reduce the mobility of prisoners, and both the physical design and the shortage of staff dictated these measures if order was to be preserved. The second dynamic operating was that, as the population soared, the staff-to-inmate ratio dropped. Although not obvious at the time, the state correctional system was becoming progressively undermanned, a problem that could be resolved only by increasing the number of staff or paying increasing overtime to the existing staff. Both meant an increase in the state's costs without any promise of resolving the basic problem. In this context, CBC represented an important alternative. If inmates serving short sentences (less than one year) could be transferred from the highly secure and therefore costly environment at the state prison to the less restrictive and less costly environment of CBC, this would both relieve the tension at the institution and significantly reduce the state's costs. Add to this the finding that sentencing policy was a major contributor to the overcrowding and the implication that the number of inmates eligible for CBC was an artifact of policy and that a reductive effect on recidivism rates was at least possible, and CBC becomes an extremely attractive option.

The CBC initiative received further impetus. Throughout the period of overcrowing (1971-1977), the inmates repeatedly filed suit in federal court charging the state with permitting cruel and inhuman conditions to exist in its prisons. These efforts finally bore fruit in the 1977 ruling by the Third District Court in favor of the inmate class action against the Delaware prison system.[11] The state was ordered to immediately reduce the population at the new prison, and suggestions were included in the opinion as to how the state might comply with this order. These suggestions drew heavily from the study cited and supported its central finding that current state policy had caused the overcrowded conditions because of its exclusive focus on incarceration.

These circumstances collectively provided an unusually supportive environment for the implementation of CBC programs. However, the potential in these circumstances was never realized.

After taking office in 1977, the new governor implemented several measures that would bring the state's system into compliance with the federal order: greater utilization of work release, work service, and parole, and the establishment of an extended furlough program. These measures were followed with proposals for half-way houses, one to be located in the state capital and another in the state's largest city. The CBC initiative seemed to be well under way. However, two subsequent events brought this initiative to an abrupt halt. The first was community resistance encountered to the half-way-house proposals. Given national experience, such resistance was by no means exceptional. There are, however, two distinctive aspects of the resistance in the case of Delaware that should be noted. First, the opposition to the governor's proposals came from overwhelmingly Democratic constituencies. Since the new governor was a Republican, the political cost of ignoring this opposition was, at the least, uncertain if real at all. Secondly, the primary argument used by the communities against the governor's proposal was that it would result in the addition of still another community-based facility in communities already overburdened with several such facilities.

The real importance of this resistance was not in the political cost it might carry or even its implications for community acceptance of CBC. Rather, its importance was in the opportunity it gave the legislature once again to assert itself in correctional policy. The Democratic majority in the legislature was of a decidedly different opinion as to what was needed to cope with overcrowding. They advocated the construction of a super-maximum-security wing and additional dormitories on the existing prison campus. The legislative majority used the community resistance as a wedge to press the governor for support of their program and backed up this strategy with the threat to withhold funding for two key positions in the corrections department, which were vital to implementation of the governor's CBC proposals. After modest efforts to dissuade community groups from their opposition, the governor elected to drop the half-way-house plans and thereby deprive his legislative opponents of at least one opportunity to attack his policies.

But the most significant event that undermined the governor's initiative was a wave of rapes in the summer of 1977 that were traced to an inmate free on extended furlough. The opposition to the governor's CBC initiative seized this event to denounce CBC as a danger to the public and to call for a more stringent sentencing policy. CBC, which had originally been proposed as a fiscal panacea, now became the focus of an emotionally charged controversy.

Curiously, the circumstances surrounding this inmate's release to furlough were given little attention, namely, that he was released to the custody of a prison guard and that this release, like many before, was in gratitude for information he had provided guards about recent prison disturbances. Thus, in one of the several ironies in the Delaware case, an event that reflected the failure of traditional corrections came to be regarded as a failure of CBC.

After meeting community resistance to his half-way-house plans and increasingly vocal political opposition as a result of the one-man crime wave of a furloughed inmate, the governor retreated from his advocacy of CBC. The basic problems of the prison system remained, however, as the inmate population continued to grow. In response to these continuing problems the governor submitted in 1978 a master plan for corrections which had as its centerpiece the construction of a 300-bed minimum/medium-security prison in the state's largest city.[12] This plan was hailed by the governor as a "new direction" in corrections policy. The governor felt compelled to address the question of whether this new direction did not contradict his original advocacy of CBC. He chose to characterize the new prison as part of his CBC initiative and to dismiss the possibility of contradiction by pointing to the substantial diagnostic and treatment focus in the design of the new facility and to the fact that it would be located in an urban center rather than a corn field.

There are a number of ways to interpret these events. The most obvious of these would suggest that the CBC initiative in Delaware was a casualty of politics. From the most cynical perspective, the governor's accommodation of his CBC initiative with the building of a new prison represents a masterful use of political language to obscure and sanitize an otherwise offensive compromise. And there is some evidence to support this interpretation. For example, passage of the master plan made this governor, who had campaigned against constructing new prisons, responsible for the largest prison-building program in the state's history. Furthermore, to secure Democratic support for his plan, the governor had to concede to their demand that a "super-max" wing be built on the grounds of the campus-style prison. With this concession the governor effectively endorsed the shift in security at the old prison that had originally been forced on it by overcrowding. Finally, it should be noted that considerable community resistance accompanied the governor's new prison proposal and yet, unlike the half-way-house case, this opposition had no influence whatever on the governor's support.

In a more generous posture one might argue instead that CBC was a casualty of expected and necessary political compromise rather than deception. In this light, it could be argued that CBC initiatives are never advanced in a political vacuum; that compromise is a natural part of the process of implementing CBC programs; and that the governor's deal compares well with several of the alternatives with which he was faced. Moreover, the definitional boundary of CBC is problematic: CBC has meant many things to many people. In this regard, the governor's proposal incorporates a number of attributes frequently associated with CBC: a much higher proportion of diagnostic and treatment personnel than found in traditional prisons; better access between inmates and community members than ordinarily permitted in prisons; an explicit objective of decreasing the pretrial-detention population by locating a full-time magistrate in the facility to speed bail hearings. Indeed, what would seem to be the major objection to characterizing the new facility as a CBC initiative is its scale, and, if so, it is not at all clear whether this is a satisfactory basis for denying such a characterization. In any case, from this perspective the governor would be perceived as having chosen the best of the alternatives available to him and having carried forward his advocacy of CBC as far as was politically feasible.

Both of these interpretations explain the events in Delaware as a manifestation of politics as usual. Although we would not deny that political deception and compromise played important roles in determining the fate of CBC, such interpretations skirt a more fundamental issue. If the explanation of the events in Delaware is to be a political one, then we believe that their essential political character is not primarily a function of deception or compromise but of ideology. Our objection to such interpretations is that they ignore the domination of American corrections by a particular correctional ideology—an abiding commitment to incarceration as the only appropriate response to crime. The traditional interpretations imply that if political deception and compromise were removed, substantial prison reform would be possible—that what is needed to bring about prison reform is simply adequate political support for initiatives such as CBC. If our interpretation is correct, however, merely removing the aspects of deception and compromise is unlikely to create the basis for real prison reform.

The association of CBC with the construction of new prisons, as occurred in Delaware, is not as bizarre as it might seem. Insofar as CBC must be accommodated to a system dominated by an incarceration ideology, then, as we shall argue, its substantive promise will of necessity be dissipated and a bastardized version substituted. The events in Delaware magnify the basic dilemma of correctional reform: whether reforms such as CBC are compatible with a general correctional ideology of incarceration. We think not. With all the favorable circumstances surrounding the CBC initiative in Delaware, it is nothing less than remarkable that an isolated one-man crime wave and mild community resistance were sufficient to scuttle the effort. Remarkable, that is, if one sees the problem not as the compatibility of CBC with the philosophy of incarceration but as a technical one of implementation. The outcome in Delaware, however, is not remarkable if one takes into account the two-hundred-year history of American corrections and its focus on incarceration to the exclusion of all substantive alternatives.

The Ideology of Incarceration

American corrections is built on an ideology of incarceration. This ideology derives from a cultural understanding of crime as a basic threat to the survival of society and is sustained by an institutionalized and bureaucratic commitment to prisons as the only viable means to protect society.

Cultural attitudes toward crime and justice, symbolized by the phrase *law and order*, frequently have been employed to explain the character of American criminal justice. This explanation can be overgeneralized and result in monistic vision in which all events are rationalized by a single idea. Nonetheless, the attitudes symbolized by law and order have importance for understanding the political and psychological dimensions of American corrections.[13] The maintenance of law and order has become the domestic equivalent of national defense, enjoying the highest political and budgetary priority and signifying the preeminence of concerns for social control even when it conflicts with the rule of law.[14] Crime is equated with social disruption and its perpetrators are society's "enemies" who stand outside of and are threatening to the dominant culture. The role of the criminal-justice system, and especially prisons, is to protect society's lawful members and the values of the dominant culture. To carry out this special role, corrections officials historically have been extended substantial discretion in the formulation and execution of corrections policy. Courts have traditionally adopted a "hands-off" policy toward prison conditions and operations, and the virtual absence of judicial review has encouraged prison administrators to presume that they operate with immunity from legal prosecution.[15] This has prompted some authors to characterize prisons as "lawless agencies," and, indeed, some degree of lawlessness is necessary.[16] Without the extension of immunity, the social-order function of prisons would be jeopardized: "To require that charges be proven before a prisoner can be punished, for example, is to introduce far more than a procedural change. Requiring a hearing implies that a guard can be wrong and an inmate right; it conveys an implicit promise that an inmate can refuse a guard's order or challenge his veracity and get away with it."[17] Immunity from the rule of law is thus rationalized by the fear of penal institutions run by inmates. The irony of this posture is that we must depend on a lawless agency to protect the law abiding.

The maintenance of law and order is seen to require that the criminal be regarded as a social deviant and that crime be regarded primarily as a psychological-moral problem and not a legal problem. What is needed, from this viewpoint, is an institution largely free of interference that can modify or at least incapacitate persons. The result has been that the correctional business is conducted outside of the public eye but with at least tacit public consent.

The maintenance of law and order delivers a rationale for correctional policy that is built around incarceration and that exempts the institution from responsibility for the consequences of its policies. It furnishes the foundation for a doctrine of political immunity in which prison officials are held minimally accountable, if at all, for their actions, and it predisposes correctional administrations to adopt an "ideology of form" in which the requirements of organizational order are the primary concern in establishing and implementing policy.[18]

Within this environment a certain type of penal institution has flourished. The central feature of this institution has been characterized by Erving Goffman as "a human environment from which there is no escape and over which the (person) has no control."[19] Where an inmate lives, what time he goes to bed, what time he gets up, the people with whom he eats, works, socializes, and sleeps are chosen for him. He is denied the opportunity to affect even the most mundane features of his life. It is this complete absence of control and responsibility that makes prisons total institutions. By their very nature, they are places in which individuals are denied the most basic political and economic freedoms. They are institutions opposed to choice and liberty, built on a totalitarian and despotic system of governance and an economic system based on indentured servitude. As Paul Keve, a former corrections commissioner of Delaware and one of the most respected penologists in America, has observed:

> It is not necessary to look for a venal warden, or even a merely inept one. It is not necessary to look for sadistic guards, political chicanery from the governor's office, inadequate food, or stingy budgets from an uncaring legislature. . . . When we look for such factors we are missing the real guts of the problem, which is that in the best of prisons with the nicest custodians and the most generous of kitchens, the necessary minutiae of management tend to deny and even insult the basic needs of the individuals.[20]

Totalitarian, despotic, and indentured attributes of prisons are the inescapable requisites of effective total-institution management. Yet, satisfying these requisites creates a basic dilemma. Precisely because the American correctional system is based on extreme material deprivation and powerlessness within the inmate population, it is a system that is highly vulnerable. While such extreme circumstances enable keepers to extract obedience from the kept, they also manufacture a pressure-cooker environment. Tensions are magnified by the extraordinary difference in power and control between keeper and kept, giving prison life an extremely violent potential. These extreme conditions ensure an ever-present undercurrent of challenge and conflict. To prevent tensions from boiling over, officials must continuously maintain the precarious order. Yet, there is a contradiction implicit in this system of control: with prisons based on extreme conditions at the outset, any effort to respond to an immediate challenge will require the use of even more severe measures; their use, however, can only serve in the end to exacerbate the tensions. The ultimate irony of the situation is that these officials have no other choice but to tighten the screws, for anything less would threaten the very foundation of their authority.

The prison, in sum, is an institution that is unable to admit flexibility, unable to absorb change. As a result, American corrections has had a two-hundred-year history of reform without change. The failure of reform documented by Martinson in his review of 231 projects now awaits community-based corrections unless the focus of correctional policy is radically altered.[21] Past reform efforts have been systematically diluted by the requirement that they adapt to the requisites of total institutions. So long as total institutions are the core of corrections and community-based alternatives are the fringe, the latter will be required to adapt their goals to the organizational needs of the former. Community-based programs will not be trusted by the larger system until and unless it can be demonstrated that they do not challenge the principle of incarceration. Moreover, in such an environment inmates will likewise distrust these programs. With the bulk of their prison experience in a primary system that continuously assaults their dignity and that tells them that they cannot be trusted with the most mundane responsibilities of life, inmates are unlikely to believe the message of community-based corrections—that they are now to be trusted and respected as responsible human beings. No matter how much better community-based conditions may seem, the message remains—one's freedom is still in the hands of the keepers.

Finally, in such a system initiatives like the recent CBC initiative in Delaware will likewise be regarded suspiciously by local communities. This resistance, we believe, will stem not from public rejection of the aims of CBC per se, but from the absence of any constructive role for communities in the design of American correctional policy. Prison administrators and other criminal-justice experts create and modify policy out of the public eye. In this vacuum they have designed a system geared toward the incarceration of so-called dangerous men and have rationalized such a system as the only reliable means of ensuring public safety. The public role in this context is limited to an endorsement of existing incarceration policy without the opportunity to debate any substantive alternatives. Moreover, public debate takes place virtually only when a threat to public safety is perceived and the question is whether more, not fewer, persons should be incarcerated. Thrust into this environment; the proposal for CBC inevitably encourages negative politics—the chance to say no to the new burdens associated with policy without the opportunity to affect policy content. And indeed can the public be faulted for such a response when they have been told that the individuals who will now be resettled in their neighborhoods are the very same individuals who earlier could be restrained only by the most repressive systems of control legalized in democratic society? The public concludes, quite rightly we believe, that CBC amounts to nothing more than an administrative tool to ease the management problems encountered in the primary system of total institutions. For this reason local citizens will resist attempts to transfer the risks of existing policy from its architects to them. Unfortunately, there is ultimately no escaping these risks. The ideology of incarceration ensures that.[22]

Decarceration as a Philosophy for Community-Based Corrections

The American corrections system has exacted an extremely high cost from inmates and society alike. With its only ambition to warehouse, this system has been able to ignore what in any other context would be regarded as massive failure—a 60-percent recidivism rate among those it supposedly rehabilitates. In this system, risks are almost exclusively bureaucratically defined; the issue is whether any change upsets the manageable order of prisons and not how that change might reduce the risk to the public. The burden the public must bear for a system that does nothing to alleviate, and often increases, the dangerousness of the men it treats is not an important consideration in the modern correctional calculus. Indeed, the preferred policy is often one that reduces bureaucratic risk by increasing the risk to the community. The severe restrictions imposed on the use of programs such as work release, community-work service, and extended furlough enhance the manageability of these programs at the expense of a higher likelihood of success of inmate reentry to the community. But the most severe cost of the current system is that it perpetuates an institutional form that must function beyond the reach of justice and public accountability.

These costs have not gone unrecognized among corrections policymakers or, indeed, the public at large. Nonetheless, it is remarkable that these costs continue to be justified by the correctional establishment as inescapable; the price that must be paid if social order is to be preserved.

The foundation of American corrections must be changed. It can no longer be accepted that incarceration is successful by definition and, therefore, beyond criticism. But if not incarceration, then what is to be the primary focus of corrections? When one attempts to answer this question, it is immediately clear that we are dealing with a small part of a general societal problem. As David Rothman has observed:

> To plan for a more rational disposition of offenders after they are convicted is to do nothing about the related circumstances of poverty, racism, unemployment, and inequitable distribution of wealth and power. Indeed, what we might fear not unreasonably is that a more efficient, even more humane, system of processing people after conviction will only reinforce present inequalities, allowing the haves to control the have-nots at lower cost and with greater effectiveness.[23]

Yet, this realization cannot be allowed to stand in the way of efforts to alter the current system. As Rothman concludes:

> The wretchedness of our present system is too acute to let prisons go untouched until other social problems have been dealt with; the risks involved in making changes should not serve as an excuse to stifle attempts at amelioration. . . . (Efforts at reform) must not pretend to stand as alternatives to broader efforts at ending exploitation and racism, or at redistributing opportunity and wealth, but as parts of the overall press for social justice.[24]

To achieve the needed depth of change, decarceration must become the primary focus of corrections policy. The correctional establishment must have as its goal "getting and keeping as many people as possible out of institutions."[25] This goal is essential if public accountability is to be restored, because it is the only way to guarantee that the extent, severity, and effectiveness of incarceration are continuously evaluated. The emphasis on decarceration does not mean that confinement will disappear, rather that its use will be bound by the criterion of last resort. What is needed is a correctional system that no longer shifts the risks of incarceration costlessly to the public but instead internalizes these systematic failures. No system of correction can erase all risks to the public, but a system can be created that would balance the risks that new programs may bring against "the clear likelihood of continuing recidivism, crime, and brutalization under the existing system."[26]

Only in the policy environment of decarceration can community-based corrections avoid the cooptation that has characterized past efforts at reform. A philosophy of decarceration provides assurance that the new risks CBC brings will be weighed against those that would occur in its absence and provides the opportunity to exercise deliberate choice in the nature of the public risks we accept.

A Postscript on Delaware

A number of events of significance have transpired in Delaware since our research was concluded that further underlines the frustrations and ineffectiveness attending CBC initiatives. The new prison has not turned out to be the panacea it was intended to be. Before construction had even begun, corrections officials concluded that the facility might be overcrowded shortly after it opened, thereby threatening the viability of its diagnostic function. Reflecting on the troubling similarity between this prospect and that experienced at the previous panacea (the campus-style prison), the state's major newspaper commented: "Delaware's prison system, the perennial nemesis of smooth running government, is gnawing at the body politic again. . . . Occasionally, the monster is wounded and held at bay by sensible improvements or real reform. But never, it seems, for long."[27]

As might be expected, the plight of the prison system attracted considerable attention in the 1980 gubernatorial race. Once again, CBC was offered as the solution to Delaware's corrections dilemma. The case for CBC was made in words almost parodying those of the 1976 election:

> Our prison system is nothing more than a larger and more expensive finishing school for criminals. . . . What will be the next step when (the new facilities) become overcrowded too? . . . Prisoners should only be held in that degree of custody which assures the safety of the public. . . . As time passes and prison populations continue to rise, alternative incarceration systems will have to be developed. . . . Much as the citizenry at large wants to see criminals incarcerated, the amount of public money available to support the prison system is not infinite.[28]

Interestingly, the advocate of these positions was not the incumbent who had supported them four years earlier but his challenger.

Notes

1. David J. Rothman, "Decarcerating Prisoners and Patients," *The Civil Liberties Review* 1(Fall 1973):8–9. We owe a substantial debt to this paper, especially for the historical perspective on American corrections that it provides and for its development of the idea of decarceration. All quotes are reprinted with permission.

2. National Advisory Commission on Criminal Justice Standards and Goals, *A National Strategy to Reduce Crime* (Washington, D.C.: U.S. Government Printing Office, 1973), p. 173. It is noteworthy that this is an insider's view, as is clear from the membership of the Commission and its task forces— Norman A. Carlson, director, U.S. Bureau of Prisons, Edward M. Davis, former chief, Los Angeles Police Department, Clarence M. Kelly, former director of the FBI, Richard G. Lugar, senator from Indiana, and Arlen Specter, former district attorney of Philadelphia, among others.

3. Hans Mattick as quoted by Gordon Hawkins in *The Prison* (Chicago: University of Chicago Press, 1976), p. 45.

4. Malcolm Braly, *False Starts* (Boston: Little, Brown, 1976), p. 251.

5. Robert Martinson, "What Works?—Questions and Answers about Prison Reform," *The Public Interest* (Spring 1974):22–54.

6. Illustrative of the neoconservative movement in criminology are: Ernest van den Haag, *Punishing Criminals: Concerning a Very Old and Painful Question* (New York: Basic Books, 1975); and James Q. Wilson, *Thinking about Crime* (New York: Vintage Books, 1977).

7. See National Advisory Commission on Criminal Justice Standards and Goals, *Corrections* (Washington, D.C.: U.S. Government Printing Office, 1973); J. Joper, *Alternatives to Prison—A Thoughtful Approach to Crime and Punishment* (Washington, D.C.: National Moratoriam on Prison Construction, 1979); C.R. Dodge, *World without Prisons—Alternatives to Incarceration Throughout the World* (Lexington, Mass.: Lexington Books, D.C. Heath, 1979).

8. Then, as now, deterrence referred to making crime uneconomic while maintaining the economic status quo. In this sense, one deters crime not only by redistributing income but by raising the perceived cost to the poor of committing street crime.

9. John Byrne, Donald Yanich, and David van Tijn, *Correctional Standards for Delaware: A Cost Analysis of Present Operations and Policies of the State's Correctional System* (Wilmington, Del.: Delaware Agency to Reduce Crime, 1976).

10. The method used in the Delaware study simulated inmate population growth as a function of the average number of new arrivals per month, the average length of sentence, and the average rate of recidivism. By holding the recidivism rates constant and changing the average length of sentence and the average arrival rate to reflect the impact of new mandatory sentences (note that

mandatory sentences affect the likelihood of being sentenced and the length of sentence), it was possible to account for nearly all the growth in the Delaware inmate population between 1975 and 1976 (see table 3.9 of the study). Since inmate populations grow at a cumulative rate, such a simulation cannot be claimed to explain long-term relationships between the various growth factors.

The study showed that it was possible to reduce the sentenced population by 32 percent through the implementation of the following CBC policies: the diversion of all inmates sentenced to two months or less to work-service, half-way-house, and furlough programs; the diversion of all inmates serving sentences of two to three months to half-way houses; the diversion of those inmates serving sentences of three to six months to half-way houses and furlough programs; the diversion of 2.8 percent of those sentenced to one to two years to work-release programs commencing six months before their maximum expiration date (overnight custody); the diversion of 2.1 percent of those sentenced to two to five years to work-release programs also; and finally, the creation of a pretrial-diversion facility that would divert 4 percent of the detained population that would eventually be sentenced.

11. Anderson et al. v. Redman et al., C.A. 76-364 (D. Del. Feb. 16, 1977).

12. *A Master Plan for the Department of Corrections* (Dover, Del.: Office of the Governor, September 15, 1977).

13. For a discussion of the use of the term law and order and its application to the body politic see: William J. Chambliss and Robert B. Siedman, *Law, Order and Power* (Reading, Mass.: Addison-Wesley, 1971), pp. 186–189.

14. In a recent report on American justice, the U.S. Bureau of Prisons draws the direct parallel between the criminal-justice system and the armed services as agents of national defense. The report uses the phrase *social defense* to describe the operations of the criminal-justice system and even associates offender-rehabilitation progress with this objective. See U.S. Bureau of Prisons, *Administration of Justice in a Changing Society: Report on Developments in the United States–1965–1970* (Washington, D.C.: U.S. Bureau of Prisons, 1972).

15. Although the judiciary showed some important signs of activism during the 1960s regarding prisoners' rights, the impact of this activism is regarded by many analysts as moderate at best. See, for example, Kenneth C. Haas, "Judicial Politics and Correctional Reform: An Analysis of the Decline of the 'Hands-Off' Doctrine," *Detroit College of Law Review* (Winter 1977):795–831, which argues that recent courts have been, at most, a "hesitant ally" of prisoners' rights.

16. See, for example, David F. Greenberg and Fay Stender, "The Prisoner as a Lawless Agency," *Buffalo Law Review* 21(Spring 1972):799–838.

17. Charles E. Silberman, *Criminal Violence, Criminal Justice* (New York: Vintage Books, 1978), p. 550.

18. David Schuman, *The Ideology of Form* (Lexington, Mass.: Lexington Books, D.C. Heath, 1978).

19. Erving Goffman, *Asylums: Essays on the Social Situation of Mental Patients and Other Inmates* (Garden City, N.Y.: Anchor Books, 1961). See also Gresham M. Sykes, *The Society of Captives* (Princeton, N.J.: Princeton University Press, 1958); and Karl Menninger, *The Crime of Punishment* (New York: Viking Books, 1968). The quote is from Silberman, *Criminal Violence,* p. 512.

20. Paul Keve, *Prison Life and Human Worth* (Minneapolis: University of Minnesota Press, 1974), pp. 41–42. For a brief history and overview of American prisons see: "Correctional Institutions for Adult Offenders: An Overview," in *Corrections in America* by Robert M. Carter, Richard A. McGee, and E. Kim Nelson (Philadelphia: J.B. Lippincott, 1976), pp. 96–125.

21. Eric H. Steele and James B. Jacobs, "A Theory of Prisons," *Crime and Delinquency* 21(April 1975):149–162. The authors define community-based corrections as "small, functionally independent institution(s) with heterogeneous populations." If CBC is implemented under this definition, it us unlikely that significant change in the prison system will occur.

22. Wilkins has attributed the failure of the criminal-justice system as a whole to the absence of change in the prevailing ideology of law and order. He is convinced, as we are, that the dominance of this ideology ensures a course of "more-of-the-same." Wilkins argues that a total breakdown of the American system is likely to occur by the end of this century. See his "Crime and Criminal Justice at the Turn of the Century," in *Probation, Parole and Community Corrections,* ed. Robert M. Carter and Leslie T. Wilkins (New York: John Wiley and Sons, 1976), pp. 5–19.

23. Rothman, "Decarcerating Prisoners and Patients," p. 25.

24. Ibid., p. 26.

25. Ibid.

26. Ibid., p. 28.

27. *Evening Journal,* Wilmington, Delaware, 18 June 1979. Reprinted with permission of The News-Journal Co., Wilmington, Del.

28. *Evening Journal,* Wilmington, Delaware, 28 October 1980. Reprinted with permission of The News-Journal Co., Wilmington, Del.

3 Problems of Theory-Based Corrections Policy

Albert C. Price and
Kent E. Portney

Corrections policy, defined as the allocation of sanctions among convicted offenders, has recently become a topic of considerable political importance in the United States, especially since a growing number of state legislatures have adopted or are currently considering criminal-sentencing reform. Perhaps part of the reason for this trend is that abundant research suggests that existing programs rarely achieve their goals to any significant degree. For example, analyses have repeatedly found that various efforts to rehabilitate convicted offenders usually fail to achieve their goal[1]; and studies have often shown that the criminal-justice system does not seem to deter crime.[2] Numerous attempts have been made to explain failures to achieve specific goals, and these attempts typically concentrate on characteristics of the organizations responsible for program implementation.[3] For example, intraorganizational exercise of discretion over the implementation and operation of programs has often been explored as a major influence on the extent to which externally (legislatively) determined goals are actually accomplished.[4] In other policy areas, at least one commentator suggests that ambiguous legislation, and perhaps the lack of a clear legislative consensus regarding specific goals, lies at the root of such exercises of discretion.[5] Indeed, at a time when state legislatures are considering major changes in criminal-justice legislation, it is important to understand how the legislative process might relate to achievement of correctional goals.

From a slightly broader perspective, implementation theory might entail focusing substantially on the nature of the goal "messages" from policymakers to policy implementers.[6] Instead of deriving policy goals solely from written legislation, policy implementers often take cues from other characteristics of the political system generating relevant legislation. In the case of corrections policy, one of the more vital aspects of such messages concerns the extent to which legislators' attitudes toward the criminal sanction seem grounded in any particular theory of corrections. One might wish to entertain the possibility, for example, that when legislators are more clearly able to distinguish among the various theoretical goals of corrections policy, they will be better able to transmit the desire to achieve any single goal (or optimum mix of goals) to policy implementers. Given this possibility, this chapter examines patterns of legislators' perceptions of the goals of various criminal sanctions in four states that have recently undertaken substantial criminal-justice reform.[7]

Despite the policy relevance associated with the actual transmission of goals from legislators to implementers, that exploration is well beyond the scope of this chapter. Nevertheless, this analysis focuses on state legislators as key policy-makers and explores the interrelationships among their perceptions of the four major goals of corrections policy: rehabilitation, incapacitation, deterrence, and retribution. Additionally, this chapter discusses some policy implications resulting from the examination of the extent to which legislators can distinguish among these goals. The analysis relies on results of a survey of state legislators in Connecticut, Illinois, Indiana, and Minnesota.

The Four Major Goals of Corrections

Although a plethora of correctional philosophies exists, these may be summarized as four major goals associated with sentencing and corrections policy: rehabilitation, incapacitation, deterrence, and retribution. Although these four goals may not be mutually exclusive, they do tend to stress distinctly different ways of achieving a reduction in crime.

Rehabilitation stresses the resocialization or reformation of the offender through institutional or community programs. For example, convicted offenders may take part in vocational training, education, psychiatric counselling, or a host of other rehabilitation-oriented programs. Generally underlying the belief in rehabilitation as a goal is the notion that the offender is sick and can potentially be cured through institutional intervention.[8]

Deterrence refers to the notion that the punishment of offenders serves as an example to the rest of society; therefore potential offenders will be less likely to violate the law. This position has its roots in the utilitarian philosophy of Jeremy Bentham, and assumes that a potential criminal is a substantially rational actor who will weigh the benefit of criminal behavior against the costs of possible sanctions.[9] Deterrence-oriented public policies would presumably seek to increase the costs by making sanctions more likely and more severe.

Incapacitation, not unlike some aspects of deterrence, seeks to reduce crime through the actual physical restraint of convicted offenders. The goal of incapacitation relies on the notion that a convicted felon cannot commit crimes against others while incarcerated. Therefore, total crime would be reduced by the number of offenses that would have been committed if offenders were not incarcerated.[10]

Finally, retribution refers to corrections policy predicated on two principles: individual responsibility and proportionality.[11] That is, a convicted offender deserves to be punished because he or she is responsible for committing a specific criminal violation, and the sanction must be in proportion to the severity of the offense committed.

Although these definitions may seem oversimplified, they do illustrate the multiplicity of correctional goals that could be reflected in any particular piece of legislation. Moreover, these summaries provide a background against which some problems of theory-based policy can be examined.

Problems of Theory-Based Corrections Policy

In the abstract, each of these goals of corrections appears distinct from other objectives. However, difficulties arise when attempts are made to transfer these goals into legislatively mandated sentencing practices. Each goal of corrections would seem to require a set of sentencing statutes and administrative operations that, to some extent, directly contradict the objectives of one or more of the other goals. Several examples of the tension among the goals of corrections can be delineated.

If rehabilitation is the goal of corrections, then the sentencing policy must involve substantial administrative flexibility, as exemplified in the use of indeterminant sentences and parole. This flexibility often manifests itself in the form of substantial amounts of discretion provided to correctional authorities, who determine when an offender has been rehabilitated and is ready to return to society. Rehabilitative sentences reflect the characteristics and needs of the individual offender, and treatment aimed at reform may vary from individual to individual.[12] Consequently, sentences are not necessarily proportional to the offense committed, illustrating the tension between retribution as a goal and a pure rehabilitative goal.

Deterrence as a goal of corrections requires that the sanction in particular cases be accompanied by enhanced likelihood of apprehension, prosecution, and conviction.[13] The need of society to inhibit criminal behavior through exemplary sanctions tends to take precedence over the needs of the individual offender. Some commentators have suggested that the issue of whether an individual is factually guilty is secondary to the societal need for exemplary punishment.[14]

Correction policy based on a goal of incapacitation generally seeks to reduce crime through restraint of offenders, using a system of sentences based on the legislature's (or the court's) desire to keep off the street those offenders who might otherwise engage in criminal behavior. According to several studies, the overall crime rate could be substantially reduced by adopting and utilizing such an incapacitation orientation toward corrections.[15]

Retributive sanctions would ostensibly require a relatively inflexible sentencing system, wherein the convicted offender is penalized according to the degree of responsibility for and in proportion to the severity of the crime. Most discussions of this suggest that the relative severity of offenses and associated sanctions would be determined by legislatures and set in statute. Therefore, if retribution constitutes the correctional goal, little discretion would be permitted either at the sentencing stage or on the part of correctional authorities.[16] The notion of "just deserts" has recently begun to displace retribution as a goal of corrections, but the basic principles remain retributive.[17]

These four theoretical goals of corrections represent a variety of distinctly alternative policy formulations, even though some of the subtleties elude brief description. Often, state legislators face responsibility for selecting the desired goal or mix of goals from among these competing goals when correctional reform is contemplated. Indeed, because elements of contradiction exist in attempts to achieve multiple goals, it is important to examine legislators' perceptions of the goals of corrections. The question addressed by this research concerns the extent to which legislators' perceptions about these four correctional goals are grounded in values that imply understanding of such distinctions.

How Do Legislators View the Goals of Corrections Policy?

To examine legislators' perceptions of correctional goals, a survey of all lawmakers in Connecticut, Illinois, Indiana, and Minnesota was conducted.[18] Each legislator was asked to express the degree to which he or she agreed with four general tenets of the goals of corrections policy and the degree to which he or she agreed with four specific statements of attitudes (about behavior toward offenders) expected to be associated with goals of corrections.

Table 3-1 shows the percentage distribution of responses to questions about the general tenets of four correctional goals. The distributions on all four questions appear quite similar. These state legislators at least partially agree with each of the four tenets. For example, even though the vast majority of these legislators agree that the seriousness of the crime committed should be the most important consideration in sentencing, over half of the legislators also agree that the social environment causes crime. This, of course, does not necessarily imply that the same cohort of legislators believes in the tenets of both rehabilitation and retribution. Understanding how the four specific statements of attitudes about behavior toward offenders are related to these general tenets should provide some insight into the interrelationships among legislators' perceptions.

In general, it might be expected that legislators who believe in the specific propriety of punishment also should support the general notion of deterrence; legislators who specifically wish to keep repeat offenders in prison also should support the goal of incapacitation; legislators who believe criminals are sick people and need help should support the belief underlying a goal of rehabilitation that social environments cause crime, and oppose the goal of retribution; and legislators who believe the justice and correctional system is too hard on offenders should support rehabilitation tenets.

Table 3-1
Distribution of Responses to Statements about Tenets of Four Correctional Goals in State Legislatures
(percent)

Response Category	Deterrence: Harsh Sentences Deter Crime (n = 321)	Incapacitation: First Priority, Get Offender Off Street (n = 318)	Retribution: Seriousness of Crime Most Important (n = 320)	Rehabilitation: Social Environment Causes Crime (n = 319)
Disagree totally	5.6	6.6	0.6	12.9
Disagree partially	20.9	21.5	10.2	23.5
Neither agree nor disagree	8.4	9.1	3.7	5.3
Agree partially	49.2	43.2	57.8	53.3
Agree totally	15.9	19.6	27.6	5.0
Total	100.0	100.0	100.0	100.0

Note: Statement wordings were: a harsh sentence serves as an example to keep others from committing the same act; the first priority in sentencing should be to get the offender off the street; the seriousness of the crime committed should be the most important consideration in sentencing; most offenders commit crimes because of environmental factors, such as poverty, poor education, broken homes, and bad neighborhoods.

Utilizing the four specific statements, an attempt is made to explain attitudes toward each of the general tenets, using multiple-regression analyses.[19] The results of these analyses are presented in table 3-2.

As table 3-2 indicates, legislators who believe in the propriety of punishment strongly tend to support the notions that harsh sentences deter crime and that the first priority of corrections is to get the offender off the street. Punishment is modestly negatively related to a belief that the environment causes crime. Legislators who believe repeat offenders should be kept in prison strongly tend to believe that harsh sentences deter, that the first priority of corrections is to get the offender off the street, and that the seriousness of the crime should be the most important determinant of sentence severity. Belief that repeat offenders should be kept in prison is modestly negatively related to belief that the social environment causes crime.

However, legislators who believe that criminals are sick and need help tend not to believe that the seriousness of the crime should be most important in determining sentence severity, and they strongly tend to believe that the social environment causes crime. Finally, legislators who believe that the correctional system is too hard tend to believe that harsh sentences do not deter crime; that the first priority should not be to get the offender off the street; and that the seriousness of the crime should not be the most important consideration. And

Table 3–2
Standardized-Regression Results Explaining Tenets of Four Correctional
Goals in State Legislatures

Independent Variables: Agreement with Specific Statements	Dependent Variables: Agreement with General Tenets Reflecting Goals of Corrections Policy							
	Deterrence: Harsh Sentence Deters Crime (n = 311)		Incapacitation: First Priority, Get Offender Off Street (n = 311)		Retribution: Seriousness of Crime Most Important (n = 311)		Rehabilitation: Social Environment Causes Crime (n = 311)	
	Beta	Partial F	Beta	Partial F	Beta	Partial F	Beta	Partial F
Children should be punished	.27	31.3**	.17	9.0**	.04	0.5	−.06	0.9
Keep repeat offenders in prison	.30	35.7**	.28	24.8**	.21	12.8**	−.08	1.7
Criminal is sick, needs help	−.09	3.0*	−.06	1.4	−.15	7.3**	.22	16.5**
System is too hard on offenders	−.24	22.9**	−.12	4.2**	−.11	3.2*	.14	5.6**
R^2	.39		.20		.12		.11	
Overall F	47.8**		19.0**		10.2**		9.2**	

Note: Statement wordings were: a harsh sentence serves as an example to keep others from committing the same act; the first priority in sentencing should be to get the offender off the street; the seriousness of the crime committed should be the most important consideration in sentencing; most offenders commit crimes because of environmental factors, such as poverty, poor education, broken homes, and bad neighborhoods; if children are to learn right from wrong they need to be spanked now and then; repeat offenders should not be allowed out of prison; people who commit crimes are often sick and need to be helped; our criminal-justice system is too hard on offenders.

*Significant at .05 lvels.

**Significant at .01 level.

these legislators seem to support the notion that the social environment causes crime.

These findings contain several important patterns. First, the general expectations are upheld: legislators who believe in the propriety of punishment strongly support the tenet of deterrence; legislators who would not permit repeat offenders to leave prison strongly support the tenet of incapacitation; legislators who believe that criminals are sick support two tenets of rehabilitation, that the social environment causes crime and that the seriousness of the crime should not be the most important consideration; and legislators who believe that the system is too hard do not believe in the notion of deterrence, but they do believe that the social environment causes crime. Second, and perhaps more important, the direction of the relationships is fairly consistent for all the general tenets of correctional goals except rehabilitation. Beliefs in the propriety of punishment and that repeat offenders should be kept off the street are both positively related to tenets of deterrence, incapacitation, and retribution, but they are negatively related to the tenet of rehabilitation. Belief in the sickness of criminals and that the system is too hard are both negatively related to the tenets of deterrence, incapacitation, and retribution but are positively related to the tenet of rehabilitation. The importance of this is that legislators do not seem to draw distinctions from among three of the four goals of corrections. Deterrence, incapacitation, and retribution seem to be part of the same underlying dimension of legislators' views of correctional goals.

Implications for Specific Legislation: The Case of Definite Sentences

The patterns of legislators' beliefs underlying the four major goals of corrections, which suggest that they clearly distinguish between only two basic sets of correctional goals, have important implications for the development of criminal-justice legislation.[20] The apparent lack of a clearly perceived distinction between retribution, incapacitation, and deterrence suggests an explanation for some of the major difficulties encountered in criminal-justice reform. The way this lack of distinction manifests itself in specific policies can be illustrated in an examination of lawmakers' attempts to enact definite-sentencing legislation in the four states. This particular reform is selected because each of the states surveyed (Connecticut, Illinois, Indiana, and Minnesota) has recently experienced significant political conflict over the need for, and actual substantive details of, definite sentences. Ultimately, definite-sentencing legislation was adopted in each of the four states, and similar changes are currently being considered in many others.

Proposals for definite sentencing relate to a general restructuring of the state's sentencing policy through modification of the entire criminal code. Such proposals call, in general, for fixed sentence lengths, voluntary participation in treatment programs, and the abolition of parole. The issue of fixed sentence lengths reveals the type of problem produced by the lack of distinctions among correctional goals. It is not the only example of such problems, but it is a particularly salient one.

In each of the four states examined, a similar pattern emerged surrounding how fixed sentences were defined.[21] In each state, the relatively simple notion, derived from the concept of retribution, that any particular crime should be accompanied by a fixed sentence, was transformed into a complex system of sentences specifying a multiplicity of sentencing criteria. To some degree, the multiple-sentencing criteria tend to contradict each other in terms of correctional goals. For example, legislative action adhering to a retribution philosophy (punishment based on crime severity) varied length of sentences based upon severity and degree of responsibility (with attention, therefore, to "aggravating and mitigating" factors). At the same time, legislation permitted inclusion of the prior criminal record of felons as a criterion in sentencing. Presumably, the inclusion of prior criminal record is justified because of the belief that past criminal behavior is an important predictor of future criminal behavior. This sentencing criterion, seemingly related to incapacitation appears to conflict with the requirements of retributive justice, which stipulate that an offender should be punished only for the specific crime committed and not for previous behavior. In other words, when legislators consider specific legislation, they may wish to establish fixed sentences, but they also wish to place particular emphasis on incapacitating repeat offenders. There is no evidence that legislators understand the theoretical difficulties in such an effort.[22]

The case of definite sentences begins to demonstrate the tension between the theoretical goals of incapacitation and retribution when efforts are made to achieve both. Other examples of inherent contradictions in multiple policy goals exist, but in this case they exist because legislators are not able to distinguish between these two goals. Indeed, the situation is made more complex, and the goal of either incapacitation or retribution might be expected to be more difficult to achieve, when attempts are made to achieve other goals as well. Perhaps more importantly, the fact that legislators do not seem to distinguish among retribution, incapacitation, and deterrence as goals of corrections might help account for legislation that does not recognize contradictions in simultaneous achievement of goals.

Some Broad Implications for Corrections Policy

Why would legislators create sentencing policies that attempt to fulfill contradictory theories? Perhaps two factors are crucial: (1) the lack of understanding on the part of legislators of the contradictions in some of the theories of corrections; and (2) the overwhelming need to create a voting coalition of diverse interests. Perhaps the patterns of state legislators' attitudes, and the implications of these patterns for specific legislation (such as definite sentencing) can be expanded into a broader, albeit speculative, discussion concerning the role of legislators in corrections.

Initially, we started with the idea that when legislators are more clearly able to distinguish among the theoretical goals of corrections, they would probably be better able to transmit the desire to achieve any single goal or optimum mix of goals to policy implementers. Based on the finding that these state legislators are not able to make such distinctions, it would be difficult to argue that conflicting elements in specific legislation simply reflect conscious efforts by legislators to communicate the desire to optimize multiple, albeit conflicting, corrections goals. Rather, these findings suggest that such conflicting goals are more likely a result of legislators' inability to recognize the conflicts that they might be producing.

Legislators' inability to distinguish among the three correctional goals may have another side—it may be that such a lack of distinction facilitates the building of coalitions in support of any particular piece of legislation. Enactment of specific corrections legislation may well necessitate aggregation of such diverse interests as those associated with police, corrections professionals, and bar associations. Explicit investigation of this possibility remains a topic for future research. In the final analysis, however, if the inability of legislators to distinguish among three of the four somewhat distinct goals of corrections examined here facilitates enactment of corrections legislation, it may do so at the expense of unambiguous policy guidance to implementers. And if this set of relationships tends to exist, it may inevitably lead to the conclusion that resultant public policy is doomed to failure if judged against achievement of any one goal or against any coherent mix of correctional goals.

Notes

1. Compare Walter C. Bailey, "An Examination of One Hundred Reports" *Journal of Criminal Law, Criminology, and Policy Science* 57(1966):155-160; Charles H. Logan, "Evaluation Research in Crime and Delinquency: A Reappraisal" *Journal of Criminal Law, Criminology, and Police Science* 63(September 1972):378-387; and Robert Martinson, "What Works?—Questions and Answers about Prison Reform," *Public Interest* 35(Spring 1974):22-54.

2. Franklin E. Zimring and Gordon J. Hawkins, *Deterrence: The Legal Threat in Crime Control* (Chicago: University of Chicago Press, 1977); and William J. Chambliss, "The Deterrent Influence of Punishment," *Crime and Delinquency* 12(January 1966):70-75.

3. Compare with chapter 2 of this book; Dennis Palumbo and Elaine Sharp, "Process Versus Impact Evaluations of Community Corrections," in *The Practice of Policy Evaluation,* ed. David Nachmias (New York: St. Martins, 1980), pp. 293-294.

4. See for example, Erika S. Fairchild "Organizational Structure and Control of Discretion in Police Operations," *Policy Studies Journal,* Special Issue (1978):442-449; and Jameson W. Doig, "Police Policy and Police Behavior: Patterns of Divergence," *Policy Studies Journal,* Special Issue, (1978): 436-441.

5. Theodore J. Lowi, *The End Of Liberalism,* 2d ed. (New York: W.W. Norton, 1979), especially chap. 6.

6. Robert T. Nakamura and Frank Smallwood, *The Politics of Policy Implementation* (New York: St. Martins, 1980), pp. 39–40.

7. Estimates vary, but it is safe to say that a majority of states have actively explored sentencing reform during the past five years.

8. On the perspective see, for example, Karl Menninger, *The Crime of Punishment* (New York: Viking Press, 1968).

9. See Gilbert Geis, "Pioneers in Criminology: VII, Jeremy Bentham (1748–1832)," *Journal of Criminal Law, Criminology, and Police Science* 46 (July–August 1955):159–171.

10. David F. Greenberg, "The Incapacitative Effect of Punishment: Some Estimates," *Law and Society Review* 9(Summer 1975):541–580.

11. See J.D. Mabbot, "Punishment," in *The Philosophy of Punishment,* ed. H.B. Acton (London: Macmillan, 1969), pp. 41–54.

12. See Menninger, *Crime of Punishment,* especially pp. 228–230.

13. Geis, "Pioneers in Criminology"; aslo see Marcello Maestro, *Ceasare Beccaria and the Origins of Prison Reform* (Philadelphia: Temple University Press, 1973).

14. Ernest van den Haag, *Punishing Criminals* (New York: Basic Books, 1975), p. 50.

15. See discussion in James Q. Wilson and Barbara Boland, "Crime," in *The Urban Predicament,* William Gorham and Nathan Glazer ed. (Washington, D.C.: Urban Institute, 1976), pp. 179–230.

16. For an excellent discussion concerning the difficulties of creating "just" sentences upon retributive principles, see Edmund L. Pincoffs "Are Questions of Desert Decidable?" in *Justice and Punishment,* ed. J.B. Cedarblom and William Blizek (Cambridge, Mass.: Ballinger, 1977), pp. 75–88.

17. See David Fogel, *We Are the Living Proof* (Cincinnati: Anderson, 1975); The American Friends Service Committee, *Struggle for Justice* (New York: Hill and Wang, 1971); and Andrew von Hirsch, *Doing Justice* (New York: Hill and Wang, 1976).

18. A self-mailing questionnaire was distributed to every legislator in these four states during 1979. The response rates were: Connecticut, 48.6 percent; Illinois, 29.2 percent; Indiana, 46.6 percent; and Minnesota, 47.0 percent. Based on a number of tests, there was obvious bias in the respondents compared to nonrespondents.

19. Regression analysis was deemed appropriate, since none of the assumptions underlying its use was severely violated. The same general patterns in the directions and relative strengths of the relationships emerge when other methods, including log-linear analysis, are utilized.

20. Ideally, we would like to have used our information on legislators' attitudes to predict each individual legislator's vote on such legislation. Because of our inability to verify the actual votes, this was not possible.

21. This discussion is based on an extensive analysis of definite sentencing as found in Albert C. Price, "The Politics of Definite Sentencing in Four American States," (Ph.D. diss., University of Connecticut, 1980).

22. Some retributive theorists, such as von Hirsch, have attempted to incorporate longer terms for repeat offenders in the sentencing guidelines. See Andrew von Hirsch, *Doing Justice* (New York: Hill & Wang, 1976), especially chap. 10.

Crime and Incarceration across American States

Jack H. Nagel

Since its presentation at the 1976 Congress of Corrections and subsequent publication in a variety of locations, William G. Nagel's paper "On Behalf of a Moratorium on Prison Construction" has had substantial impact on corrections professionals and reformers.[1] Opponents of new prison construction have cited its arguments in seeking, sometimes successfully, to block or cut appropriations at the federal and state levels.

The paper has had wide appeal partly because it was written by a practitioner for practitioners. By the same token, limitations resulting from the fact that its author is avowedly not a social scientist may have reduced the attention given Nagel's research by more rigorous policy researchers. This is regrettable, since few other studies attempt to look statistically at determinants of crime and incarceration across the states, and none uses such recent (1975) data.[2]

Nagel examined statistics from the states and found no relation between crime rates and incarceration rates. Instead, he concluded, crime depends on poverty, unemployment, and urbanization. Imprisonment policies respond not to crime but to states' political climates and the relative sizes of their black populations.

This chapter corrects important methodological weaknesses in Nagel's study to determine whether his key results should be sustained, modified, or abandoned.

Methods

The greater part of the "Moratorium" paper consists of a cross-sectional comparison of all fifty states using a large number of variables. I shall improve that analysis in three ways.

1. *Level of Measurement.* Many of Nagel's conclusions are supported by graphical scatterplots charting states' rankings on two variables (for example,

Jack Schaller collected most of the data used in this chapter and provided much useful consultation. The author is also grateful for the advice, assistance, or comments of Gerard Anderson, Anthony Boardman, George F. Cole, Jameson Doig, David Franceski, John Jackson, David Luery, William G. Nagel, and James A. Spady. The author alone is responsible for interpretations and errors. An earlier report of these findings was presented in testimony to the Subcommittee on Crime of the House Judiciary Committee and published in its *Hearings on Unemployment and Crime* (1978).

unemployment rate and crime rate). These ordinal measures are weaker than the original data from which they derive, causing unnecessary loss of information and preventing use of more powerful statistical methods. Moreover, the graphical displays are vulnerable to subjective differences in interpretation.

2. *Multivariate Analysis.* Nagel did supply a matrix of correlations computed from the original data and not subject to the problems just described. However, unless we control for the effects of other variables, it is possible that these bivariate associations (or, in some cases, the absence of such associations) may be spurious.

3. *Simultaneity.* The most common method for conducting such multivariate analysis—ordinary least-squares regression—cannot, however, handle the third difficulty raised by the "Moratorium" study (and much other criminal-justice research). Nagel derived his central conclusion that incarceration rates do not affect crime from the lack of statistical association between the two variables, as indicated by both scatterplot and correlation coefficient. Conventional wisdom, however, predicts two causal relationships between crime and imprisonment: when crimes are frequent, more people are jailed; but locking up more criminals prevents crime. The first effect should produce a positive association between crime and incarceration rates, but the second should result in a negative association. If the two opposed tendencies are nearly equal in strength, they may cancel each other, producing a near-zero bivariate relation, such as Nagel observed. In principle, we might gauge the two effects by observing each state over time to see whether crime waves precede crowded jails and safer streets follow new prisons. Unfortunately, lacking adequate information for a complete longitudinal analysis, we must estimate two-way causal links simultaneously from cross-sectional data. To accomplish this, I resorted to two-stage least-square (2SLS) regression.[3]

The Reanalysis

The causal specification on which all our numerical results depend posits two endogenous variables—incarceration rate and crime rate, each presumed to affect the other. To disentangle their effects on each other and to control for other influences, we must include in each equation other, exogenous factors. Moreover, these putative causes are of interest in their own right. We would like to know their strength relative to each other and to the two central variables.

From Nagel's study, I took seven exogenous variables: liberalism, percentage of urban population, percentage of black population, unemployment rate, income per capita, percentage of low-income population, and black migration from 1960 to 1970.[4] Of the variables mentioned in the static part of his paper, I did not consider (for various reasons) four: net population change from 1955 to 1975, population density, median age, and percentage of nonwhite population.

Two-stage least-squares estimation requires that the set of exogenous variables contain at least one variable for each equation to satisfy the exclusion assumptions necessary for identification of the coefficients. These instrumental variables must significantly affect one, but not both, of the two variables in a reciprocal relation. Thus each instrument is included a priori in one estimating equation but not in the second.

In searching for satisfactory instruments, I added three more variables to those already examined by Nagel; percentage of the population who are young males and two controls for region—South-North and East-West.[5]

I first regressed the exogenous variables against crime and incarceration, using ordinary least-squares. The purpose of this step was to discover which exogenous factors had no effect and so could be dropped from the analysis and to find out whether our lists included suitable instruments.

Three variables had no significant effect on either crime rates or incarceration rates. These were percentage of young males, black migration, and percentage of low-income population. The last of these findings seems to contradict one of Nagel's conclusions—that states with a high incidence of poverty tend to have low crime but high incarceration. I found neither tendency, but my regressions included another variable highly correlated (−.77) with poverty— state per-capita income, which did have a strong association with crime (although not with incarceration). When two closely associated variables appear in the same equation, one may get all the credit for an effect they actually share.[6] In any case, I dropped the poverty variable from subsequent regressions.

A fourth variable omitted in later runs was the control for North-South region. It has no relation to overall crime rates, but southern states do have somewhat higher incarceration rates. In searching for instrumental variables, however, it became necessary to control for East-West region. Since all but two southern states are also eastern, I dropped the control for North-South region.

With the East-West variable in the equations, adequate instruments now appeared. The instrument for incarceration rate is percentage of black population, which strongly influences imprisonment but has no effect on overall crime (a finding that supports one of Nagel's key conclusions). I discovered two instruments for crime rate—percentage of urban population and income per capita. Both strongly affect crime but have no impact on incarceration.

Results

Inclusion of these three instrumental variables made it possible to proceed to the second stage of the 2SLS procedure. This stage produces estimates of the effects of crime and incarceration on each other as well as final assessments of the influence of the remaining exogenous variables. These results are summarized in tables 4–1 and 4–2 and in figure 4–1.

Table 4–1
Regression Results for Crime Rates across the Fifty States, 1975

Variable	Regression Coefficient	Standardized Coefficient	t Statistic
Percentage urban	23.4	.42	4.46
Unemployment rate	266.4	.38	4.01
Income per capita	.627	.30	3.41
East region	−1561.0	−.52	5.83
Incarceration rate	4.169	.13	1.09

Note: Constant = −1508.6
$R^2 = .68$

The tables present, for each equation, the regression coefficients, standard-ized-regression coefficients (path coefficients or beta weights) and t statistics. Figure 4-1 presents the same results in diagram form. The solid arrows stand for strong relationship in which we may place considerable confidence; all have t's greater than 3. Dashed arrows indicate weaker relationships, with t's between 1 and 2—findings that are suggestive but unimpressive and probably unreliable.[7] When no arrow joins a pair of variables, I found no (appreciable) relationship between them. Path coefficients appear beside each arrow.[8]

How do Nagel's conclusions stand up against our findings? On the whole, they do very well indeed.

His central point that heavy reliance on imprisonment fails to reduce crime is strongly upheld. The sign of the relation from incarceration to crime is ac-tually positive, the opposite of that predicted by prison advocates. The connec-tion is, however, so weak that it may be disregarded.

Table 4–2
Regression Results for Incarceration Rates across the Fifty States, 1975

Variable	Regression Coefficient	Standardized Coefficient	t Statistic
Percentage black	3.76	.67	4.96
Unemployment rate	4.40	.20	1.18
Liberalism	−.327	−.17	1.44
East region	−22.86	−.24	1.39
Crime rate	−.0003	−.01	0.05

Note: Constant = 57.59
$R^2 = .51$

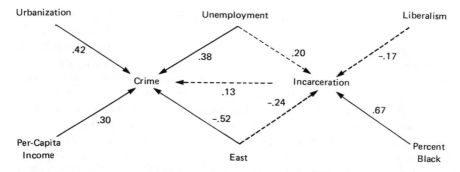

Figure 4-1. Determinants of Crime and Incarceration

Working the other way, the coefficient relating crime to incarceration rate is vanishingly small. In short, comparisons across states show that propensities to rely on imprisonment seem unrelated to variations in the prevalence of crime; and crime itself appears unresponsive in the aggregate to differences in imprisonment rates.

If crime and incarceration rates do not influence each other, on what do they depend? In our analysis, racial composition is the only important predictor of incarceration rates. Although percentage of black population has no relation to crime rates, for each 10-percent increment in black-population percentage, states tend to add 37.6 prisoners per 100,000 population. For a state with the size and black population of Georgia, this effect amounts to a prison population over 4,400 larger than it would be if the state were entirely white—enough inmates to fill five typical prisons.

This result upholds one of Nagel's major findings; but the present results somewhat undermine his emphasis on political climate as a second determinant of prison construction. Conservative states do have higher incarceration rates, but the effect is statistically weak. Additional weak ties appear for region and unemployment, with eastern states relying slightly less on imprisonment and states suffering high unemployment tending slightly to have more people in prison.

Except in one ambiguous respect, our results sustain Nagel's conclusions about the determinants of crime rates. As noted, the proportion of a state's population under the poverty level was dropped from the analysis after it had no effect in an initial ordinary least squares (OLS) run.[9] As Nagel observed, urbanized states are likely to have more crime. Even our new geographic variable (East-West region) has an effect supporting his observation that "idyllic" (most western) states actually experience more crime that the despised East. States with greater per-capita income pay a price for wealth in higher crime, a finding compatible with previous theory and evidence (Gillespie 1978).

Location and urbanization are not manipulable variables, and few would want to reduce crime by decreasing wealth, so from the policymaker's point of view, unemployment is the most important determinant of crime found in this research. The regression coefficient suggests that each 1-percent increase in unemployment may result in 266.4 more crimes per 100,000 population. More optimistically, a 1-percent decrease should reduce crimes by the same amount.

Thus, for an average state of 4 million population—about the size of Maryland—we would expect a 1-percent decline in unemployment to prevent more than 10,000 index crimes each year. If, in 1975, Maryland's unemployment had been 4 percent, the so-called full-employment level, instead of its actual 7.5 percent, citizens of the state would have suffered an estimated 32,500 fewer crimes, a 13 percent reduction.

Even more dramatic are extrapolations for large states suffering especially high unemployment. Michigan, for example, in 1975 had the nation's second-highest unemployment rate (13.8 percent), and its fifth-highest crime rate (6,771 index crimes per 100,000 population). Our results predict that, if Michigan's unemployment had been reduced to 4 percent, its crime rate would have dropped to 4160, a 39 percent decline. This means that, in one year alone, the people of Michigan would suffer about 240,000 fewer serious crimes.

Discussion

The research reported here involves a number of serious limitations. First, the crime-rate data employed are from the FBI Uniform Crime Reports. These figures are notoriously unreliable, depending as they do on local-police reports. It may be, for example, that crime seems higher in the West only because western police departments are more highly professionalized. Indeed, bad crime data may render the entire analysis useless, its only merit being to show prison advocates that they must find better numbers to support their prescriptions.

Second, we have reported our results as indicating determinants of overall crime rates, and in fact they do apply to the FBI "Total Crime Index." That index, however, as a simple summation of seven types of crime, is overwhelmingly determined by the more-frequent property crimes. Total crime rates correlate .995 with property crime but just .708 with violent crime. Therefore, our results are essentially for property crime only; in fact, when property crimes are regressed separately, the findings are virtually identical to those reported here.

I would like to be able to present a separate analysis of violent crime, which, although less frequent, causes more suffering and public anxiety. Unfortunately, I could not locate instrumental variables needed to complete the 2SLS procedure for violent crimes. The preliminary ordinary least-squares regressions do, however, indicate a somewhat different causal pattern from that which obtains for property crimes. Urbanization and unemployment affect violent-crime rates less strongly than property-crime rates. States with large black populations have more violent crime, although they have no more property crime than other states.

Third, the use of cross-sectional data weakens the inferences we can make to causation and to policy.[10] For example, we found only a weak effect of unemployment rate on incarceration rate. Previous time-series research, using both national and state data, shows that unemployment fluctuations are a strong predictor of prison admissions (Brenner 1978; Hromas and Crago 1978). A factor that changes little over time but varies markedly across states—such as percentage of black population—may dominate the cross-sectional results but not appear strongly in time-series evidence.[11] Conversely, percentage of young males, which varies little across states, has no appreciable effect in our analysis but may be an important cause of trends in the national crime rate over time.

Nevertheless, the impact we have found of unemployment on crime is quite comparable to results derived from time-series research. Brenner found that 1-percent changes in unemployment resulted in changes in crime nationally that ranged from 2.2 percent for burglary to 8.7 percent for narcotics offenses (1978, p. 15). Our corresponding cross-sectional estimate for overall index crime varies (according to the existing crime-rate base) from 3.2 percent in Arizona to 12.7 percent in West Virginia.

Finally, this study is limited by its rather crude central variables. Much of the deterrence literature, in contrast, focuses on specific categories of crime rather than on overall crime. For some policy purposes, it would also be desirable to examine the effects of the various factors that combine to determine incarceration rates—the probability that law breakers will be arrested, the probability of conviction if arrested, the probability of imprisonment if convicted, and the average length of time served. In the study most comparable to ours, Nagin (1977) did separate imprisonment risk and average length of time served. Using two-stage least-squares estimation and the frequently researched 1960 cross-section of states, he found that neither variable had a significant effect on crime rates.

In conclusion, the present study upholds Nagel's earlier analysis in throwing serious doubt on the common-sense presumptions that states build prisons in response to crime and that their reliance on imprisonment in turn reduces crime. States appear to resort to incarceration less as a solution to crime than as a response to racial divisions. As for the answer to crime, this research, like many other studies, reveals only one manipulable remedy: To reduce crime, provide jobs.

Notes

1. The initial publication was Nagel (1977).

2. For reviews of previous research in this area using state data, see Gillespie (1978) and Nagin (1977).

3. For an explanation of the method, see Heise (1975, pp. 160–195). The problem of simultaneity in criminal-justice research is discussed by Fisher and Nagin (1978).

4. Variable definitions and sources are listed in appendix 4A.

5. Barbara Boland of the Urban Institute suggested the second regional control, which turned out to be crucial.

6. See Gordon (1968).

7. A t of 1.56 is statistically significant at the .05 level (one-tailed test) for these equations; however, significance tests are not strictly appropriate here, because we are dealing with the entire population (of states) rather than with a sample. Inclusion of any variable with t greater than 1.0 increases the variance explained corrected for degrees of freedom (Haitovsky 1969).

8. See appendix 4B for a matrix of correlations among the variables.

9. See Danziger and Wheeler (1975) for an analysis of the effects of income distribution on crime across SMSAs.

10. But see Klein, Forst, and Filatov (1978) for an appreciation of some virtues of cross-sectional research.

11. Also, fluctuations in prison admissions will not strongly affect populations if authorities adaptively offset them by changing sentencing and parole practices.

References

Brenner, M.H. 1978. "Impact of Economic Indicators on Crime Indices." Statement and testimony in U.S. Congress, *Unemployment and Crime,* pp. 20–54.

Danziger, S. and D. Wheeler. 1975. "The Economics of Crime: Punishment or Income Redistribution." *Review of Social Economy* 33:113–131.

Fisher, F.M. and D. Nagin. 1978. "On the Feasibility of Identifying the Crime Function in a Simultaneous Model of Crime Rates and Sanction Levels." In National Research Council, *Deterrence and Incapacitation,* pp. 361–399.

Gillespie, R.W. 1978. "Economic Factors in Crime and Delinquency: A Critical Review of the Empirical Evidence." Report to the National Institute of Law Enforcement and Criminal Justice, reprinted in U.S. Congress, *Unemployment and Crime,* pp. 601–626.

Gordon, R.A. 1968. "Issues in Multiple Regression." *American Journal of Sociology* 73:592–616.

Haitovsky, Y. 1969. "A Note on the Maximization of R^2," *American Statistician* 23:20–21.

Heise, D.R. 1975. *Causal Analysis.* New York: Wiley.

Hromas, C.S. and T.G. Craco. 1978. "Population Projections: Past and Present." Office of Research and Evaluation, Department of Corrections, State of Colorado.

Klein, L.R., B. Forst, and V. Filatov. 1978. "The Deterrent Effect of Capital Punishment: An Assessment of the Estimates." In National Research Council, *Deterrence and Incapacitation,* pp. 336-360.

Nagel, W.G. 1977. "On Behalf of a Moratorium on Prison Construction." *Crime and Delinquency* 23:154-172.

Nagin, D. 1977. "Crime Rates, Sanction Levels, and Constraints on Prison Population." Working Paper, Center for the Study of Justice Policy, Institute of Policy Sciences and Public Affairs, Duke University.

National Research Council. 1978. *Deterrence and Incapacitation.* Washington, D.C.: National Academy of Sciences.

U.S. Congress, House, Judiciary Committee, Subcommittee on Crime. 1978. *Unemployment and Crime.* Washington, D.C.: U.S. Government Printing Office.

Appendix 4A:
Variable Definitions and
Data Sources

Incarceration rate Prisoners per 100,000 population, 1975. National Clearing-house on Criminal Justice Planning and Architecture.

Crime rate Total index crimes per 100,000 population, 1975. FBI *Uniform Crime Reports.*

Liberalism Average annual ratings of U.S. senators by Americans for Democratic Action, 1955 to 1975.

Percentage urban Percentage of population living in Standard Metropolitan Statistical Areas in 1975. U.S. Census, *Current Population Reports,* series P-25, no. 618. 1975 SMSA estimate extrapolated from 1970 to 1974 change in SMSA population.

Percentage black Estimated 1975 black population as percentage of 1975 total population. Black population projected from 1970 census figure using same growth rate as overall state population between 1970 and 1975.

Unemployment rate Unemployment as percentage of labor force. Preliminary 1975 average from U.S. Department of Labor, *Income and Earnings Magazine,* June 1976, p. 312.

Income per capita Preliminary 1974 estimate from U.S. Census, *Statistical Abstract,* 1975.

Percentage low-income Percentage of persons below poverty-income level, 1969. U.S. Census, *Census of Population,* 1970, vol. 1.

Black migration Percentage change in black population, 1960 to 1970. U.S. Census, *Current Population Reports,* series P-25, no. 460.

Percentage young males Percentage of population who were males aged 15 to 24 in 1970. U.S. Census, *Statistical Abstract,* 1975.

East-West States counted as eastern (=1– if east of Mississippi River, Minnesota and Louisiana included.

South-North States counted southern (=1) if part of the Confederacy.

Appendix 4B:
Correlation Matrix of Variables Appearing in Final Regressions

	Incarceration	Urbanization	Unemployment	Income	East	Black Population	Liberalism
Crime	.28	.58	.42	.54	−.19	−.08	.10
Incarceration	−	.09	.22	−.11	.18	.65	−.39
Urbanization		−	.43	.43	.29	.22	.27
Unemployment			−	.21	.46	.21	.07
Income				−	.02	−.20	.25
East					−	.51	.06
Black population						−	−.32

Part II
Innovations in Juvenile Corrections

5 Juvenile Justice in America

Bruce Bullington, Daniel Katkin, and Drew Hyman

Introduction

For the student of social policy the history of juvenile-justice systems provides a dramatic example of persistent failure to achieve laudable goals. The humanitarian rhetoric that gave impetus to the development of juvenile courts and reform schools for youthful offenders has always been more honored in the breech than in the observance. The turn-of-the-century reformers who campaigned to decriminalize delinquency (that is, to divest criminal courts of jurisdiction in cases involving misbehaving children) hoped to create nonadversarial, nonpunitive programs that would provide therapeutic, regenerative services to delinquents. The goal, as Judge Julian Mack put it, was to restore the child to the "right path that leads to good, sound adult citizenship" (Mack 1925, pp. 311-312).

In the years between 1899 and 1925, the social policy of reforming delinquents was enthusiastically embraced. Systems of juvenile justice were established in virtually all American Jurisdictions. Although the existence of reform schools can be traced to the early 1800s, they experienced a massive expansion as part of the development of children's courts and therapeutic justice (Rothman 1971, pp. 207-209, Katz 1968, pp. 163-212). The emerging clinical professions, including psychiatry, psychology, and social work, assumed the mandate to administer therapeutic justic to children. Yet things went awry.

In 1937, Dean Roscoe Pound of the Harvard Law School observed that the potentially abusive powers of the Juvenile Court had grown to be as awesome as those of the Star Chamber (Pound 1937). Twenty years later Dean Francis Allen of the University of Michigan Law School wrote a persuasive essay to the effect that very little helpful treatment was actually provided to delinquents and that the jargon of psychotherapy was often used euphemistically to disguise traditional punitive practices (Allen 1959). In the following decade, this viewpoint dominated the field of juvenile justice. In the 1960s and early 1970s, the administration of juvenile justice was attacked as ineffective, unfair, and even criminogenic by such respectable sources as Howard James of the *Christian Science Monitor,* Edwin Newman of the news department of the National Broadcasting Corporation, Judge Lisa Richette of the Philadelphia Family Court, Senator Birch Bayh, the President's Commission on Law Enforcement and Administration of Justice, The National Advisory Commission on Criminal Justice Standards and Goals, and the U.S. Supreme Court. Even the chairman of the National Association of

State Juvenile Delinquency Program Administrators went on record saying: "With the exception of a relatively few youths it (would be) better for all concerned if young delinquents were not detected, apprehended, or institutionalized. Too many of them get worse in our care (James 1970, p. 99)."

Amidst all this antagonism toward the status quo, professional and scholarly literature began to propose reforms that posited that the needs both of delinquents and of society could best be served by reducing the jurisdiction of traditional juvenile-justice agencies. Diversion, deinstitutionalization, and the decriminalization of status offenders were all advertised as strategies that would minimize contact between misbehaving children and the established agencies of juvenile justice.[1]

In a remarkably short time national policy on delinquency underwent major revision reflected in a great many legal documents. Between 1966 and 1971 the Supreme Court ordered significant changes in the procedures of juvenile courts in several landmark opinions. In the first of these, the Court observed:

> Some juvenile courts . . . lack the personnel, facilities and techniques to perform adequately as representatives of the State in a *parens patria* capacity, at least with respect to children charged with law violation. There is evidence, in fact, that there may be grounds for concern that the child receives the worst of both worlds: that he gets neither the protections afforded adults nor the solicitous care and regenerative treatment postulated for children (*Kent* v. *U.S.*, 383 U.S. 355, 1966).

Study commissions and agencies associated with the executive branch of the national government also endorsed the reform of juvenile justice, in two major documents. Indeed, the origins of the concept of diversion are commonly attributed to the 1967 report of a President's Commission, which concluded that: "The formal sanctioning system and the pronouncement of delinquency should be used only as a last resort. In place of the formal system, dispositional alternatives to adjudication must be developed for dealing with juveniles, including necessary control without unnecessary stigma" (President's Commission 1967, p. 171). In 1973, The National Advisory Commission on Criminal Justice Standards and Goals endorsed the development of diversionary programs on a vast scale, which might, if effected, lead to a 50-percent reduction in the number of cases coming before juvenile courts in the next decade (National Advisory Commission 1973, pp. 23-25).

The policy of restructuring the administration of juvenile justice through diversion, deinstitutionalization, and the decriminalization of status offenders was enacted into law in 1974 in a statute commonly referred to as the Bayh Act. The explicit intention of this act is to "identify those youth who are victimized or otherwise troubled but have not committed criminal offenses and to divert such youth from institutionalization" (P.L. 93-415, 1974). The law provides for developing innovative alternatives to prevent delinquency and to divert status offenders from the criminal-justice system. Moreover, the act even includes a mechanism to promote compliance among the states: the threat of withholding federal support for delinquency programs in jurisdictions that fail to pursue these goals.

Since 1974, there has been a flurry of activity by state and local governments to achieve compliance with the Bayh Act and thus ensure continued eligibility for federal funds (Sprowls 1980). For the better part of a decade, it has been indisputable that the formal policy of the United States (jointly and severally) has been to promote programs that would reduce the jurisdiction and resources of existing juvenile-justice systems in favor of innovative community alternatives.

The central thesis of this chapter is that these reforms have not been implemented. Indeed, they have been sabotaged and coopted so as to produce results directly contrary to those intended: the authority and resources of the traditional agencies of juvenile justice have actually been augmented. To a people accustomed to the idea of the rule of law this result may seem perplexing; but to policy scientists it is almost a regular affair. Studies of controversial decisions of the Supreme Court have consistently revealed imperfect patterns of implementation (Friedman and Macauley 1969; Becker and Feeley 1973); and specific studies of the reform process in juvenile-justice systems have often found resistance to change and abuses of discretion (Stapleton and Teitelbaum 1972; Sprowls 1980). It is not surprising that some observers predicted the eventual cooptation or destruction of diversionary programs almost as soon as the idea first emerged (Morris 1974). It appears that the skeptics have been right.

Perhaps the most conspicuous evidence that this is so is the simple observation that the rhetoric of reform has been enthusiastically embraced by the very agencies whose power and influence were to decrease. Judges, probation officers, police, and correctional officials have almost universally adopted the terms diversion, deinstitutionalization, and decriminalization as their own; furthermore, their established agencies administer most of the programs that claim to be based on these reforms. In short, the reform movement has not reduced the numbers of young people brought into the formal system of social control; rather it has produced a "widening of the nets" to encompass ever-increasing numbers of young people in an increasingly comprehensive system of control.

In the remainder of this chapter, we shall present evidence about each of the reforms to demonstrate the gap between the intentions of the policymakers and the reality implemented.

Rhetoric and Reality in the Reform of Juvenile Justice

Initially two observations must be made that limit the certainty with which conclusions may be drawn. The first of these is the existence of definitional ambiguity of such magnitude that a single term may take on almost contradictory meanings. Donald Cressey and Robert McDermott, for example, have noted the difference between diverting children from the formal processes of juvenile justice and diverting them to something else:

> If "true" diversion occurs, the juvenile is safely out of the official realm of the juvenile justice system and he is immune from incurring the delinquent label or any of its variations—predelinquent, delinquent tendencies, bad guy, hard core, unreachable. Further, when he walks out the door from the person diverting him, he is technically free to tell the diverter to go to hell. We found very little "true" diversion in the communities studied (Cressey and McDermott 1974, pp. 3–4).

Cressey and McDermott go on to observe that although "true diversion" does not exist, some progress has been made in developing alternative programs that may be less stigmatizing than juvenile courts and reform schools. These new programs still seem to involve elements of coerced participation. Youth-service bureaus, for example, may claim to be voluntary, but frequently their clients know that nonparticipation in programs may result in referrals back to the justice system.

The second preliminary observation is that the literature describing programs of diversion, deinstitutionalization, and decriminalization, although voluminous (a bibliography compiled by the U.S. Department of Justice lists almost 2,200 titles), is often plagued by serious methodological problems. Thus the validity of some findings can be brought into question.

Despite these qualifications, the evidence that the reform movement has been turned back in favor of business-as-usual is very persuasive. We demonstrate this by contrasting expectations for change implied by the reform rhetoric with findings about the current operations of juvenile-justice systems.

Rhetoric and Reality about the Power and Resources of Juvenile-Justice Systems

The reform movement of the late 1960s was based on a widespread perception that the juvenile-justice system had failed to achieve its social mandate. Decriminalization, deinstitutionalization, and diversion all suggest dismantling of traditional agencies. A major purpose of the reform movement was to reduce the jurisdiction and resources of juvenile courts and reform schools. Youngsters would be diverted from the juvenile-justice system to other social-service agencies. So-called hard-core youngsters who remained in the system would be kept away from institutions in favor of more normal environments. Expectations for change derived from the critical literature of the late 1960s and early 1970s embrace the following:

1. The number of cases processed by juvenile courts would decrease as a consequence of the removal of status offenders and the diversion of petty offenders.
2. The formal agencies of juvenile justice would be left with responsibility for a comparatively small number of serious offenders.
3. There would be a reduction in the number of institutionalized youths, with a concommitant reduction in the number of institutional facilities.
4. A corollary of reduced dependence on expensive institutional programs would be increased cost-effectiveness in the programs working with those delinquents who remained in the system.[2]

It appears, however, that the net effect of reform activity has been to expand the power and resources of the traditional agencies of juvenile justice. Nationwide data indicate a steady increase in the rates of young people processed by juvenile courts between 1957 and 1977 (Smith 1980). This trend was neither reversed nor halted in the most recent period for which data exist (1975–1977). Nor does it appear that the types of youths brought to court are, on average, more serious offenders than in the past. The rate of status offenders brought to court has decreased 18.2 percent (Smith 1980). The decrease seems small in light of the purposes of the Bayh Act; the numbers continue to be high, probably, because most status offenders are brought to court by their parents. Interestingly, however, the percentage of petitions filed for offenses against persons has decreased 7.6 percent and the percentage of petitions filed for property offenses has increased 12.3 percent (Smith 1980). Because the property-offense totals are far larger than the other two categories, the result is an overall net increase. In short, the population of the juvenile-justice system has expanded, and its characteristics have changed but little.

Satisfactory census data do not exist to permit certain conclusions about the size of institutionalized populations. Contradictory conclusions can be drawn from two nationwide studies. Federal-government statistics indicate a 7-percent decrease in the number of juveniles held in public facilities, combined with a 7-percent increase in the private sector, producing an overall decrease of 2 percent between 1975 and 1977 (LEAA 1979). The impact of this modest decrease is, however, sharply undermined by the observation that "the average length of stay in private long-term facilities was 58 percent greater than in their public counterparts"; these averages were 291 and 184 days (LEAA 1979, p. 1). Data of apparently comparable validity collected by the National Center for Juvenile Justice show an increase in juveniles held in public facilities and a decrease in those held in private. These data also indicate that the number of juveniles held in state prisons (the most-restrictive-possible alternative) has gone up from 1,970 in 1973 to 2,697 in 1979 (Lowell and McNabb 1980). In any event, there is no evidence that suggests a widespread decrease in the use of institutions for juveniles.

Only one jurisdiction (Massachusetts) has undertaken a large-scale deinstitutionalization in the field of juvenile justice. Despite this effort's apparent success (Ohlin, Coates, and Miller 1974), it has been attacked as ineffective by many detractors. Attempts to replicate the Massachusetts experience in other jurisdication (notably Illinois and Pennsylvania) have failed (Lowell 1978; Mattingly 1977).

Even in Massachusetts, reversion to a more traditional approach may be imminent. A special gubernatorial taskforce recently released recommendations that call for substantial changes in that state's juvenile-justice system, including doubling the number of secure beds and reinstatement of commitment powers to judges (Governor's Task Force 1981).

Nor is there any evidence nationally that the programs available in institutional facilities have improved significantly. The warehousing of young people continues to be a common policy in juvenile corrections.

In inflationary times, it may have been unrealistic to expect a reduction in costs. However, the Law Enforcement Assistance Administration (LEAA) reports a 12-percent nationwide increase in the number of employees in private juvenile facilities and a 40-percent increase in expenditures between mid-1975 and the end of 1977 (LEAA 1979). Moreover, while a study of California diversion projects found that "an average savings of $31.95 occurred for each *diversion* client who was referred from a justice system source," many clients were youths who ordinarily would not have been processed at all; thus there was a substantial overall increase in expenditures (Palmer, Bohnstidt, and Lewis 1978, p. 2). Although data about the public sector are incomplete, it seems likely that there has been a net increase in expenditures for juvenile justice.

In summary, the reform movement anticipated a withering away of traditional mechanisms of juvenile justice. Reform implementation has produced no such result. Instead, as Pabon's review of the literature led him to conclude:

> Existing research studies on diversion and deinstitutionalization . . . indicate that the principal effects of these programs are . . . : (1) greater numbers and types of juveniles contacted . . . , (2) expansion of the system, and (3) alternative encapsulation, or the removal of youths to other forms of incarceration that are as restrictive as the first (Pabon 1978, p. 493).

Rhetoric and Reality about Coercion and Stigma

It was intended that the reform movement would produce a network of community alternatives that would be more effective than the traditional agencies in pursuing the best interests of children in trouble. This policy incorporates the following elements.

1. There would be a proliferation of community-based programs to which delinquents would be diverted; they which would be noncoercive, nonstigmatizing, and most importantly, administered outside the formal institutions of juvenile justice.

2. The underlying philosophy of these new programs was advocacy for troubled youth to ensure that community institutions (schools, child welfare, health and social services, for example) would provide alternative services to children who otherwise would be caught in the juvenile-justice system.

3. Status offenders in particular would be placed in different and less restrictive environments than delinquents or adult offenders. They would cease to be processed by police and the courts.[3]

It appears that these expectations have not been fulfilled. There has been a substantial increase in the number of community-based programs, but available evidence suggests that these programs tend to be coercive, stigmatizing, and encapsulating rather than diversionary. Prior to the Bayh Act, some states had developed new official labels for status offenders, and after passage of the new federal law other states followed suit. Status offenders are no longer delinquents but are rather PINS (persons in need of supervision), CHINS (children in need of supervision), or JINS (juveniles in need of supervision). The purpose of these changes was to encourage less stigmatizing and less restrictive treatment of children who had committed no criminal acts (for example, runaways). Nevertheless, "recent studies indicate that despite the nondelinquent status accorded children in need of supervision," from 25 to 40 percent of the boys and some 70 percent of the girls in jails, detention homes, and correctional institutions are in this category. Also, they report that such children generally remain longer in institutions than those committed for acts of delinquency" (Ward 1979, p. 46). Hickey (1977) concludes a nationwide study of status offenses in the juvenile court by noting that despite the separate legal category, a juvenile who has committed a status offense will often be handled the same as serious offenders. These youngsters continued to be handled through the same juvenile courts, with virtually identical processing and results.

Thus, it appears that the condition of status offenders has not been substantially ameliorated by the development of community-based programs. It is questionable whether being labeled PINS, MINS, or CHINS is less stigmatizing than being labeled delinquent, particularly since the processing and treatment are so similar. Indeed, it can be argued that the total amount of stigmatization induced by agencies of juvenile justice has increased.

This line of argument is derived not only from the perspective that the stigmatization and coercive treatment of status offenders are as extensive as ever (and these noncriminal youngsters were the first priorities of the reform movement), but also from the evidence presented earlier about the expansion of the juvenile-justice system.[4] As the number of youths committed to institutions has not decreased appreciably, and there has been a proliferation of new diversionary programs, it appears that the clients of these programs are youths who might genuinely have been diverted in the past. Much of the literature reflects this point. Don Gibbons and Gerald Blake, for example, concluded an evaluation of nine diversion programs as follows: "Diversion, growing out of the sociologist's recommendations of 'radical nonintervention,' 'benign neglect,' or 'judicial nonintervention,' has become perverted in practice into a strategem that swells the population of acted upon offenders" (Gibbons and Blake 1976, p. 413). Andrew Rutherford and Osmar Bengur take the same position: "The development of community corrections is not associated with reduced rates of institutional incarceration. States that place more offenders in community-based programs do not place fewer in training schools although there are exceptions. In general as the number of offenders in community-based facilities increases, the total number of youth incarcerated increases" (Rutherford and Bengur 1976, p. 30).

In short, it appears that the net effect of the reform movement has been to leave institutional facilities intact with populations of roughly the same size as ever, to leave status offenders in the same conditions as ever (albeit under new labels), and to create a network of new agencies and borrowed services for youths who in the past would probably have been left alone. Often these youngsters (and their families) are brought into diversion programs under the threat that noncooperation will result in juvenile-court litigation. Thus, it appears that the population at risk is more than ever subject to coercive and potentially stigmatizing treatment from the juvenile-justice system.

Conclusion: The Failure of Reform

Having demonstrated that the implementation of the national policy to develop programs of diversion, deinstitutionalization, and decriminalization has produced results directly contradictory to those anticipated, it is appropriate to speculate about the causes of this anomaly.

Definitional Ambiguity

In the absence of definitional precision the agencies of juvenile justice have been able to coopt the movement to their own ends. The terms diversion, deinstitutionalization, and decriminalization, as used by the reformers, refer to a process of divesting traditional agencies of responsibility for youngsters in favor of diversion to other community resources, including noncoercive counseling, family, and being left alone. In practice, however, existing structures have been able to seize on the opportunities offered by new legislation and funding to enhance their own positions. Several studies point out that many, perhaps most, of the new programs are run by police and probation officers and other traditional-system professionals. Furthermore, this has happened with few changes in traditional practices. Malcolm Klein found few structural changes in police departments to accomodate diversion: "In most instances, new units are not established, additional staff are not assigned, work routines are not substantially altered, lines of supervision are not shifted, etc. Diversion has been appended rather than incorporated" (Klein 1976, p. 127). And Thomas Blomberg concluded that "organizationally, diversion became an extension of informal probation" (1977, p. 276). Although this involves comparatively few restrictions for most clients, it nevertheless invariably involves the possibility of coercive intervention for behavior that probation officers consider inappropriate.

Financial Inducements to Almost Everyone

The implementation of these reforms was largely dependent on block grants to state and local governments. This practice occurred without appropriate safeguards to ensure that applicants using the reform labels actually embodied reform goals, it allowed differences in state systems to be continued, and it gave an advantage to existing agencies with expertise in grantsmanship. Furthermore, as the funds flowed through agencies closely aligned with existing-system personnel (for example, governor's justice commissions, which include members of the existing criminal-justice departments of the state government), the review and approval process was influenced in the direction of traditional points of view.

Organizational and Interorganizational Pressures

It is not surprising that existing agencies, under the pressure to survive, were compelled to compete for the new resources. In addition, innovative-service vendors had to meet the approval of judges, police, and probation personnel to ensure that their facilities would be utilized and to secure political support for funding applications. These processes inhibited genuine reform by forcing assimilative pressures on would-be innovators, who often find themselves needing the support and assistance of agents of the status quo.

The National Mood

The conservative tone of national politics and the abandonment of the rehabilitative ideal in adult-justice systems in favor of fixed, determinate, just-deserts sentencing also appear to have influenced the juvenile-justice system. The emphasis in the media on dangerous and violent youth encourages a punitive public response—despite the fact that statistics reflect a decrease in arrests for youthful crimes of violence (Smith 1980).

Inappropriate Evaluation Criteria

One might expect that policymakers and officials responsible for implementation would have criteria for tracking and evaluating the progress of the reforms. As it happens, however, most programs have been evaluated not in terms of their capacity to promote diversion but in terms of recidivism, a questionable evaluative standard in most circumstances, especially when the central research question involves the system's behavior, not its clients' failures. Furthermore, it is worth noting that, although the preponderance of evaluative-research evidence on programs of diversion, deinstitutionalization, and decriminalization shows that little diversion has occurred, this information has had little impact on shaping policy or the pattern of its implementation.

A Tentative Proposal for Reform

The absence of an external watchdog agency with oversight responsibility allows the many agencies in a fragmented system to interpret policy and to implement programs in their own best interests without fear of review. Thus, there has been no authoritative barrier to the process of cooptation by traditional agencies. Given this conclusion, it seems safe to predict that little meaningful change can take place in the present system. The attempts of the last decade to minimize the reach of the juvenile-justice system have had the net effect of actually broadening its power and authority.

Given this reality, it seems unrealistic for reformers to expect that the present system can be successfully circumvented. If circumventing the official juvenile-justice system is impracticable, then the task for researchers and reform-oriented policymakers is to explore changes that will generate greater responsiveness within the existing system to the goals espoused in relevant legislation.

Some agency must emerge with sufficient power to secure compliance with the law and to monitor the activities and interactions of the cooperating and competing elements of juvenile-justice systems. A new watchdog agency might be contemplated; however, unless this agency had extensive budgetary control its influence would be limited. In existing juvenile-justice systems the greatest concentration of power generally resides in the juvenile-court judiciary. Judges are powerful local politicians, they have prestige, they are often able to secure compliance through persuasion, and when persuasion fails coercion (for example, through the contempt power) is possible. The key to successful reform may lie in increasing the power of the judiciary and expecting the courts to see that the agencies with which they work are in compliance with legislative standards.

Since past research indicates that juvenile-court judges do not always implement the law precisely as it is written (Stapleton and Teitelbaum 1972; Sprowls 1980), it may be thought that increasing their authority is like putting the fox in charge of the hen house. Additional changes will be necessary. We suggest that active and broad appellate review of juvenile-court decisions be considered. Specifically, a judicial commission would set clear guidelines for juvenile judges to follow, and the appellate courts would apply these guidelines in reviewing the decisions of the lower courts, thus generating organizational pressures toward compliance. In this manner fragmenting juvenile-justice systems might gradually be rationalized and brought more fully within the rule of law.

Notes

1. *Diversion* has been important both in juvenile-justice and mental-health systems. The central idea is that interactions with these systems are actually damaging to clients and that the best interests of misbehaving children and or emotionally disturbed young persons are served by minimizing formal interventions. Thus, doing nothing is often preferred to doing anything, and community-based interventions are preferred to institutional treatment (See, for example, Schur 1973). *Deinstitutionalization* generally refers to the process of reducing the size of incarcerated populations by expanding community-based resources, by utilizing institutional commitments only in the cases of very serious offenders, and by providing shorter sentences for those who are incarcerated. In a more radical sense the term refers to the actual closing of whole institutions and institutional systems (as in the case of Massachusetts) in favor of less restrictive alternatives, such as community-based advocacy efforts. The deinstitutionalization movement has been concerned not only with juvenile justice but also with adult corrections and mental-health facilities. *Status offenses* refer to acts for which children can be adjudicated delinquent but for which adults could not be convicted. Most states include a number of these offenses in their juvenile codes; truancy, runaways, incorrigibility, curfew, and underage drinking are typical examples.

2. Among the important works of this type are: Nicholas Kittrie, *The Right to Be Different* (Baltimore: Johns Hopkins, 1971); National Advisory Commission on Criminal Justice Standards and Goals, *A National Strategy to Reduce Crime* (U.S. Government Printing Office, 1973); Lisa Richette, *The Throwaway Children* (Philadelphia: J.B. Lippincott, 1969); Kenneth Wooden, *Weeping in the Playtime of Others* (New York: McGraw-Hill, 1976).

3. Some works on this theme include: C. Wilson Anderson, *Juvenile Justice: A Stance for Cooperation* (State College, Penn.: Pennsylvania State University,

1974); "The Rights of Children," *Harvard Educational Review,* vols. 43 and 44 (November 1973 and February 1974), Daniel Katkin, Drew Hyman, and John Kramer, *Delinquency and the Juvenile Justice System* (North Scituate, Mass.: Duxbury Press, 1976); Lisa Richette, *The Throwaway Children* (Philadelphia: J.B. Lippincott, 1969).

4. The nature of stigmatization and its psychosocial effects have been most sensitively explored by Erving Goffman. See, for example, *Asylums* (Chicago: Aldine, 1968), and *Stigma* (Englewood Cliffs, N.J.: Prentice-Hall, 1963).

References

Allen, Francis A. "Criminal Justice, Legal Values, and the Rehabilitative Ideal." *Journal of Criminal Law, Criminology and Police Science.* 50(September-October 1959):226–232.

Anderson, C. Wilson. *Juvenile Justice: A Stance for Cooperation.* State College, Penn.: Pennsylvania State University, College of Human Development, 1974.

Becker, T.L. and M.M. Feeley. *The Impact of Supreme Court Decisions,* 2d ed. New York: Oxford University Press, 1973.

Blomberg, Thomas, "Diversion and Accelerated Social Control." *Journal of Criminal Law, Criminology and Police Science* 68(June 1977):274–282.

Cressey, Donald R. and Robert A. McDermott. *Diversion from the Juvenile Justice System.* Washington, D.C.: National Institute of Law Enforcement and Criminal Justice, 1974.

Friedman, L.M. and S. Macauley, eds. *Law and the Behavioral Sciences.* Indianapolis, Ind.: Bobbs-Merrill, 1969.

Gibbons, Don C. and Gerald F. Blake, "Evaluating the Impact of Juvenile Diversion Programs." *Crime and Delinquency* 22(October 1976):411–420.

Goffman, Erving. *Asylums.* Chicago: Aldine, 1968.

_____. *Stigma.* Englewood Cliffs, N.J.: Prentice-Hall, 1963.

Hickey, William L. "Status Offenses and the Juvenile Court." *Criminal Justice Abstracts* 9(March 1977):91–123.

James, Howard. *Children in Trouble: A National Scandal.* New York: D. McKay, 1970.

Juvenile Justice and Delinquency Act of 1974, 93rd Congress, 2nd sess.; 42 U.S.C. section 5633 (Supp. IV, 1974).

Kaplan, John. *Criminal Justice: Introductory Cases and Materials.* New York: Foundation Press, 1973, pp. 217–219.

Katkin, Daniel, Drew Hyman, and John Kramer. *Delinquency and the Juvenile Justice System.* North Scituate, Mass.: Duxbury Press, 1976.

Katz, Michael B. *The Irony of Early School Reform.* Boston: Beacon Press, 1968.

Kent v. United States, 383 U.S. 541, 1966.

Kittrie, Nicholas. *The Right to be Different.* Baltimore: Johns Hopkins, 1971.

Klein, Malcolm W. "Issues in Police Diversion of Juvenile Officers: A Guide for Discussion." In *Juvenile Justice Management,* edited by Gary B. Adams, Springfield, Ill.: Charles C. Thomas, 1973, pp. 375-422.

———. "Issues and Realities in Police Diversion Programs." *Crime and Delinquency* 22(October 1976):421-427.

Law Enforcement Assistance Administration (LEAA). *Children in Custody: Advance Report of the 1977 Census of Private Juvenile Facilities.* no. 50 JD-5B, September, 1979.

Lowell, Harvey D. and Margaret McNabb. *Sentenced Prisoners under 18 Years of Age in Adult Correctional Facilities: A National Survey.* Washington, D.C.: The National Center on Institutions and Alternatives, 1980.

———. "Policy Implementation and Organizational Change: The Case of the Camp Hill Project." Doctoral dissertation; Pennsylvania State University, 1980.

Mack, J. "The Changing Procedures in the Juvenile Court." in *The Child, the Clinic and the Court,* edited by J. Addams, New York: New Republic, 1925.

Mattingly, John. "The Management of Change: Juvenile Justice and Social Policy Innovation." Doctoral dissertation; Pennsylvania State University, 1979.

Morris, Norval. *The Future of Imprisonment.* Chicago: University of Chicago Press, 1974.

National Advisory Commission on Criminal Justice Standards and Goals. *A National Strategy to Reduce Crime.* Washington, D.C.: U.S. Government Printing Office, 1973.

Ohlin, Lloyd, Robert B. Coates, and Alden D. Miller. "Radical Correctional Reform: A Case Study of the Massachusetts Youth Correctional System." In *The Rights of Children.* Boston: The Harvard Educational Review, 1974, pp. 120-157.

Pabon, Edward. "Here We Go Again—The Child Savers." *Juvenile Justice* 28 (February 1977):41-45.

———. "Changes in Juvenile Justice: Evolution or Reform." *Social Work* 23 (November 1978):492-497.

Palmer, Ted, Marvin Bohnstedt, and Roy Lewis. *The Evaluation of Juvenile Diversion Projects: Final Report.* Sacramento, Calif.: Department of the Youth Authority, 1978.

Pound, R. Foreword to Young, *Social Treatment in Probation and Delinquency.* New York: McGraw-Hill, 1937.

President's Commission on Law Enforcement and the Administration of Justice. *The Challenge of Crime in a Free Society.* Washington, D.C.: U.S. Government Printing Office, 1967.

Richette, Lisa. *The Throwaway Children.* Philadelphia: J.B. Lippincott, 1969.

Rothman, David. *The Discovery of the Asylum.* Boston: Little, Brown, 1971.

_____. *Conscience and Convenience.* Boston: Little, Brown, 1980.

Rutherford, Andrew and Osmar Bengur. *Community-Based Alternatives to Juvenile Incarceration.* Washington, D.C.: Law Enforcement Assistance Administration, 1976.

Schur, Edwin. *Radical Nonintervention.* Englewood Cliffs, N.J.: Prentice-Hall, 1973.

Skolnick, Jerome. *Justice without Trial: Law Enforcement in a Democratic Society.* New York: Wiley, 1966.

Smith, Daniel, D.; Terrence Finnegan; and Howard N. Snyder. *Delinquency 1977: United States Estimates of Cases Processed by Courts with Juvenile Jurisdication.* Pittsburgh, Penn.: National Center for Juvenile Justice, 1980.

Sprowls, James T. *"Discretion and Lawlessness: Compliance in the Juvenile Court."* Doctoral dissertation, Pennsylvania State University, 1980.

Stapleton, W.; Vaughan Teitelbaum; and Lee E. Teitelbaum. *In Defense of Youth.* New York: Russell Sage, 1972.

Ward, Frederick. "Prevention and Diversion in the United States." In *The Changing Faces of Juvenile Justice,* edited by V. Lorne Stewart. New York: New York University Press, 1979.

Wooden, Kenneth. *Weeping in the Playtime of Others.* New York: McGraw-Hill, 1976.

6

A Statute Backfires: The Escalation of Youth Incarceration in England during the 1970s

Andrew Rutherford

The Children and Young Persons' Act of 1969 was intended to herald a less punitive approach to juvenile offenders in England and Wales. One of the act's key sections, section 7, removes from courts the power to sentence "young persons" (aged 14-16) to detention centers and borstals (reform schools).[1] The provisions under section 7 were to be activated once local government had developed adequate sentencing alternatives. Over the next decade virtually no progress was made by local government in this regard, and section 7 was not brought into effect. During this period the incarceration of young persons in detention centers and borstals, institutions administered by the Prison Department of the Home Office, continued to escalate both numerically and as a percentage of all sentences.[2] The number of young persons sentenced to detention centers and borstals between 1960 and 1978 increased at a rate three times that of the increase in offenses recorded by the police, and at a rate nearly three times that of the increase in known offenders aged 14-16. The details are set in table 6-1.

In October 1980, the government announced its intention to repeal the two provisions of the 1969 act, a part of its legislative proposals with regard to young-adult and juvenile offenders (White Paper 1980). This chapter explores the failure to implement these provisions of the act and examines why the legislation as a whole was so singularly unsuccessful in reducing the number of young persons sentenced to Prison Department custody.

Background to the 1969 Act

The 1960s were characterized by a mood of qualified optimism about reducing juvenile delinquency. First, there were socialist critiques of the legal process as a means of handling the problems of youth in trouble and their families.[3] There was some disappointment that the Ingleby Report (1960) had endorsed the existing formal apparatus of the juvenile court, and a growing expectation that a future Labour government would be more bold.[4] The Longford Report (1964)—a Labour-party review of criminal-justice problems, published just a few months before the general election—called for the replacement of juvenile

The author is grateful to Tony Bottoms for comments on an earlier version of this chapter.

73

Table 6–1

Young Persons Sentenced to Detention Centers and Borstals, Known
Offenders (Aged 14–16), and Offenses Recorded by Police, 1960–1978

	Detention Center		Borstal		Known Offenders (Cautions and Guilt Findings)	Offenses (Recorded by Police)
	Number	Percent of All Sentences	Number	Percent of All Sentences		
1960	605	1.7	171	0.6	32,350	800,323
1965	952	2.5	151	0.3	45,428	1,243,463
1971	2,061	4.4	1,285	2.4	74,989	1,665,663
1975	4,296	7.1	1,680	2.5	106,871	2,105,631
1978	5,528	8.5	1,860	2.5	116,171	2,395,757

Source: *Criminal Statistics*, England and Wales, 1960–1978.
Note: Figures refer to indictable offenses only.

courts by procedures providing "treatment" that was "without stigma." A
second, and separate, line of criticism of traditional practice was levelled by
members of the emerging social-work profession, which was to have more direct
impact in Scotland than in England and Wales (Kilbrandon 1964).[5] Once Labour came to power, in October 1964, officials in the Home Office began to
synthesize the socialist commentaries with social-work concepts.[6]

This attempted fusion found its first expression in a white paper that immediately encountered a hostile reception from the magistracy and probation
officers (White Paper 1965). The disagreements on this issue between probation
officers and social workers (employed by local-government children's departments) were in part substantive (issues such as due process) but also territorial,
with anticipated gains by social workers at the expense of probation and the
courts. Such was the strength of the opposition that the white paper was with-
drawn, to be replaced three years later by another white paper (1968), which
formed the basis of the 1969 act. The juvenile court was retained, but the new
statute removed the power of the judge to issue an "approved school order"—
that is, an order that specifically sentenced a youth to an approved school.
Instead, under the 1969 law the magistrate could only issue a "care order,"
which gave the local authority (and its social-work department, in effect) the
discretion to decide where to send an errant juvenile—back to home, to foster
care, or to a residential school. Magistrates were especially concerned that their
power to sentence youths to approved schools was being ended.

The white paper also contained important new proposals to remove powers
to sentence young persons to detention centers and borstals, but it suggested
that this would best be achieved through a sequential strategy as new alternatives

became available. Consequently, section 7 (and certain other provisions) of the 1969 act were not brought into force when most of the act took effect on 1 January 1971.[7]

Successive governments have been totally unsuccessful in the implementation of this sequential strategy. Far from reducing the number of young persons sentenced to Prison Department institutions and eventually activating section 7 of the act, the number of borstal and detention-center sentences have escalated. These are four principal reasons for the failure of the 1969 act to reduce the incarceration of young offenders:

1. The issue of incarceration was sidestepped.
2. Central government is, at best, able to exert only a marginal influence on the sentencing decisions of the courts.
3. The reformers erred in starting at the so-called shallow end of the juvenile-justice process.
4. There was no clear allocation of responsibilities and resources between central and local government.

In examining these reasons some comparison with recent developments in the United States is appropriate. The most striking general difference between the two countries in the 1960s was the pressures in the United States to move the juvenile court toward an increasingly legalistic stance, culminating in Supreme Court rulings that insisted on certain due-process protections. It is ironic, as A.E. Bottoms notes, that these American developments were little known in Britain, and were not referred to by opponents of the 1969 act (1974, p. 345). In the United States efforts have been made to deal separately with young offenders and categories of nondelinquent children (such as dependent, neglected, or status offenders), and a series of strategies has been undertaken since the early 1970s to remove status offenders from institutions.[8] In contrast, the 1969 act sought to blur the distinctions between juveniles who were before the court for delinquency and other reasons or were placed under the supervision or care of the local authority.

Sidestepping the Issue of Incarceration

The 1969 act and the discussions and debates that preceded it did not directly address the issue of incarceration. Indeed, the issue as such did not exist. Certainly the term *incarceration* was not used, and there was a general blurring of issues around the use of custody. The key distinction was not between custody and its alternatives but between treatment (which might entail custody) and punitive methods (which might include noncustody).[9]

Although proponents of the act sought to end the use of the central government's Prison Department institutions, which were regarded as punitive, they did not object to custody at the local level of government. Indeed, the 1968 White Paper stated: "These proposals will not diminish the need for residential facilities. In particular, the retention of the seventeenth birthday as the upper age limit for the juvenile courts means that all the existing approved schools, including the senior schools, will probably be required for the accommodation of children and young persons in care" (p. 12). The approved schools did, however, get a new name, now designated CHEs (Community Homes with Education on the premises). Furthermore, plans had been underway since 1967 to establish a small number of youth-treatment centers (YTCs) to be administered by central government.[10] These YTC facilities were to be therapeutic communities, and admission of children in care was to be made not by courts but by social workers using care and treatment criteria.[11]

The ambivalent perspective on institutions for young offenders, which is reflected by the 1969 act, contrasts with the more direct and specific approach to incarceration in the United States, exemplified in the Juvenile Justice and Delinquency Act of 1974.[12] This federal legislation was influenced by the view that youth institutions are beyond reform and by the events in Massachusetts during 1971–1972, when state and county training schools were closed.[13] In 1973 the National Advisory Commission on Criminal Justice Standards and Goals recommended that states should build no more institutions for juveniles and that they should phase out existing institutions over a five-year period (1973, p. 121).

There are several reasons why the British position on youth institutions was less coherent than that in the United States. There was less general public disquiet about juvenile institutions in Britain. Although there were inquiries into the administration of certain approved schools during the 1960s,[14] scandals regarding abuse were less dramatic than in the United States, as revealed by litigation against juvenile correctional agencies or by the exposures of investigative journalists and other writers.[15] The issues in Britain concerned the need for better management, staff recruitment and training, and for more sophisticated treatment programs. The notion of the therapeutic community, which had earlier received little support in England, now took hold in the planning of the so-called new-look institutions and came to serve as a rationale for custody and as a means of modifying and often masking the realities of institutional life.[16] The director of the first YTC declared: "Treatment is the total living situation, all the waking hours of the young person and particularly those immediately before he goes to sleep, when he is warm, comfortable and surrounded by those adults with whom he has warm and secure relationships" (Edwards 1976, p. 9).

The English uncertainties about youth incarceration also have to be placed in the context of an increased capacity and means to place youth in custody, an evolution that commenced in the 1950s. At the local level, secure units were established, the first in 1964, and by January 1980 there were more than 350 secure beds at the local level in England and Wales and a further 200 under construction or planned.[17] The secure units were in part intended for youth regarded as too troublesome to hold in other settings. This rationale had also been used in 1961 to justify reducing of the minimum age of sentence to borstal from 16 to 15.[18] The most significant development, however, was that of the detention center. The Criminal Justice Act of 1948 abolished corporal punishment as a sentence of the courts and introduced detention centers as an alternative form of what was to be termed the "short sharp shock." The first detention center, a facility for 14–16-year-old boys, was opened in 1952, and by 1968 there were six detention centers for this age group, with catchment areas covering the whole county.[19] The increase in detention-center capacity reflected, in part, concern about increased reported crime, which at least in the Conservative party still meant pressure to reintroduce corporal punishment.[20]

Magistrates, resentful of the loss of approved-school orders, were hardly likely to welcome any move to further reduce their sentencing powers. The ambivalence within the act on the question of custody persisted through much of the 1970s and enabled the initiative to remain with pressure groups such as the Magistrates' Association. This is exemplified in the evidence to the House of Commons Expenditure Committee during 1974–1975. The Magistrates' Association stated: "The essential problem is to provide the courts with greater powers and facilities where they are clearly needed for persistent young offenders."[21] Most other groups giving evidence to the committee sidestepped the custody issue. Only the National Association for the Care and Resettlement of Offenders (NACRO) specifically urged the implementation of section 7(1) and (3) (Expenditure Committee, vol. 2 1975, p. 150). The Expenditure Committee's recommendations largely reflected the ambiguity and lack of clearly defined objectives in much of the evidence it received. In the final paragraph of its report the committee stated: "We strongly recommend, within the framework of the Act, a major shift of emphasis away from custodial and punitive techniques and towards intermediate schemes, supervision, and a much greater use of non-residential care, especially fostering" (vol. 1 1975, p. xlix). But the bipartisan committee blunted the impact of this language by recommending that secure accommodation at the local level be increased,[22] and that courts be enabled to impose secure care orders and sentences to detention centers very much shorter than the existing minimum of three months.[23] The Expenditure Committee rejected NACRO's argument that detention centers and borstals be replaced by the 200 secure beds planned for YTCs and commented: "A considerable change in the attitude of magistrates, and of society as a whole, to the containment of delinquent youngsters would be necessary before such a total number of secure places could suffice." (vol. 1 1975, p. xlx).

The ambivalence and ambiguities associated with the use of custody severely retarded the development of a coherent policy position on limiting incarceration. It was not until 1977 that the issue of custody was squarely faced and a decarceration strategy was spelled out. The Jay committee, which was set up by NACRO, estimated that secure places were required for no more than 400 juveniles in England and Wales and argued that no other institutional provision be made (Jay 1977, pp. 49–54).[24] Similar logic was applied two years later to the situation in Northern Ireland by an official committee, which recommended that secure capacity for the Province be limited to 120 places and that other institutions be closed (Black 1979, pp. 44–49). It was not until the decade closed that the issue of incarceration was directly recognized and the specifics of decarceration strategies set forth.

This analysis raises the question of whether a direct and specific decarceration strategy would have worked had it been spelled out in 1969. Such an approach may have had some success if it had included the systematic provision of some secure facilities by local government. The ceiling on this secure capacity no doubt would have been a contentious issue, but there was no reason why it need have been much larger than 350–550, the secure provision at the local level that was, in fact, established during the 1970s. The absence of a decarceration strategy and the unsystematic development of policy by both central and local governments enabled the Magistrates' Association to perpetuate the myth that their hands were tied and to obscure the reality of the rapid rise in the number of young persons in custody at the local and central level.

Central-Government Difficulties in Influencing Sentencing Decisions

The failure of the 1969 act to reduce the sentencing of young persons to borstals and detention centers must also be seen in the context of the general problem faced by government in influencing sentencing practice. It has been explicit Home Office policy since the early 1970s to reduce the size of the prison population. Despite a variety of exhortations and the provision of new noncustodial sanctions the prison population has continued to grow. In 1977 the Home Office commented: "There is an inconsistency between the publically avowed policy of using custody only as a last resort for the really serious offence or dangerous offender, and actual practice. One manifestation is the presence of increasing numbers of juvenile offenders in the prison system" (Home Office 1977, p. 7). As is evident from table 6–1, there was an increasing use of borstal and detention centers by the courts in the decade before the act. The escalation in the use of custodial sentences, especially the detention center, since the act in part reflected the dismay of many magistrates concerning both the loss of the approved-school order and the nebulous quality of the new care order. The care order locates with social workers the discretion as to where to place the juvenile, which might or might not be away from home. The Magistrates' Association has continued to press for restoration of the judge's power to remove the juvenile offender from home without resorting to a sentence to borstal or detention center. The proposed "residential care order" in the 1980 White Paper meets this demand, and it is especially ironic that this new measure is to be accompanied not by the activation but by the repeal of section 7 of the 1969 act. Although approved schools had many empty beds in 1969 and the custodial sentencing of young persons to more secure institutions was increasing throughout the 1960s, it is the perception of magistrates that the problem resulted from the act. It seems likely, however, that the act intensified a view already held by magistrates that the courts had an insufficient range of powers for dealing with serious and persistent young offenders.

The structure of central and local-government finances has contributed to the failure at the local level to develop alternatives to custody. A particularly important feature of the central-agreement–local-government relationship is that the costs of incarcerating youth in Prison Department facilities are met in full by the Home Office.[25] No effort has been made by central government to have local government meet some of the costs involved. Indeed, there has been a striking lack of public discussion of the question of costs and resource allocation.[26] Central government has no systematic information on variations in the use of custody across local government and does not appear to have given consideration to subsidy programs linked to rates of incarceration.[27] With central government meeting the costs in full there is a counterincentive for local authorities to develop and administer their own alternatives. The position of central government is that actual expenditures are under the control of local authorities, and central government has remained reluctant to seek a uniform pattern.[28]

The Error of Starting at the Shallow End of the Juvenile-Justice Process

Successive governments reiterated the point that section 7 of the act, which would terminate the sentencing of juveniles to borstal and detention centers, could be brought into effect only after local governments had developed alternative resources and programs. With the failure to activate section 7, the approach during the 1970s was that of a shallow-end strategy to reforming the juvenile-justice process. By first dealing with youth on the periphery of the process it was hoped that reform at the deep end, via section 7, would follow. The lessons from the decade following the act strongly suggest that the required change is more likely to be achieved if the strategy commences at the deep end.

The shallow-end strategy, pursued through the 1970s, had three components—police cautioning, intermediate treatment, and alternatives to remand in custody.

Police Cautioning

One of the most significant developments during the 1970s, which was encouraged but not initiated by the 1969 act, was the rapid increase in the number of juveniles officially cautioned by the police as an alternative to prosecution.[29] Table 6-2 shows that the sharpest increase in the police cautioning of young persons occurred in the five years after passage of this statute.

The concept of diversion has remained much less developed in England than in the United States.[30] Virtually all the diversionary activity has involved the police, who are responsible for both arrest and prosecution policy.[31] Despite the increasing tendency of the police to caution juveniles, there is little reason to suppose that this had much impact on the number of juveniles reaching custody. Although one effect of the increase in police cautioning has been to divert juveniles from the juvenile court (who might otherwise, in many cases, have received discharges from the court), it is also likely that cautioning has brought to official notice many juveniles who would in earlier years have been ignored or handled with the proverbial "clip around the ear."[32]

Intermediate Treatment

The second principal component of the 1969 act's shallow-end strategy involves the many activities with delinquent and other young people under the umbrella term *intermediate treatment* (IT). The 1968 White Paper called for a new legal and administrative framework, which would encourage ". . . the development of a variety of forms of intermediate treatment for children and young persons

Table 6–2
Young Persons Cautioned and Found Guilty
(thousands)

Year	Cautioned	Found Guilty	Percentage Cautioned of Total Cautioned and Found Guilty
1964	15	67	18.2
1969	20	65	23.5
1974	47	84	36.1
1978	51	89	36.4

Source: *Criminal Statistics and Supplementary Statistics,* England and Wales, 1964–1974, and *Criminal Statistics,* 1978.

Note: Figures include indictable and nonindictable offenses, excluding motoring offenses.

placed under supervision by the courts." The white paper added that these resources should also be available for persons who had not been before the courts,
that they might take residential and nonresidential forms, and that "When adequate facilities for short-term residence are provided under a scheme, existing
powers to commit to a junior detention center will lapse" (1968, pp. 9–11).

The reality has been far removed from the white paper's expectations. The
emergence of IT activities, which are the responsibility of local government, has
been slow and uneven. Where IT has gotten off the ground, it has generally
focused on delinquency prevention and has steered well clear of youth at the
deeper end. Indeed it has been estimated that only 1,500 of the 12,000 youths
participating in IT activities during 1978 were involved because of a court order
(*New Society,* 18 January 1974). There was an absence of strategic planning
with reference to intermediate treatment by both central and local government.[33] At the central level, little thought was given to linking IT with the
eventual activation of section 7 of the act. At the local level those involved in
setting up projects have showed little inclination to work with more difficult
youth. As a consequence IT has remained firmly located at the shallow end of
the juvenile-justice process, dealing with youths considered to be at risk of getting involved in offenses rather than at risk of being committed to custody. Only
a tiny minority of IT programs have focused on serious young offenders with the
explicit goal of reducing the number of youths in custody. The irrelevance of IT
to the problem of custody is but one facet of the facile assumption that the development of alternative sanctions will necessarily prompt the withering of custodial arrangements. Unlesss the alternatives are tightly connected with the deep
end of the process, they simply supplement rather than replace custody. The
piecemeal strategy explicit in the 1969 act contrasts sharply with the approach
followed in Massachusetts in the early 1970s. It was only after closing its main
institutions that the Department of Youth Services set up a purchase-of-services
budget and an array of alternative programs emerged.

Alternatives to Remand in Custody of the Prison Department

The third component of the general strategy that has been pursued through the
1970s has addressed the remanding of juveniles in Prison Department custody.
Remand encompasses both pretrial detention and detention of those convicted
but not yet sentenced, and, under the 1969 act, powers were provided to end
the use of Prison Department facilities for the first of these purposes. Perhaps
because some juveniles on remand have continued to be sent to prisons, the issue
of remand has been more often highlighted than the use of custody as a final
court disposition. Much of the Expenditure Committee's enquiries during 1974–
1975 centered on remand, and it has been an explicit part of central-government
strategy to eliminate the remanding of juveniles to Prison Department facilities

before dealing with borstals and detention centers. In 1977, by executive order under the 1969 act, the remanding before trial of 14-year-old girls in adult prisons was ended, and the ban was extended to cover all juvenile girls in 1979.[34] Even this modest step did not meet with unreserved enthusiasm by local authorities, who became responsible for these juveniles.

The sequence of tackling the remanded category first contrasts with the Massachusetts strategy, where detention facilities were excluded from the institutional closures that took place in the early 1970s.[35] The sequential strategy moved so slowly in England, however, that it is not possible to conclude whether it was a wise judgment to commence with the remand population. It took eleven years after passage of the act before it was even proposed by the government that boys awaiting trial be barred from Prison Department institutions, and even this step was limited to 14 year olds (White Paper 1980).

None of these three approaches, then, has helped develop the capacity to divert juveniles from borstals and detention centers. The sharp rise in police cautioning has touched only those on the periphery. Intermediate-treatment activities, focusing as they have on youth at the shallow end of the process, have had no impact on the custodial arrangements they were intended to replace. Intermediate treatment has served not to divert youth away from institutions but to divert community resources away from youth at the deeper end of the juvenile-justice process. Finally, the rather limited steps that have been taken with regard to remanding have had very little impact on the problem of custodial sentencing.

Allocation of Responsibility and Resources between Central and Local Government

The 1969 act and the events that followed did little to bring about a more coordinated approach to young-offender problems at either the central or local level of government. At the central level, it was agreed after considerable infighting that the Children's Department (which was responsible for drafting the act) should be transferred from the Home Office to the Department of Health and Social Security (DHSS).[36] However, the Home Office retained responsibility for certain crucial areas, including the overall administration of juvenile courts and for juveniles sentenced to Prison Department institutions. During the 1970s the DHSS's sphere of influence gradually declined, and the drafting of proposals for legislation during 1979-1980 was largely undertaken within the Home Office. The uncertainties as to ministerial responsibility have contributed to the absence of a clear lead from central government in the implementation of the 1969 act.[37] It is probably not without significance that full implementation of the act would have narrowed the Home Office sphere of influence.[38]

The confusion and uncertainty at the central level regarding responsibility for young offenders have been mirrored at the local level of government. In part this was because of major reorganizations. Single departments of social services were created within local authorities in 1970 (bringing together services for children, the elderly, and handicapped persons, but not probation), and this was followed in 1974 by the redrawing of local-authority boundaries. The considerable upheaval associated with these developments retarded the ability of local authorities to respond to the new challenges posed by the 1969 act.

The situation in England and Wales (but not Scotland) was further complicated at the local level by a split in responsibilities between social-service departments and probation.[39] The original intention was that responsibility for juveniles would be assumed by social-services departments, commencing with the younger age group. The split has remained very uneven across the country, but, nationally, probation has retained primary responsibility. Both probation and social services have argued for sole responsibility (in the case of probation for young persons only), and the local situation somewhat resembles the Home Office/DHSS territorial tussle.[40] Full implementation of the 1969 act would, of course, move resources from probation to social-services departments.[41]

Conclusion

Judged against the intention of ending the incarceration of young persons in Prison Department institutions, the Children and Young Persons' Act of 1969 has been a total fiasco. No attempt was made during the 1970s to bring into effect those parts of section 7 of the act that would have ended the sentencing of young persons to borstals and detention centers. Between 1 January 1971 (when most provisions of the act came into effect) and 31 December 1978, the number of young persons sentenced to Prison Department institutions increased by 130 percent. Moreover, the proportion of young persons so sentenced, of all 14–16 year olds sentenced for indictable offenses, almost doubled over the same period. The incarceration of young persons during this period increased at a greater rate than did the number of young persons who were cautioned or found guilty and at an even greater rate than the increase in indictable offenses recorded by the police.

The sequential approach to the implementation of the act took little account of the interest groups advocating the use of custody or of the powerful inertia that supports ongoing institutional arrangements. The act did nothing to disturb the financial disincentive for local government to take responsibility for juvenile offenders. From the standpoint of party politics this escalating drift into custody is a bipartisan responsibility.[42] The political will at central and local government throughout the decade to reduce custodial capacity has been missing.

With the announcement in October 1980 that certain sections of the 1969 act are to be repealed, including section 7's provisions on the sentencing of juveniles to borstals and detention centers, the reform effort has reached its desultory and dismal finale. The new proposals will, if acted on, increase opportunities for the courts to impose custodial sentences (White Paper 1980).[43] There is, as a new decade begins, little doubt that what Michel Foucault has called the "carceral archipelago" is alive and well for juveniles in England.

Notes

1. Children and Young Persons' Act 1969, section 7(1) and (3). The jurisdiction of the juvenile court is from ages 10 to 16; this age range is encompassed by the term *juvenile*. The term *children* refers to persons aged 10 to 13; *young persons* to persons aged 14-16; and *young adults* to persons aged 17-20.

2. The minimum age for detention center is 14, and it is available for boys only. In Britain, the detention center is an institution for sentenced youths, and the sentence is generally for 3 months. The minimum age for borstal is 15, and the sentence is 6 to 24 months, with the release decision made by the Prison Department. In 1978 the average length of time served was 8.7 months.

3. See Donnison, Jay, and Stewart (1962) and Longford (1964).

4. The Ingleby report did propose that the age of criminal responsibility be raised from 8 to 12. In 1963, through a legislative compromise, the age was set at 10.

5. For a review of juvenile-justice developments in Scotland see Morris (1978).

6. As Bottoms has described in his analysis of events leading up to the 1969 act, senior civil servants in the Children's Department of the Home Office played a particularly crucial role in shaping the legislation (1974, pp. 331-334).

7. The main provisions of the 1969 act were as follows:

a. Juvenile courts lost the power to make an "approved school order," and instead were able to make a "care order," committing the child to the care of local government (took effect on 1 January 1971).

b. Twelve regional-planning committees were set up to plan a system of local-government "community homes" to replace "Home Office approved schools" and children's homes (took effect on 1 April 1973).

c. "Probation orders" were replaced by "supervision orders," which did not have reasons defining when a juvenile might be brought back to court (took effect on 1 January 1971).

d. The Home Secretary was enabled by the act to raise the age below which the child may not be prosecuted for a crime (other than homicide) from 10 to 14 (although raising it above 12 would require the express approval of Parliament). Below this age, a child was only to be dealt with by care proceedings in which the offense was only one of a number of factors taken into account. (Through 1980, the Home Secretary had taken no action under this provision.)

e. For 14-16 year olds there was to be a preference for noncriminal care proceedings instead of prosecution. (Although this section of the act was brought into effect on 1 January 1971, it has not been much used.)

f. The powers of the courts to order boys of 10 and over to attend at an attendance center, and boys of 14-16 to be sent to a detention center were to be phased out. It was also intended to deprive the courts of the power to send young persons to a borstal. (These provisions have not been activated.)

8. The decarceration of status offenders is a major thrust of the Juvenile Justice and Delinquency Prevention Act of 1974; see chapter 5 of this book.

9. One of the act's purposes, for example, was to phase out the use of attendance centers (a court order whereby juveniles report for evening or weekend activities organized by the police). This intention had been explicitly dropped in 1976. "The Government's existing policy for junior attendance centers is to see them as a useful sanction and the Expenditure Committee's endorsement of this policy is welcome" (White Paper 1976, p. 12).

10. Provision for these institutions was provided by section 64 of the 1969 act. On 1 January 1971, when most of the act's provisions were brought into effect, responsibility for youth-treatment centers was transferred from the Home Office to the Department of Health and Social Security (DHSS). Two centers, with a total of sixty-two beds, were in operation in October 1980.

11. An official document decreed that within youth-treatment centers, "treatment will be through the child's experience of the whole therapeutic environment" (DHSS 1971, p. 12). Youth-treatment centers are secure facilities, whereas community homes with education are open, although some do contain small secure units.

12. Juvenile Justice and Delinquency Prevention Act of 1974, P.L. 93-415.

13. See Rutherford (1974) and Ohlin, Coates, and Miller (1974).

14. See, for example, *Disturbances at the Carlton Approved School on 29 and 30 August 1959,* Report of Inquiry, Cmnd. 937, 1960; *Administration of Punishment at Court Lees Approved School,* Report of Inquiry, Cmnd. 3367, 1967.

15. For cases of litigation see: Nelson v. Heyne, 355 F. Supp. 451 (N.D. Ind. 1972), aff'd 491 F. 2d 353 (7th Cir. 1974) and Morales v. Turman, Memorandum and Order, 383 F. Supp. 53 (E.D. Tex. 1974). See James (1971) and Wooden (1976) for examples of investigative exposures.

16. See, for example, Home Office (1970).

17. House of Commons reply, 7 January 1980. For an account of the development of secure units see Millham, Bullock, and Hosie (1978, pp. 24-32); see also Cawson and Martell (1979).

18. See *Criminal Justice Act,* 1961, 5.1.

19. This was described as a pilot scheme and was evaluated by Dr. Max Grunhut of Oxford University, see Grunhut (1955). For a review of how Grunhut's conclusions were used by the Home Office and other interested parties see Land (1975, pp. 331-337).

20. Hilary Land observed: "The introduction of detention centers was the price paid for the abolition of corporal punishment at a time when there was much concern about crime rates among the young. Their expansion, when criminal activities of the young were again causing alarm and the prison system as a whole was under great pressure, was the 'civilized alternative' to its re-introduction." (1975, p. 368). As the corporal-punishment issue lapsed during the 1970s, detention centers placed more emphasis on education and counselling. However, in 1979 the new Conservative government selected one junior and one senior detention center as so-called pilot projects in a reversal to a more rigorous regime.

21. The Magistrates' Association also recommended repeal of 7(3) of the 1969 act, which provided for the phasing out of detention centers (Expenditure Committee, vol. 2, 1975, p. 129).

22. Under the Children's Act of 1975 the central government commenced direct grants for the provision of secure accommodation at the local level. Nearly £8,000,000 was made available by central government for local secure-unit capital costs between 1975-1976 and 1979-1980 (House of Commons, written answer, 21.2.1980).

23. These recommendations were rejected by the government in its response to the Expenditure Committee, see White Paper (1976, pp. 8-10, 12). In 1980 the Conservative government revived the short-detention-center-sentence proposal as well as that of the residential care order (but not with the secure prefix), see White Paper (1980). Shorter detention-center minimums are likely to increase usage of this custodial sanction by the courts, see Rutherford (1981).

24. Since the mid-1970s there has been a growing interest in Britain in the events surrounding the closure of the training schools in Massachusetts. Accounts of these events had a marked impact on the Jay committee's decarceration strategy.

25. In contrast with youth-treatment centers, where DHSS exacts a charge to local authorities of 60 percent of the weekly cost.

26. Remarkably, the issue of costs hardly arose in the examination of the workings of the act by the House of Commons Expenditure Committee during 1974-1975.

27. The earmarked finance that central government has made available to local authorities has been for capital expenditure on secure custody. This has amounted to about £2,000,000 per year, compared with £100,000 set aside for capital expenditure arising with intermediate-treatment programmes.

28. J.W. Stackpoole, assistant under-secretary at DHSS told the Expenditure Committee: "The Act does provide a framework for treatment; it does not

lay down more than that, and that I am sure is right. There ought to be scope for each institution to develop its own treatment methods and for each authority to give effect to its own views on treatment in the community and for the children from its community." Expenditure Committee, vol. 2 (1975, p. 32). This view might be compared with the issue of new federalism that arose during hearings on the implementation of the Juvenile Justice and Delinquency Prevention Act of 1974; see U.S. Senate, Sub-committee to Investigate Juvenile Delinquency (1976), pp. 32-36.

29. *Children and Young Persons' Act of 1969,* section 5(2) gave statutory recognition to police cautioning of juveniles. Virtually all the increase in police cautioning since 1969 has concerned juveniles. See Ditchfield (1976) and Priestley, Fears, and Fuller (1977, pp. 60-80).

30. There have been some attempts at transatlantic transplantation. See, for instance, Zander (1975).

31. One commentary on the 1969 act argued that: "The police, alone, amongst the major agencies involved, emerged from the proceedings with fresh powers they had never solicited" (Priestley, Fears, and Fuller, 1977, pp. 34-35).

32. For a review of evidence pointing in this direction see Ditchfield (1976, pp. 7-12) and Farrington (1980). The probability that police cautioning is widening rather than contracting the juvenile-justice net is all the greater now that cautions are increasingly a matter of court record in subsequent hearings and thereby are regarded as the first notch on the sequence of sanctions. See, for example, Home Office Circular 70/1978 (The Citing of Police Cautions in the Juvenile Court).

33. The regional-planning committees set up by the act have largely neglected nonresidential sanctions and have failed to generate comprehensive strategy at the local level. See White Paper (1968, pp. 3-14), and White Paper (1976, p. 17).

34. The Expenditure Committee recommended in 1975 that all remanding of young persons to adult prisons should cease forthwith; but the Government moved more slowly. During 1978, 4,615 young persons were remanded to Prison Department institutions; this was 22 percent more than in 1971.

35. A study of juvenile-detention facilities in Massachusetts quotes the former commissioner of the Department of Youth Services as saying in 1979: "We had closed the training schools. It would have been political disaster to close the detention centers as well." Massachusetts Advocacy Center (1980, p. 13). The detention facilities, which house both pretrial and convicted unsentenced juveniles, have yet to be closed.

36. Richard Crossman, who was secretary of State for Social Services from 1968-1970 provides an interesting insight into the way in which the fate of the Children's Department of the Home Office was handled: "I know that he [James Callaghan, Home Secretary] and his whole Department are anxious to keep the Children's Department as part of the Home Office and not see it mopped

up in my new Ministry and I have always realized that as long as Callaghan is Home Secretary I can't take the Children's Department out of his hands. It could only happen under a new Home Secretary who would come into the Home Office on condition that he accepted the transfer. So I said straightaway, 'I'm not hoping to grab this from you Jim. I promise you I shan't!' 'Is that a deal?' he asked. 'Well', I said, 'it's not a deal. I am just telling you what my attitude is.' " This was 24 September 1968, but by July 1969 Callaghan had conceded the Children's Department to Crossman (Crossman 1977, pp. 198, 561).

37. In contrast, the issue of where to locate this area of responsibility was more successfully laid to rest in the United States. Although there was a struggle during debate on the Juvenile Justice and Delinquency Prevention Act of 1974 as to whether the new federal office should be located in HEW or the Justice Department, the legislation placed the office firmly in Justice, leaving HEW with responsibility only for funding some prevention programmes.

38. This consideration was partially explored during a session of the House of Commons' Expenditure Committee in 1974. Mr. F. Hooley, M.P.: "If, in fact, all these various powers, which I gather exist under the 1969 Act and have not been exercised in one way or another, are exercised by some government in the near future, would this not push the whole system over towards the DHSS and local government and away from the Home Office inextricably?" Mr. F.L.T. Graham-Harrison, deputy under-secretary for State at the Home Office: "It would shift the balance." To which Mr. Horley commented: "As it shifts, presumably the question of resources in local government and social services will become more and more important on that side and less and less important to you?" Expenditure Committee, vol. 2 (1975, p. 95).

39. Probation departments receive 80 percent of their funding from central government and do not fall within the formal local-government structure.

40. See Chief Probation Officers' Conference, *A Report by the Children and Young Persons Act 1969 Committee* (mimeo, 1980), and Association of Directors of Social Services, *Children and Young Persons' Legislation in 1980, Observations and Proposals* (mimeo, 1980).

41. The use of supervision orders, which was declining prior to the 1969 Act, fell from 23 percent of all boys' sentences for indictable offenses in 1969 to 14 percent in 1978.

42. The 1969 act was enacted during the final months of a Labour government, and it was a Conservative government that brought only certain provisions into effect on 1 January 1971. The next Labour government, in office between 1974 and 1979, was generally tardy in further implementing the legislation and prior to leaving office was suggesting that 16 year olds might, for disposition purposes, be best regarded as "young adults" (Green Paper 1978, pp. 42–46). In broad policy terms the emphasis of Labour has been on encouraging local government to increase the range of its activities and responsibilities, whereas the Conservative emphasis has been to strengthen the powers of the courts. Neither

party has attended to detailed policy on young offenders, and the decade has been more characterized by drift than design.

43. For a review of the 1980 White Paper see Rutherford (1981).

References

Black, H. 1979. *Report of the Children and Young Persons' Review Group.* Belfast: H.M.S.O.

Bottoms, A.E. 1974. "On the Decriminalization of English Juvenile Courts." In *Crime, Crimonology and Public Policy,* edited by R. Hood. London: Heinemann.

Cawson, P. and Martell, M. 1979. *Children Referrred to Closed Units.* Department of Health and Social Security Research Division, Research Report, no. 5.

Crossman, R. 1977. *The Diaries of a Cabinet Minister,* vol. 3. London: Hamish Hamilton and Jonathan Cape.

Department of Health and Social Security. 1971. *Youth Treatment Centers.* London: H.M.S.O.

Ditchfield, J. 1976. *Police Cautioning in England and Wales.* Home Office Research Study, no. 37. London: H.M.S.O.

Donnison, D., Jay, P., and Stewart, M. 1962. *The Ingleby Report: Three Critical Essays.* London: Fabian Research Pamphlet No. 231.

Edwards, S. 1976. *Treatment in Security.* London: Institute for the Study and Treatment of Delinquency.

Expenditure Committee. 1975. *Eleventh Report from the Expenditure Committee, The Children and Young Persons' Act, 1969 Report,* vol. 1. London: H.M.S.O.

Expenditure Committee. 1975. *Eleventh Report from the Expenditure Committee, The Children and Young Persons' Act, 1969, vol. 2, Minutes of Evidence and Appendices.* London: H.M.S.O.

Farrington, D. 1980. "Juvenile Diversion in England and Wales." *Deviance et Societe* (forthcoming).

Green Paper. 1978. *Youth Custody and Supervision: A New Sentence.* Cmnd 7406. London: H.M.S.O.

Grunhut, M. 1955. "Juvenile Delinquents under Punitive Detention." *British Journal of Delinquency* 5.

Home Office. 1970. *Care and Treatment in a Planned Environment: A Report on the Community Homes Project.* London: H.M.S.O.

Home Office. 1977. *A Review of Criminal Justice Policy 1976.* London: H.M.S.O.

Ingleby. 1960. *Report of the Committee on Children and Young Persons.* Cmnd 1191. London: H.M.S.O.

James, H. 1971. *Children in Trouble: A National Scandal.* New York: Pocket Books.

Jay, P. 1977. *Children and Young Persons in Custody, Report of a NACRO Working Party.* Chichester and London: Barry Rose.

Kilbrandon. 1964. *Children and Young Persons, Scotland.* Cmnd. 2306. Edinburgh: H.M.S.O.

Kobrin, S. and Klein, M. (forthcoming) "National Evaluation of the Deinstitutionalisation of Status Offender Programs."

Land, H. 1975. "Detention Centers: The Experiment Which Could Not Fail." In *Change, Choice and Conflict in Social Policy.* edited by P. Hall; R. Parker; H. Land; A. Webb. London: Heinemann.

Longford. 1964. *Crime: A Challenge to Us All.* Report of the Labour Party's Study Group. London.

Massachusetts Advocacy Center. 1980. *Delinquent Justice: Juvenile Detention Practice in Massachusetts.*

Millham, S.; Bullock, R.; and Hosie, K. 1978. *Locking up Children.* Farnborough: Saxon Press.

Morris, A. 1978. *Juvenile Justice?* London: Heinemann.

National Advisory Commission on Criminal Justice Standards and Goals. 1973. A National *Strategy to Reduce Crime.* Washington, D.C.: U.S. Government Printing Office.

Ohlin, L.; Coates, R.; and Miller, A. 1974. "Radical Correctional Reform: A Case Study of the Massachusetts Youth Correctional System." *Harvard Educational Review* 44:74-111.

Priestly, P.; Fears, F.; and Fuller, R. 1977. *Justice for Juveniles, The 1969 Children and Young Persons' Act: A Case for Reform?* London: Routledge and Kegan, Paul.

Rutherford, A. 1974. *The Dissolution of the Training Schools in Massachusetts.* Columbus: Academy for Contemporary Problems.

_____. 1981. "Young Offenders: Comments on the White Paper on Young Adult and Juvenile Offenders." *British Journal of Criminology* 21.

Thorpe, J. 1979. *Social Enquiry Reports: A Survey.* Home Office Research Study, no. 48. London: H.M.S.O.

U.S. Senate. 1976. *Hearings before the Subcommittee to Investigate Juvenile Delinquency of the Committee of the Judiciary, Assessment of Implementation of the Juvenile Justice and Delinquency Prevention Act of 1974.* Washington D.C.: U.S. Government Printing Office.

White Paper. 1965. *The Child, the Family and the Young Offender.* Cmnd 1742. London: H.M.S.O.

White Paper. 1968. *Children in Trouble.* Cmnd 3601. London: H.M.S.O.

White Paper. 1976. *Observations on the Eleventh Report from the Expenditure Committee on the Children and Young Persons' Act 1969.* Cmnd. 6494. London: H.M.S.O.

White Paper. 1980. *Young Offenders.* Cmnd. 8045. London: H.M.S.O.
Wooden, K. 1976. *Weeping in the Playtime of Others.* New York: McGraw-Hill.
Zander, M. 1975. *Diversion from Criminal Justice in an English Context.* Report of a NACRO Working Party. Chichester and London: Barry Rose.

Part III
Conditions in Prisons and
Strategies for Change

7

American Jails: Still Cloacal after Ten Years

Karen A. Reixach and
David L. Weimer

More than ten years ago, in an article titled "the Cloacal Region of American Corrections," Hans Mattick and Alexander Aikman (1969) described how the historical legacy of obsolete buildings, inadequate local resources, and absence of widespread public concern combined to make local jails inappropriate settings for isolating and rehabilitating convicted criminals. Since the early 1960s public concern has focused more on the problems of pretrial custody caused by the money-bail system than on the role of the local jail as a correctional institution. By 1970, the use of own-recognizance release had greatly increased, reducing the percentage of defendants held in pretrial custody. Continuation of this process with the introduction of additional pretrial-diversion programs may have resulted in a further shift during the 1970s in the composition of the inmate population. In 1970, 48 percent of the inmates in local jails on any given day were serving postconviction sentences, whereas by 1978 preliminary census figures showed that the fraction had risen to at least 50 percent and perhaps to as high as 58 percent (LEAA, 1971: 1979a). During the same period the total number of inmates increased by 12 percent, so that the number of inmates serving postconviction sentences on any given day in local jails may have increased by as much as 35 percent.

It thus appears that reductions in jail populations through increased use of alternatives to pretrial custody are being more than offset by the increased use of jails for postconviction sentences. Consequently, jail conditions (and alternatives to the use of local jails for postconviction sentences as well as pretrial custody) continue to warrant attention and concern. To what extent, then, have the conditions under which at least one million (and perhaps as many as three million people) serve annually, improved over the last decade?

After briefly reviewing the available evidence, which indicates that any progress made over the last decade in improving jail conditions is minimal compared to the problems remaining, we consider policy changes that might be made at the state level to accelerate improvement in local jails or reduce their use as a sentencing option. State-set standards for local jails, the prevalent approach in recent years, will not lead to substantial change unless accompanied by other state actions. We conclude by suggesting a research agenda that will lay the groundwork for more effective state policies.

National Overview

Jails are local facilities that hold people for more than forty-eight hours but usually no more than a year, according to the census definition. They include places that house only sentenced misdemeanants, but most jails are multipurpose institutions, housing pretrial detainees, convicted prisoners, and miscellaneous detainees (such as material witnesses and people awaiting transfer).

By all accounts jail conditions have been and continue to be deplorable. However, rigorous national comparisons over time are impossible. Jail records are notoriously bad, and the best studies of jails have relied on specially conducted jail-by-jail surveys (Mattick and Sweet 1969, for Illinois; Wayson et al. 1977, for Washington State; and Milin 1979, for New Jersey; see also Johnson and Kravitz 1978, for listing of further studies). These are statewide rather than national studies, use varied criteria, and are single views of one state's jails rather than repeated pictures of the same jails over time.

Two national overviews analyzed jail conditions in the late 1960s and early 1970s (Mattick 1974; Goldfarb 1975). These help pull together the dreadful catalogue of inadequacies in state after state.

The only recent national data are those gathered by the U.S. Bureau of the Census. Two separate questionnaires, one administered to a sample of jail inmates and the other sent to all local jails, were circulated in 1972 and 1978. The 1972 results have been reported in summary form (LEAA 1975a; 1975b), but the 1978 data are still being analyzed (U.S. Department of Justice 1980).

There are several problems with the data, however. First, much information is missing. The design of questions sometimes makes it hard to tell whether a jail actually lacks staff or program in a given area or simply skipped the question. When this can be distinguished, it sometimes turns out that two thousand jails did not answer while a hundred or so admitted to having no program. Also, researchers who wish to pursue leads will find that the inmate data cannot be readily matched state by state or by jail size with the institutional data. And cost data are available only in a third survey (U.S. Department of Justice and U.S. Department of Commerce 1979). Therefore, the job of reconciling these three sources of information is enormous. Nonetheless, these censuses represent an underutilized source of insights about prisoners and jails in the United States. Table 7-1 is an example of some of the comparions that can be made; it presents the jail programs measured by both the 1972 and 1978 surveys of institutions. Only in the use of weekend sentences had dramatic change occurred; nearly two-thirds of all jails now have such programs. Although there are some other encouraging signs of improvement in programs in the large jails, the majority of jails have no rehabilitation staff and no medical facilities.

The 1972 census of institutions included twelve questions on jail programs, out of a total of forty-three questions. The report on this census showed a high percentage of all jails with no programs at all (LEAA 1975b, p. 43). Unfortunately

Table 7-1
Indicators of Jail Conditions by Jail Size

	50 or less		51-249		250-499		500+		Total	
	1972	1978	1972	1978	1972	1978	1972	1978	1972	1978
Number of jails	3439	2876	368	491	67	74	47	52	3921	3493
Utilization (crowding)[a]	.21	.33	.63	.75	.85	.80	.96	.89	.25	.39
Staff size[b]	16,504	28,770	11,262	18,852	5,631	8,505	10,899	14,290	44,298	70,517
Percentage of jails without rehab staff	85.5	86.7	37.2	24.6	6.1	0.0	6.4	0.0	78.7	74.9
Percentage of jails without medical facilities	94.2	89.0	49.3	25.0	9.4	0.0	9.1	0.0	87.6	76.8
Percentage of jails without work release	58.2	59.4	51.8	47.9	55.4	51.3	57.4	56.6	57.5	57.6
Percentage of jails without weekend sentences	54.5	39.0	48.2	32.2	36.9	26.3	46.8	38.9	53.6	37.8

Source: Tapes of the data collected by the U.S. Bureau of the Census for the Law Enforcement Assistance Administration were provided by the Inter-University Consortium for Political and Social Research. Neither the collectors of the original data nor the Consortium bear any responsibility for the analysis or interpretations presented here.

Note: Jail size is calculated by size of prisoner population rather than capacity. The 1978 Census affords at least three measures of prisoner population: average daily-population weekdays, average daily-population weekends, and population on 2-15-78; 1972 Census measured only "population today," so to maintain comparable measure, jail size for 1978 is calculated using population 2-15-78, even though other measures are more accurate. The cutoffs (50 or less, and so on) will be used by the Census in its analysis of 1978 data.

[a] 1972 utilization is based on estimated capacity, including drunk tanks and counting all three- or four-person cells as holding four people. Utilization rates for 1972 probably represented a lower boundary. This figure is extremely soft, not only because of capacity estimation but also because of the number of missing values. 1972 and 1978 utilization rates are medians.

[b] 1978 staff-size figures raise questions about comparability with 1972. The marked increase in staff may be due in part to more accurate reporting of employees whose duties include but are not limited to jail activities.

comparable questions about most programs were not asked on the 1978 census survey of institutions, so that detailed comparisons cannot be made. Instead the 1978 census explored the details of medical care available in local institutions. What the 1972 survey demonstrated for educational and counselling programs, the 1978 survey confirmed for medical care: small jails—those housing fifty inmates or less—are deplorably deficient. These small jails are greatly underutilized, and this oversupply of small jails is one of the central jail problems of the 1980s. The numbers of jails contracted significantly between 1972 and 1978, and this trend should be encouraged. Small jails with bad conditions should not be repaired or replaced—they should be eliminated.

Larger jails are more likely to have programs. However, the census data show that these jails are at capacity or overcrowded. Crowding begins not at 100-percent utilization but rather at about 80 percent, because of the need for special areas for holding different classes of prisoners; by this criterion 69.2 percent of the largest jails were overcrowded in 1978. Given the high prisoner populations, the rehabilitation staff (such as teachers, social workers, psychologists, and doctors) is stretched very thin. Rough calculations of inmate-to-rehabilitation-staff ratios show in 1978 that even the larger jails had roughly forty to fifty inmates to every rehabilitation staffer. These ratios do not take into account that rehabilitation staff often work part-time. Since education, counselling, and medical care generally rely on face-to-face interaction, these ratios raise serious doubts about the quality of programs that do exist.

These problems are not new; they were the problems of the 1970s as well. And the solutions of the 1970s were only a start.

State-Set Standards: The Improbable Dream

During the 1970s state correctional agencies, federal commissions, and national organizations invested millions of dollars in developing standards for local jails (Allinson 1979). Hopes that these standards would bring about substantial improvement in jail conditions have not been realized for several reasons:

1. Meeting the standards often requires major capital investment. Decrepit physical plants can be brought into compliance only by outlays so large as to deter action. For example, the Correctional Economics Center study of Washington State jails found that it would take $44.5 million (in 1975 dollars) of capital investment alone to bring the forty-five jails in the state up to minimum standards. This expenditure is over 600 percent of the annual operating costs of the state's jails (Wayson et al. 1977, pp. 45–74). In light of such costs, it is not surprising that local officials have not rushed to meet state-set standards.

2. Standards challenge the existence of widely dispersed and underutilized jails. For example, 60 percent of the jails in Washington State are at 55-percent capacity or less (Wayson et al. 1977, p. 100). Hans Mattick (1974) has pointed

out that simply bringing existing jails up to standards makes little sense when rural jails tend to stand empty while urban jails bulge with prisoners. Implicit in the implementation of standards is some consolidation and reorganization of corrections. However, sheriffs and other local officials are unlikely to yield control of local jails, which are often a source of patronage, without a fight.

3. Agencies that set standards lack credible threats to force compliance. The closest approximations of national standards come from the American Correctional Association; they are enforced through voluntary accreditation. Federal mechanisms include the Bureau of Prisons inspection of jails holding federal prisoners and the withholding of federal funding to substandard jails; neither of these would touch the majority of local jails. State mechanisms include grand-jury oversight, inspections, and condemnation of jails. A look at experience in one state suggests these may be empty threats.

New York State: The Case of Health Standards

Not all standards require huge capital outlays. With some ingenuity health standards can be met largely without altering the physical plant. The history of health standards in New York State demonstrates that even such improvements are difficult to bring about through standards. (For another overview of New York health standards and their lack of impact, see Resnik and Shaw 1980.)

Projects to draft health-care standards specifically for correctional institutions have been conducted by the American Medical Association (AMA) and the American Public Health Association (APHA). The AMA adopted 170 separate standards for medical services and health care in prisons and jails, running to over 30 typescript pages (1979); the APHA standards are published in a 112-page book (APHA 1976). The New York State Commission of Correction, which has had authority since 1965 to promulgate rules and regulations, has issued medical standards that fit on a single page for local jails and penitentiaries and half a page for lockups (New York State Commission of Correction 1976); the jail standards are reproduced in appendix 7A. The gaps in the Commission's standards are glaring: there is no guarantee of the right to attend sick call and, in fact, no mention of regular medical services being available. The appointment of a jail physician is mandated, but there is no outline of duties. There is no mention of mental-health or dental services, drug detoxification, or prenatal care.

Even these minimal standards have not been fully enforced. (The Commission staff did draft twenty-two pages of medical standards in 1976, but these died quickly. The Commission also neglected to prompt the state medical society to apply for LEAA/AMA funding to upgrade local jails; not until 1980 did New York jails begin to participate in this widely publicized AMA project.) Gaps in enforcement can be documented not only by anecdotal material from various jail conditions suits but also from the 1978 jail census and a state audit.

The 1978 National Jail Census devoted seventeen of its thirty questions to health care and provides an overview of conditions in New York jails.

The major mandate in the Commission's medical standards is an admission examination. Six jails in the state out of seventy-two surveyed by the census responded that none of the people admitted was given a health interview or screening on admission, and six more examined some of, but not all, those admitted. Moreover, the responses to the screening question overstate the degree of compliance. In response to a census question about an actual physical, as opposed to an interview, twenty-six jails said that none of the people admitted was given a physical examination, and nine more replied that some received an exam on admission. Only twenty-four said that all who were admitted received a physical. (The other thirteen jails either failed to reply or answers could not be coded.) Thus more than half of the jails that responded provided no physical examination. The census delved into the quality of these exams. Height, weight, blood pressure, heart beat, and pulse were most often taken. Only nine jails said they gave a tuberculin test, only seven took a blood sample for hepatitis, and fifteen took a blood sample for venereal disease. Of the thirty-three jails responding to the census questions about diagnostic tests for alcohol and drug use, twenty-seven said they did not administer drug tests, and twenty-nine did not administer alcohol tests. Failure to provide adequate physical examinations means inmates will suffer from lack of treatment. It also exposes the jail population unnecessarily to individuals who have such communicable infections as hepatitis and venereal disease. Although dismal, the New York performance is probably above the national average (Comptroller General of the United States 1978; Anno 1977).

Several factors explain the failure of the Commission to fully implement health standards. Political signals from the legislature opposed aggressive enforcement. Although in 1975 the legislature had issued a strong legal charter to the Commission, it refused to confirm the governor's first appointment as Commission chairman—a law professor with a record of activism on prisoners' rights. The Commission was also opposed by the sheriffs, who brought a suit challenging six of the eight standards issued by the Commission in 1976-1977. Law suits surrounding the standards are still pending and have prevented aggressive enforcement as well. Additionally, eventual compliance will be difficult for the large number of small and underutilized jails outside of New York City that currently have little or no medical staff or facilities.

The Policy Research Agenda

Standards alone will not lead to substantial improvements in jail conditions. Unless states adopt more aggressive policies, local jails will still be cloacal ten years from now. Criminal-justice researchers can make contributions of potentially great importance by shifting somewhat the focus of research away from the study of jails as local criminal-justice institutions toward an investigation of the advantages and disadvantages—including political and economic feasibility—of the various policies and intervention strategies that might be adopted by the states. Here we briefly outline some of the avenues that deserve exploration.

Recognizing that rural jails typically have too few inmates to permit the econominal provision of professional and rehabilitative services, and that over-crowded urban jails—even though more likely to have professional as well as custodial staffs—usually can do little more than warehouse inmates, researchers have repeatedly advocated the creation of regional jails for sentended misde-meanants (Mattick 1974: p. 833). By concentrating large populations of sen-tenced inmates, regional jails would facilitate the provision of education, medical care, and other services.

Although this is probably the simplest answer to the problem of dreadful rural and urban jails, it has not proved extremely popular in practice. First, without some consolidation of detainee populations, the locality is compelled to support both its own jail for pretrial prisoners and a new regional facility.

Second, the question of efficient jail size still needs to be answered. Reli-able cost data comparable from jurisdiction to jurisdiction must be compiled before any marginal analysis is possible; such data are scarce. Douglas McDonald, for example, found that the New York City Department of Correction budget for its jails reflected only 64 percent of the city's actual jail costs during fiscal 1978. [See McDonald (1980) on problems with federal, New York State, and local compilations of costs.] The most recent study that attempted to look at optimal jail size found constant returns to scale for jails in California (Block and Ulen 1979; see also Block 1976, and Mikesell 1974). However, because this study focused on the costs of incapacitation, the researchers eliminated all re-habilitation costs. The inclusion of such costs, although more difficult, has bearing on decisions about how large or small jails should be.

Third, possible cost savings from large-scale facilities may be offset by the negative impacts of taking inmates far from their communities. Additionally, it is important to determine how regional jails do, and should, differ from state prisons.

A systematic review of studies dealing with regional jails would be an im-portant initial step for answering these questions. Although most have not been published in academic journals, over fifty studies dealing directly with regional jails are catalogued by the National Criminal Justice Reference Service. Inter-state and intrastate comparisons between multipurpose jails and jails solely for sentenced prisoners can also provide an empirical base for decision making about regionalization. For example, North Carolina operates prison camps for mis-demeanants with sentences of over thirty days, and several counties in New York have separate facilities for sentenced and unsentenced inmates.

The most neglected questions, however, relate to how regional jails would be established and administered: Should they be operated by the state agencies that administer prisons? By separate state agencies? By selected counties that would serve surrounding counties on a contractual basis? How would costs be financed, and to what extent could local jails still be used for sentenced inmates? The administrative and financial system should be structured so as to provide correct incentives to local jurisdictions. For example, charging per-diem fees to counties for inmates sentenced by their courts to regional jails would, if set sufficiently high, encourage investment in probation services as an alternative to incarceration. Such a fee, however, would have to be coupled with restrictions on the use of local jails for sentenced inmates. One option would be to prohibit local-jail sentences except for inmates in work-release or weekend-sentence programs.

The construction of regional jails, even if funded entirely by states, is likely to be highly controversial. Local correctional officials may view the regional jails as a threat to their autonomy, and political leaders may reject such jails because they will reduce the number of locally controlled patronage jobs. Reform groups, which generally advocate community-based alternatives to incarceration, may object to the creation of additional jail capacity and the removal of inmates from their local communities. Even when agreement can be reached to construct regional jails, implementation may be delayed indefinitely by fights over locations. If regional jails are to be a realistic option for reform, strategies to increase their political feasibility must be developed.

Inducements for reform might be created through restructuring the financial incentives facing local correctional officials. States would create incentives for meeting standards by offering per-diem inmate subsidies at rates proportional to levels of compliance. Such subsidies, despite providing steady incentives for gradual improvement, would not readily encourage regionalization or other alternatives to incarceration in local facilities. A stronger approach would be to fine local jurisdictions for inmates held in substandard conditions. To enhance political feasibility, the fines could be coupled with block grants so that in the initial year of the program, jurisdictions not altering their behavior would be neither fined or subsidized. For example, a jurisdiction with n_0 inmate-days per year in substandard condition when the program is initiated would receive a grant each year of $\$Xn_0$ where $\$X$ is the fine that is to be imposed on inmate days in subsequent years. In the ith year, if the jurisdiction had n_i inmate-days in substandard conditions, the net funds received from the state would be $\$X(n_0 - n_i)$. Local jurisdictions could increase the amount they receive by reducing the number of inmates held, bringing their facilities up to standards, or transferring inmates to facilities in neighboring jurisdictions that meet standards. The transfer option would represent a gradual movement toward a decentralized system of regional jails.

Other forms of state subsidy have been suggested. For example, states could provide medical services directly to inmates held in local jails (Wayson et al. 1977, pp. 103-104). A similar approach might be taken with other professional services that could be provided by state employees who visited jails on a rotating basis. Research is needed to determine the conditions under which such noncash subsidies would be economically and politically feasible.

Although our attention has focused on the role of jails as facilities for sentenced prisoners, research directed at improving and expanding pretrial diversion, release on own recognizance, and other alternatives to money bail continues to be warranted, not only on grounds of fairness but also because of the potential for improving conditions by reducing overcrowding in urban jails. Sentencing alternatives also must be kept in mind to avoid building regional jails that provide services better offered in the community. The emphasis on alternatives, however, must not obscure the real, and perhaps growing, problem of sentenced prisoners in the inadequate jails of the United States.

References

Allinson, Richard S. "LEAA's Impact on Criminal Justice: A Review of the Literature." *Criminal Justice Abstracts* 11(December 1979):608-648.

American Medical Association (AMA). *Standards for Health Services in Jails.* Chicago, 14 May 1979.

American Public Health Association (APHA), Jails and Prisons Task Force. *Standards for Health Services in Correctional Institutions.* Washington, D.C., 1976.

Anno, B. Jaye. *Analysis of Jail Pre-Profile Data: American Medical Association's Program to Improve Medical Care and Health Services in Jails.* Chicago, June 1977.

Bish, Frances. "Adult Pretrial Detention." In *Patterns of Metroplitan Policing,* edited by Elinor Ostrom, Robert Parks, and Gordon P. Whitaker. Cambridge, Mass.: Ballinger, 1978, pp. 207-242.

Block, Michael. *Cost, Scale Economies and Other Economic Concepts.* Washington, D.C., Correctional Economics Center, 1976.

Block, Michael, and Thomas S. Ulen. "Cost Functions for Correctional Institutions." In *The Costs of Crime* edited by Charles M. Gray. Beverly Hills, Calif.: Sage, 1979.

Comptroller General of the United States. *Conditions in Jails Remain Inadequate Despite Federal Funding for Improvements.* Washington, D.C.: U.S. General Accounting Office, 5 April 1976.

_____. *A Federal Strategy Is Needed to Help Improve Medical and Dental Care in Prisons and Jails.* Washington, D.C.: U.S. General Accounting Office, 22 December 1978.

Criminal Justice Research Center. *Sourcebook of Criminal Justice Statistics 1978.* Washington, D.C.: U.S. Government Printing Office, June 1979.

Goldfarb, Ronald. *Jails: The Ultimate Ghetto.* Garden City, N.Y.: Anchor Press/Doubleday, 1975.

Johnson, Carolyn and Marjorie Kravitz. *Overcrowding in Correctional Institutions: A Selected Bibliography*. Washington, D.C.: National Criminal Justice Reference Service, Law Enforcement Assistance Administration, February 1978.

Law Enforcement Assistance Administration (LEAA). *National Jail Census—1970*. Washington, D.C.: U.S. Government Printing Office, 1971.

_____. *Survey of Inmates of Local Jails: Advanced Report*. Washington, D.C.: U.S. Government Printing Office, 1975a.

_____. *The Nation's Jails: A Report of the Census of Jails from the 1972 Survey of Inmates in Local Jails*. Washington, D.C.: U.S. Government Printing Office, 1975b.

_____. *Prisoners in State and Federal Institutions*. Washington, D.C.: U.S. Government Printing Office, February 1979a.

_____. *Census of Jails and Survey of Jail Inmates 1978: Preliminary Report*. Washington, D.C.: National Criminal Justice Information and Statistics Service, February 1979b.

Levine, Mark and Marjorie Kravitz. *Jail-Based Inmate Programs*. Washington, D.C.: National Criminal Justice Reference Service, December 1979.

_____. *Standards of Care in Adult and Juvenile Correctional Institutions: A Selected Bibliography*. Washington, D.C.: National Criminal Justice Reference Service, February 1980.

McCrea, T.L. and D.M. Gottfredson. *Guide to Improved Handling of Misdemeanant Offenders*. Washington, D.C.: LEAA, January 1974.

McDonald, Douglas. *The Price of Punishment: Public Spending for Corrections in New York*. Boulder, Colo.: Westview Press, 1980.

Mattick, Hans W. "The Contemporary Jails of the United States: An Unknown and Neglected Area of Justice." In *Handbook of Criminology,* edited by Daniel Glaser. Chicago: Rand McNally, 1974, pp. 777–848.

Mattick, Hans W. and Alexander B. Aikman. "The Cloacal Region of American Corrections." *The Annals of the American Academy of Political and Social Science* 381(January 1969):109–118.

Mattick, Hans W. and R. Sweet. *Illinois Jails: Challenge and Opportunity for the 1970s*. Chicago: University of Chicago Law School, 1969.

Mikesell, John. "Local Jails Operating Cost and Economic Analysis: Scale Economics in Local Jail Operations." Paper presented at the Southern Economic Association, Atlanta, 15 November 1975.

Milin, Richard Kolb. *Report of the Task Force on the County Jails*. New Jersey Association on Correction, Citizen Action Division, March 1979.

New York State Commission of Correction. "Mecial Services." *Minimum Standards and Regulations for Management of County Jails and Penitentiaries,* subchapter A, part 7010. Promulgated in 1968 and repromulgated 1 October 1976.

New York State Comptroller, Division of Audits and Accounts. *Selected Operating Practices, Executive Department, State Commission of Corrections, March 31, 1978.* Albany, N.Y.: State Comptroller, 29 December 1978.

Resnik, Judith and Nancy Shaw. "Prisoners of Their Sex: Health Problems of Incarcerated Women." in *Prisoners Rights Sourcebook: Theory, Litigation and Practice,* edited by Ira Robins. New York: Clark Boardman, 1980.

Singer, Neil M. "Economic Implications of Standards for Correctional Institutions." *Crime and Delinquency* 23(January 1979):14–31.

Singer, Neil M. and Virginia B. Wright. *Cost Analysis of Correctional Standards: Institutional-Based Programs and Parole.* Washington, D.C.: American Bar Association Correctional Economics Center, January 1976.

Skolar, Daniel L. *Organizing the Non-System: Governmental Structuring of Criminal Justice Systems.* Lexington, Mass.: Lexington Books, D.C. Heath, 1977.

Thomas, Wayne H. *Bail Reform in America.* Berkeley, Calif.: University of California Press, 1976.

U.S. Department of Justice and U.S. Department of Commerce. *Expenditure and Employment Data for the Criminal Justice System, 1976.* Washington, D.C.: U.S. Government Printing Office, April 1978.

U.S. Department of Justice, Bureau of Justice Statistics. *Profile of Inmates of Local Jails—Sociodemographic Findings from the 1978 Survey of Inmates of Local Jails.* Washington, D.C.: U.S. Government Printing Office, 1980.

Wayson, Billy L.; Gail S. Funke; Sally F. Familton; and Peter B. Beyer. *Local Jails: The New Correctional Dilemma.* Lexington, Mass.: Lexington Books, D.C. Heath, 1977.

Appendix 7A:
Minimum Standards and Regulations for Management of County Jails and Penitentiaries

PART 7010
HEALTH SERVICES

Section 7010.1 Health services. (a) The county legislature, board of supervisors or similar county governing unit shall appoint a properly registered physician for the county jail and/or county penitentiary. (*Note:* See Correction Law, § 501, relative [to] appointment of physician to a county jail.)

(b) Each prisoner should be examined by the physician at the time of admission or as soon thereafter as possible and, preferably, no prisoner should be placed in a regular housing area or allowed to be in physical contact with other prisoners until such examination has been completed. Every prisoner admitted on a charge of public intoxication should be examined by the physician. (*Note:* Experience has firmly established that an alcoholic odor emanating from a prisoner can obscure a serious physical deficiency such as narcotic drug addiction, stroke, diabetic coma, heart attack, etc., or an abnormal mental condition.)

(c) No medication or medical treatment shall be given to a prisoner unless authorized or prescribed by the duly appointed facility physician.

(d) All medications shall be stored in a secure manner to insure control by authorized personnel. If it is considered that a supply of narcotic drugs, barbiturates, amphetamines or similarly sensitive or potentially dangerous drugs is to be kept at the county jail or county penitentiary, particularly secure storage facilities and adequate records of dispensing including a perpetual inventory record are required.

(e) To the extent possible, facility personnel should receive training in approved first aid and emergency life saving techniques including the use of emergency equipment, e.g., pulmotor, resuscitator, etc.

(f) Definite arrangements shall be made which will insure the prompt transportation of a prisoner to a hospital in emergency situations and provide the necessary supervision by duly authorized facility personnel during the period of hospitalization. (*Note:* See Correction Law, section 508, regarding removal to a hospital of a prisoner while confined in a county jail.)

Source: New York State Commission of Correction, "Health Services," *Minimum Standards and Regulations for Management of County Jails and Penitentiaries,* subchapter A, part 7010. Promulgated in 1968 and repromulgated 1 October 1976.

(g) Maximum use should be made of community medical and mental health facilities, services and personnel.

(h) Adequate health service and medical records shall be maintained which shall include but shall not necessarily be limited to such data as: date, name(s) of prisoner(s) concerned, diagnosis of complaint, medication and/or treatment prescribed; a record shall also be maintained of medication prescribed by the physician and dispensed to a prisoner by a staff person; under no circumstances shall a supply of medicine or medication be issued to or allowed to be in the possession of a prisoner.

8 Should Prisoners Be Classified by Sex?

Judith Resnik

Introduction

In the United States, female and male prisoners are generally consigned to separate institutions. The physical separation by gender corresponds to notions that women and men are different "kinds" of prisoners and "need" different kinds of facilities.[1]

These concepts are relatively modern. Prior to the early 1870s, prisoners were not classified by sex—nor, in most instances, by other criteria—and they were not housed in separate facilities. However, with the advent of the prison-reform movements in the late nineteenth century, women's institutions were created.[2] The articulated rationale was the protection of women, and the reform was greeted with praise. As one commentator wrote: "[t]here is ... no one living in this enlightened age who will not willingly concede that prisons for women should be separate from those of men."[3]

Once again, we are in an age of some prison reform—or at least in an age in which we express increased concern about prison conditions. In this "enlightened age," should we also readily concede that "prisons for women should be separate from those of men"? Are women's and men's prisons different? If so, what explains the differences, and should the distinctions be perpetuated? What is the relevance of the sex of a prisoner to the decision about the place of detention?

My conclusion is that sexual segregation of prisoners does not advance any appropriate purpose that underlies incarceration. The sex of a prisoner does not reveal the degree of culpability of an inmate nor the amount of supervision an individual requires. Furthermore, sexual segregation does harm to the emerging, but still fragile, societal value of sexual equality. The policy of separation works to deprive both female and male inmates of a full range of facilities, services, and opportunities. Moreover, segregation is generally rationalized as necessary for women, the objects and victims, who must be removed from men. Even if equality of services were achieved in sex-separated facilities, the continuation of gender-based classifications would continue to cause harm by perpetuating sexual stereotypes that degrade both sexes. Finally, correctional administrators justify and rely on sexual segregation as a principal technique for solving the problems of intra-inmate victimization and exploitation. However, separating women and men only avoids intersexual exploitation, it does not prevent the many acts of victimization that occur in single-sex facilities. Sexual segregation produces an illusion of safety that diverts attention from this substantial problem.

Women's Prisons: Changing Descriptions

The vision common to both popular and scholarly authors is that prisons are principally occupied by men. That image is accurate. Of the 329,000 prisoners in state and federal prisons in the United States in 1980, about 4 percent were women. Of the 26,000 federal prisoners, approximately 1,300 were female.[4]

Not surprisingly, the public receives far more information about prisons for men than about institutions that house women. The portrayals of men's institutions—in autobiographies, novels, sociological analyses, films, newspapers, and judicial opinions—generally describe fortresses, secured by steel-barred windows, walls, fences, concertina wire, and metal gates. Inside, unruly, fear-inspiring men spend endless hours in dark, damp cells.

In contrast, there is a vague impression that life for women in prison is not as difficult as it is for men. After all, there are no women in Attica, San Quentin, Leavenworth, and Marion. Rather, institutions for women are called "campuses," "farms," or "reservations," and such places have, presumably, less steel and more flowers. Women are housed in "cottages" and sleep in "rooms," which they are encouraged to decorate. Since the so-called "girls" are less frightening than male inmates—who, if white, are never described as "boys"—many assume that the controls imposed on women are correspondingly less stringent.

However, a new consciousness, forged by concern about women's rights and influenced by reports of the "forgotten" female offender, has brought attention to women's correctional facilities. Researchers have discovered that conditions for women inmates are woefully impoverished; lawsuits challenging the inadequacy of such conditions are increasingly successful. Women's prisons are abysmal, and, in contrast to common perceptions, facilities for women often provide fewer services and impose more restrictions than do those which house men.[5]

Two recent reports of the Comptroller General of the United States articulate the emerging themes. "With few exceptions, neither jails nor prisons . . . today does more than warehouse its female inmates; physical plant, staffing services, and programs are . . . sadly inadequate."[6] "Women in correctional institutions do not have access to the same types of facilities, job training, jobs in prison industries, and other services as [do] men prisoners."[7] According to this research, women prisoners have profoundly restricted opportunities for visitation, for health care, for recreation, for vocational and educational training, and for participation in work-release programs.

Judicial accounts of conditions in women's prisons confirm these conclusions. Two cases, *Todaro* v. *Ward*[8] and *Glover* v. *Johnson,*[9] are illustrative of complaints that led courts to intervene on behalf of female prisoners. In *Todaro,* women in Bedford Hills prison in New York challenged an entire health-care-delivery system as unconstitutional; they alleged that the system violated the Eighth Amendment's prohibition against cruel and unusual punishment. In the summer of 1974, Bedford Hills employed no full-time physician to treat the almost 400 women housed there. At the time of the trial in 1976, continuous medical care was unavailable, the x-ray machine was hazardous to health, and screening for medical problems was inadequate. Medical records were in disarray; laboratory test results were not delivered to patients, follow-up care was sporadic. After reviewing many instances of medical neglect that caused or exacerbated diseases, the district court concluded, and the Court of Appeals for the Second Circuit affirmed, that New York had failed to provide the inmates with adequate medical services and that such failure constituted "cruel and unusual punishment." The exacting standard of "deliberate indifference to known medical needs,"[10] rarely demonstrated, had been met. In 1977 the implementation of court-ordered changes began; in 1981 the restructuring of the medical-care system at Bedford Hills is still in process.

A second class-action lawsuit, *Glover* v. *Johnson,* brought by women imprisoned in Michigan, documents failures in other basic elements of prison life. In *Glover,* women claimed that they were permitted fewer job-training opportunities—and only in five limited and minimally remunerative areas such as food service and building maintenance—while men had access to some twenty vocational programs. Men printed a newspaper; women made personal calendars. Men learned welding, women did small handicrafts—again for personal use. Men apprenticed as machinists, tool-and-die makers, and electricians and were then permitted to practice those trades in prison industries. There were no apprentice programs for women and no industries in their prison. Based on the constitutional right to equal protection, guaranteed by the Fourteenth Amendment, the federal court concluded that "significant discrimination against the female prison population" existed.[11]

The problems of comparative disadvantage for women are not limited to Michigan. Data from the federal-prison system demonstrate comparable problems. The U.S. Bureau of Prisons operates some forty facilities for convicted inmates. Eleven of these are "camps," which are the least-restrictive settings available to federal prisoners. As of this writing, no women are housed in camps, despite the fact that in 1978, the Bureau had estimated that some 70 percent of the women met the eligibility requirements for assignments to camps. Further, although the Bureau's studies indicate that the preponderance of its female inmates comes from the Northeast, the Great Lakes region, and Southern California, all these women are placed in one of four facilities—in Alderson,

West Virginia; Lexington, Kentucky; Fort Worth, Texas; or Pleasanton, California.[12] Most women are, inevitably, at great distance from the communities in which they have lived, and their visitors—children, friends, and family—if they come at all, must travel at great expense.

The growing information about facilities for women leads to the conclusion that these prisons should not be described as environments designed especially for anyone, of either sex. To the extent that separate women's facilities held out any promise of providing services specifically to assist women, that promise is unfulfilled.

When requested—by researchers, courts, or Congress—to explain why women have received poor treatment, administrators of state and federal correctional facilities often point to the small number of women prisoners as the principal justification. With a large number of men, it is—purportedly—economically defensible to provide a number of prisons with varying custodial restrictions and with different educational, vocational, and recreational opportunities.[13]

This argument falls easily. No reason is provided for why limited resources should be allocated by sex, why services cannot be provided jointly to both sexes, or why economic burdens should be borne disproportionately by one sex. Moreover, an economic-efficiency justification—even if substantiated—could not be the guiding principle for the allocation of resources. Rather, prison administrators have recognized that the concern for equality, reflected in the Constitution, transcends arguments premised solely on efficiency. The program statement of the U.S. Bureau of Prisons is illustrative: "Inmates may not be discriminated against on the basis of race, religion, nationality, sex, handicap, or political belief. Each warden shall ensure that administrative decisions and work, housing and program assignments are nondiscriminatory."[14]

In sum, the concept of equality of the sexes has displaced precepts of the nineteenth century, which relegated women to a special, different, and lower status and which assumed that women play a very limited societal role. Today, parity between the sexes is accepted as appropriate, and parity should be the goal in prisons as elsewhere.

Reflective, in part, of this new ideology of equality, a few states and federal prisons have altered their policies of absolute sexual segregation and have begun placing women and men in the same institutions. In some twenty mixed, or cocorrectional facilities, women and men share dining, recreational, and working spaces and use them simultaneously.[15] Reports from these prison administrators suggest that such institutions are not substantially more difficult or costly to manage than are many single-sex facilities.

Despite these experiments, segregation by sex remains the more prevalent practice. That practice prompts this chapter. Given what we have learned about the impoverishment of single-sex prisons, should prisoners be housed in sexually segregated institutions? And, even assuming that equality of services and opportunities might be attained in separate facilities, should there continue to be "women's" and "men's" prisons?

Are There Justifications for Placing Women in Separate Institutions?

There are several possible methods by which to consider whether sexual segregation in prisons makes sense. To do so, it is necessary to explore the assumptions that underlie such segregation and to consider whether society at large, correctional administrators, or female and male inmates benefit from the current arrangements. Is sexual separation justified by the societal purposes and goals of incarceration, by administrative necessity or convenience, or by biologically or environmentally induced differences between the sexes?[16]

The Purposes of Incarceration

The commonly acknowledged justifications for imprisoning people after conviction include the societal interests in punishment, deterrence, incapacitation, and rehabilitation. Putting aside the propriety of incarceration as opposed to other sanctioning techniques, the question becomes: Are any societal aims furthered by having different prisons for women and men?

Punishment. The ways in which we determine how much punishment to impose are complex and unclear, but there is some agreement that two critical factors are the seriousness of the offense and the culpability or blameworthiness of the offender. Some assessment of these elements—with attention paid to other, mitigating factors—yields a decision on a sentence. To incarcerate either women or men in more oppressive or limited prisons, as we do currently, requires a judgment that either sex deserves a greater punishment. Although men are clearly apprehended and incarcerated more frequently than are women, both women and men commit the entire range of offenses, from victimless crimes to the most violent.

Is a crime any more evil, more deserving of punishment, because it is committed by a woman or a man? Historically, the answer may have been a qualified yes. Women who "sinned" fell from a higher pedestal than did men, but women were also viewed as more childlike, less responsible, and more redeemable than men.[17] Whatever the past perceptions, modern consciousness rejects the idea that the sex of the actor, any more than the race of the actor, is inculpatory or exculpatory. Further, to the extent that the vogue in sanctioning is shifting from individuated, subjective judgments to decisions made according to presumably objective guidelines, none of the current models relies on the sex of an offender as the basis for altering the kind of punishment imposed.[18] However, by placing prisoners in institutions by sex, we often accomplish such results.

A second justification may be that segregation of the sexes in prison is a punishment in itself. Segregation could be a vehicle by which prisoners are prevented from having contact with members of the opposite sex. A little imagination would simply add to a statute imposing no more than five years in prison and no more than a $10,000 fine the words, *and no intercourse—social or sexual—with members of the opposite sex.*

This artificial sexual separation may, in fact, increase the pain and discomfort of incarceration, since it underscores the distance between normal life and prison. However, if segregation is intended as a technique of punishment,[19] it is not an appropriate one. Segregation has resulted not only in isolation of the sexes but also in substantial inequities in treatment. Moreover, even if the disparities were lessened, I question the wisdom of imposing social-sexual deprivation. Segregation leads to sexual objectification, by making that which is generally unavailable—the company of a member of the opposite sex—per se desirable. Sexual stereotyping and rigid sex-role identifications may well result.[20]

Moreover, the physical separation of women and men inmates does not, in itself, prevent them from engaging in sexual activities. Homosexual behavior is not precluded. Further, virtually no institutions for women are run by—or perhaps can legally be run by[21]—single-sex staffs; by evidence of pregnancy and anecdote, we have ample proof that heterosexual activity occurs at single sex prisons. Moreover, as those with experience in administering sexually mixed prisons report, women and men prisoners can be confined in the same institutions, and share many facilities and programs, while the prohibition on sex remains intact.[22] Thus, sexual behavior is not precluded by the existence of single-sex institutions, and a decision to prohibit sexual behavior does not lead, inextricably, to the conclusion that inmates have to be segregated by sex.

Deterrence. Another reason to put criminals in prison is to deter either specifically the individual to be incarcerated or generally other individuals who may commit crimes in the future. Certain generalizations about the sexes would have to be made to justify, as a matter of deterrence, the creation of different facilities for women and men. For example, if women learned less readily or differently than do men, deterrence of specific females would require that they be placed in worse or different conditions than men. Of course, such a gross generalization is inaccurate. Sex is simply not a characteristic that conveys precise information about what will deter individuals.

Moving from the issue of specific deterrence to that of general deterrence, the question becomes whether female or male members of the community perceive themselves only as similar to members of their own sex and thus their behavior is affected only when one of their own number is punished. No research to date firmly supports this hypothesis. Moreover, there is substantial debate over whether general deterrence works at all, and, if so, how it functions.[23] Given its own theoretical and empirical shakiness, deterrence is a weak support on which to rest the logic of sex-segregated prisons.

Incapacitation. A third reason to incarcerate criminals is not to affect them but to protect ourselves. Incapacitation rests on predictions of an individual's future actions. Once a prediction is made that an individual is dangerous to society because the likelihood of future criminal acts is substantial, that person is placed in a setting designed both to prevent escape and to control behavior while that person is imprisoned. Is societal protection enhanced by using sex as the predominant predictive tool?

Reliance on sex would be useful if the sex of an offender were an accurate barometer of whether that individual was likely to commit criminal acts in the future, or to escape, or to endanger other inmates. But, sex is not that kind of forecasting tool. Empirical studies do not tell us that a woman who has robbed a bank three times is any more likely to rob a fourth time than a three-time male bank robber nor that a woman who has attempted escapes or has committed numerous acts of violence is more or less likely to repeat her behavior than would be a man. Nor does the data from mixed facilities suggest that sexual integration leads to increased escape attempts or to more frequent violence in prisons.[24]

Moreover, correctional administrators do not, in their classification systems, use sex as if it conveyed such information. Rather, when they decide how secure a setting is needed for an inmate, they assess other factors, including the past criminal record, the nature of the offense that led to the current imprisonment, the duration of the sentence, disciplinary problems while incarcerated, and personal history.[25] However, after making initial assessments based on such criteria, prison administrators then abandon their classification system and use the sex of an inmate as the ultimate and determinative factor. By insisting on sexual segregation, they override and nullify their own attempts at coherent classification, premised on predictions about the need for incapacitation and control.

Rehabilitation. A fourth justification for imprisonment is to provide criminals with a place in which they can receive treatment, support, and guidance so as to become rehabilitated. Although many now repudiate this goal as either unworkable or inappropriate,[26] rehabilitation has survived fluctuations in its popularity in the past; its relationship to sexual segregation is worth exploring here. Can the rehabilitative ideal justify different places of confinement for women and men? To respond affirmatively, one must conclude that biologically or environmentally induced differences in women and men require either different rehabilitative services or single-sex institutions.

The different-services thesis hinges on a belief that women and men do and should continue to carry out different roles in society and should be prepared for these roles while in prison. In an age when women were seen primarily as homemakers and caretakers, with fixed economic, intellectual, and personal horizons, it might have been plausible to advance the proposition that separate prisons for women could best train females for their assigned roles. But, with the large number of women in the workforce and with the growing understanding of the diversity of roles open to both sexes, the argument is specious.

A second possibility is that single-sex facilities provide a more conducive setting in which rehabilitation might occur. Given the historical disabilities imposed on women, retreat to an all-women's environment might be helpful in fostering women's growth. Single-sex colleges advance this thesis; might not the same apply for single-sex prisons?

Colleges are poor and inexact models for prisons. Placement in universities occurs by voluntary and mutual selection, rather than involuntary, unwilling designation. Further, college women are not prohibited from having regular contact with men. Moreover, when working well, schools support growth, independence, and individualization by requiring students to progress from required to elective curricula, from structured to more individualized assignments. In contrast, as currently organized, prisons require rigid conformity. Prisons are places for infantilization—paternalistic at their kindest and castrating when most brutal.

Nevertheless, some individuals may well do better in single-sex environments, others in small, rather than large, facilities, some in urban settings, others in rural. If these factors were considered, segregation by sex would no longer be automatic but would be decided on an individual basis. Therefore, to rest the continuing existence of women's prisons on the assumption that they are "good for the girls" is a suspect justification, plainly at odds with other prison practices and suggestive of a demeaning paternalism.

Governmental Needs: Economy, Efficiency, and Ease

A second set of justifications for single-sex facilities comes from the government's interest in maintaining and administering correctional facilities as inexpensively and efficiently as possible. Do administrative concerns dictate single-sex facilities?

In part, the answer rests on earlier sections of this analysis. If women and men deserved different treatment, it would simplify the delivery of those services to segregate the populations. But, having rejected the notions that women and men are incarcerated for different reasons or need different kinds of prisons, societal goals in themselves cannot necessitate separate facilities. Nevertheless, prison administrators do have additional and discrete interests, and it is often those interests that are advanced in support of single-sex facilities.

The dominant concern is cost. Prisons are operated on limited budgets. Is it more or less expensive to separate women and men in different prisons? Sometimes, to achieve separation, a jurisdiction must build a new facility; in those instances, separation will increase costs. However, rather than build or maintain separate facilities for women, a few jurisdictions send women to prisons elsewhere and pay both transportation and per-diem costs. Although this contracting avoids the expense of building an additional prison, it adds the cost of long-distance transportation to that of maintenance. In addition, there are substantial hidden costs when women are incarcerated outside their home jurisdictions. Those costs include the reduction of opportunities for family visits, the absence of personal contact with parole officials, and the increased difficulty in obtaining legal assistance for problems jurisdictions-away.

In the majority of states, new construction or transportation is not required because there are existing, separate facilities for women. Comparing the cost, per day, per inmate at women's and men's facilities is unenlightening, because prison costs vary with the size of an institution, the level of security maintained, the access to and use of community resources, the services provided, and the number of staff employed. It is difficult to find female and male institutions that are comparable, but what research there is does not suggest that separate institutions for women and men provide substantial monetary savings.[27]

If women in segregated prisons are to be afforded equal opportunities for educational, vocational, and recreational services, additional expenditures will be required at the many women's prisons where opportunities are disproportionately limited. In these instances, economies of scale may dictate mixing the sexes. For example, in *Glover,* the state argued that it could not afford to duplicate for 400 women the range of service available to the more than 16,000 men who were imprisoned in Michigan.[28] Permitting both sexes access to the same programs would be directly responsive to Michigan's fiscal concerns.

Of course, women and men may need some services, such as specialized medical care or places in which to nurse infants, that are exclusive to their sex. But gynecological and obstetrical services can be provided, by contract, wherever women are incarcerated. And, unfortunately, institutions that are designed for women do not have distinguished records of providing such necessary services to their population. Gynecologists were not members of the full-time medical staff at Bedford Hills when women sued that prison. And, today, there are still no full-time staff gynecologists at F.C.I. Alderson, the one federal prison exclusively for women. Only if separation of the sexes is accompanied by the absence of services does the maintenance of separate facilities result in fiscal economy.

A second way to assess the efficiency of separate facilities is to compare the expense of running a mixed facility with that of administering an institution for one sex. Conclusions are limited by the absence of controlled studies, but preliminary reports from mixed facilities do not indicate that the joining of the sexes greatly magnifies the expense of administration. Nor do the very limited data support a conclusion that intra-inmate violence increases when members of both sexes share facilities.[29]

In sum, maintaining single-sex prisons does not appear to be less expensive or easier than running mixed facilities. There has been no demonstration that a single-sex prison results in substantial savings. And, although there are soft-spoken fears of disorder when the sexes are mixed, thus far integrated institutions have provided no evidence to support this thesis.

The Inmates' Needs

A final support for sexual segregation comes from concern for those who are incarcerated. Although prisoners are not asked to choose conditions of confinement, some assume that prisoners prefer or are better off in single-sex facilities. Is that assumed level of comfort real, and, if so, should institutional arrangements be structured to permit it?

To the extent that the sexual-celibacy rule is a feature of imprisonment, some argue that it is unfair to place women and men in reach of each other. In accordance with traditional stereotypes, men may be driven by "irresistable urges," while women are at risk of exploitation. However, some report the easing of sexual tension when women and men share facilities.[30] Moreover, the potential for frustration and abuse is not unique to nor clearly generated by sexually mixed prisons; victimization is relatively common in all closed institutions.[31] The concern about inmate abuse—by cohorts or by staff—is substantial; the problem of protecting the victim, regardless of sex, must be addressed. Regardless of whether women and men are housed in the same or separate facilities, if, as a matter of public policy, society believes that the discomforts of imprisonment should not be aggravated by sexual tensions, then some forms of sexual expression must be permitted.[32] But neither of these issues—victimization or sexuality—intrinsically justifies maintaining only single-sex facilities.

A related concern is that mixed facilities would do violence to social mores about privacy. However, placing women and men prisoners in the same facilities does not mean they have to watch each other disrobe. Private spaces can easily be arranged, separate sleeping and bathing facilities provided. Further, inmate privacy is an ironic justification for single-sex facilities, since most correctional facilities provide prisoners with little privacy from either other inmates or staff.

Women and Men Together in Prisons: The Policy Implications

In sum, scant justification exists for the dominant practice of placing women and men in separate prisons. But the absence of persuasive rationales may be inadequate to reorder the status quo. Would the joining of women and men in facilities alleviate those problems described? Or would it cause other problems?

Substantial evidence has been accumulated that segregation works to deprive women of comparable opportunities for job training and education. However, it must be admitted that comparison can only be made between degrees of deprivation. No one in prison is advantaged; some are simply less disadvantaged than others.

However, a greater—and less easily eradicated—harm is caused by single-sex facilities. In some facets of our society, we are recognizing that gender-based classifications are offensive.[33] Sex, like race, is no longer seen as an innocuous technique for categorization but rather as one with pernicious effects. In oft-cited psychological studies, attributes of the ill and the infantile are associated with women; in contrast, the healthy adult and the male are described with identical adjectives.[34] Many prison administrators share the common cultural biases against women. Some officials openly seek to reform their errant "girls" and teach them to be docile and ladylike. Sexual segregation in prisons gives outlets for and buttresses the negative images of women.

What would happen if the world of prisons, like the world at large, became sexually mixed—if women and men were placed in prisons on the basis of criteria other than sex? In the federal system, for example, an obvious result would be the end to the concentration of women in four prisons in the country. Their dispersal—potentially to more than forty prisons—might lead to the placement of approximately thirty-five women in each facility. If such transfers occurred, some women, such as those from New York City, would benefit by being placed closer to their homes—at prisons in Lewisburg or Allenwood, Pennsylvania, or Otisville and Lake Placid, New York. Integration in the state systems would generally have similar results. Women would be able to learn trades and work in industries not now available to them. Moreover, in the federal system some women would be released earlier because, by virtue of being at prison camps, they would be automatically entitled to camp "good time"—extra statutory reductions on the length of time to be served.[35]

The prisons would, of course, have to change in some respects. Allenwood, Lewisburg, Otisville, and Lake Placid would have to contract—as do the four federal prisons that currently house women—with gynecologists and obstetricians. These institutions might also consider expanding child-visitation programs and thereby provide opportunities appropriate for parents of either sex.

The shift to a mixed prison society would not be without problems. Competition for jobs within the institutions might result in some traditional allocations. Women might be sent to the kitchen, although men were selected for jobs as auto mechanics. Concern for maintenance of sexual taboos might also increase staff surveillance of inmates.[36] These problems would have to be addressed; those who run mixed facilities have made initial efforts to deal with these issues by special training programs for both staff and inmates.[37]

Aside from these surmountable difficulties, two related concerns emerge from the exploration of a classification system independent of sex. First, because of the comparatively small number of women prisoners, placement irrespective of sex would result in their dispersal in small groups to institutions predominantly populated by men. Thirty-five "integration pioneers" might be locked into a prison with seven hundred men. Second, females have so often been victims that they might be given or assume that role in these mixed institutions. Women might be given too much attention from their male cohorts and too little from the staff; women might be beset by social pressures, feel isolated, and be in that situation for years. Given this spectre, some might assume women would be safer and more comfortable in their "own" institutions, even if far away from home and offering minimal programs and activities.

This hypothetical brings into focus the most substantial argument for grouping imprisoned women—but not men—by sex. Women prisoners are few in number and therefore vulnerable to attack. However, this concern does not lead unalterably to a single conclusion—the fixed landscape of sexual separation. Once it is understood that the problems are numerical ratios and victimization, rather than the sexual identity of prisoners, attention must shift to the questions of how many inmates of any minority are needed to comprise a "critical mass" and of how the weak can be protected. These are not "women's" or "men's" issues. They are problems that potentially implicate all members of prison populations, and other institutions, and that should be addressed by reference to anyone who may be harmed because of isolation or fragility. These are problems that merit the energy and attention of correctional administrators. Sex disguises rather than illuminates these issues.

Notes

1. Data for this chapter have been drawn from my field research, described in part in J. Resnik and N. Shaw, "Prisoners of Their Sex: Women's Health in Correctional Facilities," in *Prisoners' Rights Sourcebook: Theory, Litigation, and Practice,* edited by I. Robbins, vol. 2 (New York: Clark Boardman, 1980), and in J. Resnik, "Testimony about Women Incarcerated in the Federal System," U.S. House, Committee on the Judiciary, Subcommittee on Courts, Civil Liberties, and the Administration of Justice, *Hearings on Female Offenders,* 96th Cong., 1st sess. 106(1979). U.S. Department of Justice, Bureau of Justice Statistics, "Prisoners in State and Federal Institutions on December 31, 1978" (1979); J. Chapman, *Economic Realities and the Female Offender* (1980): C. Griffiths and M. Nance (eds.), *The Female Offender* (1980); J. Smykla, *Co-Corrections: A Case Study of a Coed Federal Prison* (1979); R. Glick and V. Neto, *National Study of Women's Correctional Programs* (1976); "Note, The Sexual Segregation of American Prisons," 82 *Yale L.J.* 1229 (1973), in the weekly reports, "Monday Morning Highlights," and the research of the U.S. Bureau of Prisons; and in many unpublished court decisions and judgments. Full reference materials are on file at the University of Southern California Law Center.

2. See, *e.g.,* Barrows, "The Reformatory Treatment of Women in the United States," in *Penal and Reformatory Institutions* (New York: Russell Sage, 1910), and E. Freedman, *Their Sisters' Keepers* (Ann Arbor, Mich.: University of Michigan Press, 1981).

3. Sara F. Keely, "The Organization and Discipline of the Indiana Women's Prison" in *Proceedings of the Annual Congress of the National Prison Association of the United States* 275 (Shaw Brothers, 1899).

4. U.S. Department of Justice, Bureau of Justice Statistics, *Bulletin: Prisoners in 1980* 4. U.S. Department of Justice, *Monday Morning Highlights* (1980) (weekly). Estimates of the exact number of women in prison vary from 3 percent to 5 percent.

5. See U.S. General Accounting Office, *Women in Prison: Inequitable Treatment Requires Action* (GGD-81-6, 10 December 1980) (hereinafter *Women in Prison*), and Glover v. Johnson, 478 F. Supp. 1075 (E.D. Mich. 1979).

6. U.S. General Accounting Office, *Female Offenders: Who Are They and What Are the Problems Confronting Them?* (GGD-79-73, 23 August 1979) (hereinafter *Female Offenders*), 31.

7. *Women in Prison, supra,* n. 5 at i.

8. 431 F. Supp. 1129 (S.D.N.Y. 1977), *aff'd.*, 565 F.2d 48 (2d Cir. 1977).

9. Glover, *supra,* n. 5.

10. See Estelle v. Gamble, 429 U.S. 97, 104 (1976).

11. Glover, *supra,* n. 5, 478 F. Supp. at 1083.

12. Minor and Bergsmann, *Long Range Facilities Plan for Female Offenders* (Washington, D.C.: U.S. Bureau of Prisons, July 1978). In 1980, the Bureau of Prisons announced its intention to open a camp for women at Danbury, Connecticut. See its *Federal Prison System, Report to Congress: Feasibility Study of Alternative Uses for the Federal Correctional Institution, Alderson, West Virginia* (1980).

13. See, *e.g.,* Glover, *supra,* n. 5, *passim.*

14. 28 C.F.R. section 551.90 (1980). See also, U.S. Department of Justice, *Federal Standards for Prisons and Jails* (1980) No. 1.02.

15. The actual number fluctuates. In 1980, according to National Institute of Justice, *American Prisons and Jails,* vol 1-3 (1980–1981) at 55 (hereinafter *American Prisons*), 26 of 559 institutions surveyed describe themselves as "co-ed."

16. One question is whether sexual segregation of prisoners is lawful under current constitutional norms. If such a challenge were raised, a court would explore the government interests advanced to justify sex-segregated institutions and would weigh their import against the detrimental effect, if any, of such segregation on either sex. If a court found that classification by sex, as by race, were so violative of constitutional values as to be "suspect," then the state's justifications would have to be "compelling." However, if sex were not perceived as a "suspect" classification, the state's explanations would be judged on a lower, less-demanding scale. Of late, the federal courts have used an intermediate-level approach when deciding whether gender-based classifications are permissible. See Rostker v. Goldberg, 453 U.S. 57 (1981) and Michael M. v. Superior Court, 450 U.S. 464 (1981). One of the few courts to address the constitutionality of gender-based classifications in correctional facilities is the *Glover* court, *supra,* n. 5. However, the issue in that case was not whether integration was required but whether equal opportunities had to be provided to women and men inmates. The district court applied an intermediate-level test

and found that "parity of treatment" was required. *Cf.* Lee v. Washington, 390 U.S. 333 (1968) (racial segregation of prisons is unconstitutional).

17. In several states, women were given indeterminate sentences so that they might be released only after they were "rehabilitated," whereas men were given fixed terms. See, *e.g.*, Commonwealth v. Butler, 328 A.2d 851 (Pa. 1974); State v. Chambers, 63 N.J. 287, 307 A.2d 78 (1973).

18. See, *e.g.*, United States Parole Commission, "Adult Guidelines for Parole Decision-Making," 28 C.F.R. section 2.20 (1980).

19. As M. Foucault argues; see *Discipline and Punish* 73–131 (New York: Pantheon, 1977).

20. See V. Gornick and B. Moran, *Woman in a Sexist Society* (New York: Basic Books, 1971).

21. See Gunther v. Iowa State Men's Reformatory, 612 F.2d 1079 (8th Cir. 1980), *cert. denied*, 446 U.S. 966 (1980); Forts v. Ward, 621 F.2d 1210 (2d Cir. 1980). *Cf.* Dothard v. Rawlinson, 433 U.S. 321 (1977).

22. See reports of the U.S. Bureau of Prisons on their facilities at Fort Worth, Lexington, and Pleasanton, in which women and men share educational, recreational, vocational, and dining facilities. See also Mabli et al., "Co-Corrections Evaluation: Preliminary Data," 2 *Offender Rehabilitation* 303 (1978); and J. Ross et al., *Assessment of Coeducational Corrections* (Washington, D.C.: Law Enforcement Assistance Administration, 1978).

23. A. Blumstein et al., *Deterrence and Incapacitation: Estimating the Effects of Criminal Sanctions on Crime Rates* (Washington, D.C.: National Academy of Sciences, 1978).

24. Researchers have not focused much on this issue; however, none of the commentators argues that sexual integration leads to a marked increase in security problems. See, *e.g.*, J. Smykla, *Coed Prison* (New York: Human Sciences Press, 1980).

25. See, *e.g.*, U.S. Bureau of Prisons, *Security Designation and Custody Classification Manual* (P.S. 5100.1).

26. See N. Carlson, "Striking a Balance in Corrections," in *Prisoners Rights Sourcebook: Theory, Litigation, and Practice;* and Martinson, "What Works?— Questions and Answers about Prison Reform," 35 *The Public Interest* 22(Spring 1974).

27. See U.S. Bureau of Prisons, *Report of the Task Force on Confinement of Female Offenders* 23(1979). In fact, some of the impetus for mixing the sexes came from a desire to utilize existing beds. Ross, *Assessment of Coeducational Corrections, supra,* n. 22 at 74.

28. Glover v. Johnson, *supra,* n. 5, 478 F. Supp. at 1077.

29. See Smykla, *Coed Prison, supra,* n. 24 and Ross, *Assessment of Coeducational Corrections, supra,* n. 27.

30. *Id.*

31. Carriere, "The Dilemma of Individual Violence in Prisons," 6 *New Eng. J. Prison Law* 195 (1980); L. Bowker, *Prison Victimization* (Amsterdam: Elsevier, 1980).

32. For example, inmates could be given furloughs from prison or conjugal visits could be allowed. See Simpson, "Conjugal Visiting in United States Prisons," 10 *Col. Human Rts. L. Rev.* 643(1978–1979).

33. See, *e.g.,* Orr v. Orr, 440 U.S. 268 (1979). But see Rostker v. Goldberg, *supra,* n. 16.

34. McKee and Sherriffs, "The Differential Evaluation of Males and Females," 25 *J. Person.* 356(1957). See, generally, E. Macoby and C. Jacklin, *The Psychology of Sex Differences* (Stanford, Calif.: Stanford University Press, 1974).

35. 18 U.S.C. section 4162.

36. Interviews at F.C.I. Pleasanton (1980). Since some sexual exchanges would occur, provision for birth control would be necessary to protect women from unwanted pregnancies.

37. For example, the National Institute of Corrections has provided funds for such programs.

Designing Effective Transitions for New Correctional Leaders

Thomas N. Gilmore and
Joseph E. McCann III

A leadership transition in a corrections department is an opportunity for significant change. A transition can destabilize accepted organizational routines, remove supports for entrenched attitudes, and alter existing power relationships. As Edgar Schein (1973) suggests, such opportunities are rarely present in the normal working environment.

The high uncertainty inherent in a transition also poses significant risks. For example, unresolved transition issues at several levels may prevent new leaders from gaining the requisite control over a department, thereby increasing the likelihood of major problems. Recent accounts of the riot in New Mexico cite personnel changes—four correctional secretaries in five years, four wardens in four years—as a major contributor to the conditions that led to the riot (State of New Mexico 1980, p. 23).

Transitions can be designed and managed to maximize opportunities and minimize risks posed by a change. When well designed and managed, a transition represents a "natural point of entry" for desired change (Yin 1976). An effective *transition* is thus defined as a leadership change that meets the more or less explicitly stated objectives of the new leader and his or her appointor.

Despite the significance of a leadership change, there is a limited formal literature and shared understanding of what does or does not lead to an effective transition. The informal, folklore quality of the lessons accumulated about transitions is striking.

This chapter identifies a number of recurrent problems that arise during leadership changes, suggesting that a more formalized, shared approach to transitions would be highly valuable. The chapter also argues that all transitions have many shared characteristics, so that a general transition model can be formulated. One such model follows. Finally, we outline two sets of strategies, with examples of their use, for better managing a transition.

Throughout the article a model situation is assumed. The focus is on new corrections commissioners who have been recruited from outside the

Two commissioners and two cabinet-level secretaries from three states appointed in the last two years contributed many helpful ideas to this chapter. Our thanks also to their staff members who reviewed an earlier draft. A promise of confidentiality precludes thanking them all by name. The American Correctional Association helped by providing us with data on leadership changes.

department. The department is also assumed to be in need of significant reform. The obviously critical issue of leadership development is not directly considered. Effective executive search and recruitment strategies are only briefly considered.[1]

The main questions are, given a competent appointment, how can the opportunity for constructive change be maximized and the costs to career employees in the department be better managed? A transition is not simply a disruptive period to endure and wait out. Nor should the fate of employees be dependent more on the unmanaged dynamics of a transition than the individual strengths and weaknesses of those employees.

Transition at the top of correctional agencies is in a sense a limiting case. If the model and strategies are useful at that level, with some modification they can guide leadership changes within departments involving wardens, regional directors, and bureau chiefs. Leadership turnovers at major institutions and offices often follow changes at the top of the department and pose many of the same opportunities and risks.

To become effective, any new policy initiatives must eventually encounter the powerful culture of the major institutions. Changing or transferring wardens is a frequently used method to introduce these initiatives. Yet if the transition is not effectively managed, not only do the initiatives remain unimplemented but there is the potential of increased disorder among prisoners and prison staff.[2]

Recent Patterns of Commissioner Turnover

Figure 9–1 illustrates the pattern of leadership change in the six and one-half years from 1974 to mid-1980 for top adult-corrections jobs. Data for the figure are for all fifty states plus New York City and Washington, D.C. Figure 9–1 reveals that only eight states enjoyed the same leadership over the time period. Ten states had three or more changes. The average tenure, based on these data, is currently between two and three years; it is our impression that this is a significant decrease from earlier periods.

Informed sources of information suggest that the following shifts are also occurring: (1) leadership changes in corrections are increasingly linked to changes in the governorship; (2) confirmation hearings are becoming less routine; (3) the average age of a new commissioner at the time of appointment is decreasing, making it more likely that the person will be significantly younger than many of his or her senior superintendents; (4) the expectation of how long a new commissioner would serve, even if asked to continue indefinitely, has dropped as awareness of executive burnout increases; (5) more are chosen from outside a department, outside corrections, and outside a state; and (6) more new commissioners have served previously as a commissioner in other states.

Given the data in figure 9-1 and the six trends just noted, the image that emerges is one of increasing turbulence and transition at the top of many agencies and departments. Given the critical need for effective, coherent management

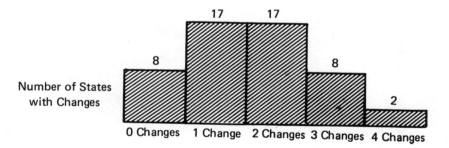

Figure 9-1. Numbers of States by Number of Leadership Changes—1974 to Mid-1980

at this strategic level, this image is disturbing. A greater appreciation of transition issues and dynamics is clearly needed.

Transition Issues and Dynamics

Two core assumptions can build a better appreciation of the dynamics of a transition. First, a transition is a process and not a discrete event. A transition has at least four more-or-less distinct, overlapping phases. Each phase poses its own difficulties and opportunities. The overall effectiveness of the process depends on when and how well each phase is managed. The managing of later phases is dependent on how well earlier phases are managed. Opportunities may exist in later phases for overcoming earlier mistakes, but these opportunities are at considerable cost in energy and political credit.

Second, a transition is a process of mutual accommodation (Gouldner 1954; Schein 1979). There are two sets of perspectives and expectations in every transition: the successor's and those of other stakeholders in the transition, most notably the views of the governor and those of department staff. The expectations of stakeholders like the heads of other departments—the successor's peers—and public-interest groups are far from insignificant as well. Each stakeholder has expectations that are grounded both in reality and in fantasy (Louis 1980, p. 227). Their expectations may or may not be compatible; some expectations will be met, some will not be met, and many will be altered during the transition.

The Four Transition Phases

Four phases are postulated: selection and contracting; entry; initiatives; and pattern setting. Figure 9-2 illustrates the relations among these phases.

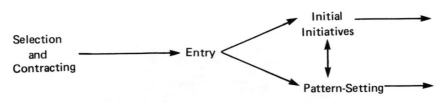

Figure 9-2. The Four Phases of a Transition Process

Selection and Contracting

This phase focuses on the screening and selection of a successor and the quality of the contracting between the successor and his or her superior (the governor or cabinet secretary). Three selection issues are present: (1) the motivations for the change in leadership; (2) the formality of the selection process; and (3) the successor's attributes.

The motivations for a change in leadership can vary greatly. Motivations affect the speed and extent of changes undertaken. If the office is vacant or a crisis climate prevails, the pressure for speedy selection and action may preclude far-reaching searches for successors. The formality of the selection process also determines the reach of the search; the use of "old-boy" networks tends to narrow the search and to stereotype the successor (Levinson 1974). Formal search processes require time and resources, but they build the legitimacy of the selection. Interrelated with these elements are the successor's credibility and desirability, which determine the amount of policy and political leverage allowed the new leader. If the successor is a second or third choice or consensus about the choice is limited, leverage will be similarly limited.

The psychological contract between the successor and his or her selector is also of critical importance, yet practice suggests that early discussions and exploration of philosophies are often neglected. For example, at his initial press conference one newly appointed secretary was asked his views about the death penalty. He glanced nervously at the governor who was present and said that he would resign on moral grounds rather than carry out a sentence of death—the secretary and governor had never discussed this issue in their prior conversations. Judging from current practice, contracting can differ greatly in its explicitness. Minimally, mutual agreement should be sought about the following: initial policy postures; the action agenda, including timing of its implementation; access to the governor or secretary; the level of support that can be expected in a pinch; and the degree of flexibility and discretion available to the new executive in taking action within the department, including replacements of staff. Opportunities for continual discussion and revisions in these five areas need to be created and maintained.

Entry

This stage is an encounter period in which initial expectations are also verified or redefined (Louis 1980, p. 227). Long-term orientations are shaped in this phase. The phase formally begins at the moment of selection. The testing and redefinition of expectations is done with staff and peers through briefings, workshops, and one-on-one interactions. Symbolic action is acutely important in this phase; everyone seeks any type of information about changes in the norms for behavior and about the areas where initiatives will begin (Rumsfeld 1979).

A core group of staff begins to emerge in this phase as the successor's expectations about staff performance are verified or rejected. As a result, issues of in-group/out-group membership become salient. It is also during this phase that a tentative agenda for action emerges, based on the preliminary intelligence gathered through briefings, task forces, and workshops.

Entry effectiveness depends on the type and amount of resources available to the new leader and the amount of pressure for immediate action present in the situation. Limited resources and intense pressure for action prematurely shorten and limit this critical phase. There is also a tendency to cut this period short, since it is uncomfortable for everyone; many expectations remain untested and implicit as a result.

The effectiveness of this phase can also be limited for a reason extraneous to the corrections agency. A prolonged disengagement from a previous position and unresolved family issues like housing and schools for children and absorb the executive's scarce energy and needed attention. Because exits are underappreciated, they tend to be undermanaged. A transition design must necessarily consider ways to bring a satisfying closure to the successor's exit from a previous position.

Initial Initiatives

This phase, blending in from entry, includes three areas of action. First, strategic replacements of staff are undertaken (Ewing 1979; Gouldner 1954). Second, major programmatic changes, including renegotiation of relations with external stakeholders, are begun. Third, internal department relations and processes are restructured to make responsibilities of units and staff consistent with the programmatic innovations.

The executive and staff may well differ about the timing and extent of the desired changes. Time horizons, for example, may differ—the former may focus on the next election, the latter on life-time careers and carryover interests. Moreover, the successor may view the status of existing plans and programs as open, while staff will be committed to protecting existing activities that they value.

Finally, how quickly the new leader can make strategic staff replacements may also depend on the quality of intelligence gathered about staff competency and the tolerance of the department to sustain the turnover.

In general, there is a tendency to move quickly into the initial-initiatives phase. Some of the difficulties encountered in implementing changes during this phase are commonly attributed by new executives to unwarranted staff resistance to innovations and to miscalculations regarding the department's capacity to shift direction rapidly. An alternative hypothesis is offered. Such difficulties are often due to unresolved transition issues within earlier phases and a premature entry into the initial-initiatives phase.

Pattern-Setting

This fourth stage runs parallel with the initial-initiatives phase. Pattern setting is concerned with the reinforcing or institutionalizing of desired norms and interpersonal relations (Gabarro 1979). Pattern setting attempts to create a predictable work climate and tone for the department, particularly about behaviors that are rewarded and expected. A noticeable routine emerges during this phase, even though major programmatic and staff changes may be underway. However, pattern setting is disrupted by surprises and may become impossible when action agendas are concealed. A clear trade-off exists between initial-initiatives and pattern-setting phases: premature routinization may block innovation and change, but prolonged change-induced turbulence can also limit the organization's capacity to institutionalize new approaches and adopt and maintain innovative routines. The tension between these two phases must be present but actively managed.

Proposed Transition Strategies

An increased appreciation of phases and issues is a critical first step toward a better-designed transition. Explicit strategies are also needed to build additional transition-management capacity. Two sets of strategies are offered. The first set builds a new commissioner's personal capacity to manage entry-phase issues by bringing external resources and expertise to the situation. The second set generates several internal department activities and events. By engaging both the new commissioner and staff, the second set of strategies builds overall department capacity. Both sets emphasize entry, initial-initiatives, and pattern-setting phases.

Collegial Strategies

Collegial strategies draw on the expertise and resources provided by a new commissioner's peers—those commissioners and secretaries in other states. More specifically, this peer group is composed of: (1) new commissioners or secretaries going through similar experiences, and (2) experienced commissioners with several years of tenure. Members of this latter group are particularly valuable because they have had the opportunity to observe the longer-term consequences of their own initial transition decisions. Collegial strategies use this peer group in two ways: for an initial support network and for individual peer consulting around specific issues.

A Support Network Strategy

Many of the most critical initial decisions confronting a new commissioner are difficult to share within the agency because of uncertain, untested loyalties. There is therefore no effective sounding board available for exploring the ramifications of a difficult personnel decision or a major policy shift. These problems are exacerbated if the new commissioner has not brought along one or two trusted staff from his or her previous position. In some cases the governor's office can serve this function, but often that forum is not available for tentative, trial brainstorming.

Ideally, the newly appointed executive would be part of a national professional network that is composed of peers who can be called on as needed. In reality, few professionals are connected with well-developed networks of this kind. A conscious effort is needed to build this kind of support network. One useful step would be an annual or semiannual national meeting of corrections secretaries, commissioners, and deputy commissioners, which would bring new executives and veterans together. Part of the agenda for such a meeting would be to identify common problem areas and develop relationships through which ongoing informal and formal assistance can be provided. Subsequently, exchanges of visits and informal telephone consultations would be more feasible. Recently the authors of this chapter were present at a meeting of this kind with seasoned leaders and new appointees in a field other than corrections; the differences in the two perspectives were noteworthy. For example, the seasoned leaders had a very different time perspective. They were also able to offer excellent advice on how to get off on a right track with key external constituencies.

A Peer-Consulting Strategy

New executives often use inappropriate strategies in their early weeks on the job; but their subordinates commonly leave them in the dark regarding such errors. For example, in three different organizations subordinates we interviewed expressed concerns about the way in which their new leaders made references to their former organizations and experience. To some, stories about the prior job suggested that the leader was still not engaging with his new department and its unique culture and climate. The new executives may well have thought that such references lent credibility to their arguments when, in fact, the opposite was true.

Peer-consulting efforts can help overcome the initial unwillingness of subordinates to discuss openly substantive issues and leadership style with a new leader. Even under stable leadership, openness is difficult to create (Steele 1978); but transitions are inherently destabilizing to power relationships, and information exchanges are colored by perceptions of who is benefiting and losing. In this situation, one useful option would be for two or three new leaders to contract with each other to gather information within each other's departments. A new commissioner from state A, for example, would interview another new commissioner's staff in state B. Information would be gathered confidentially from a diagonal slice of state B's officials and reviewed with the state-B commissioner, along with overall impressions. Specific interview questions could be designed in advance. For example, the state A commissioner might gather information in state B about initial initiatives desired by staff.

The contracts among the participating new leaders would need to confront issues of staff confidentially. In general, it is probably better to avoid a commitment to total confidentiality; with few exceptions, staff should make only those comments that they are willing to have repeated.[3] Experience suggests that there is a considerable amount of information that staff would like to communicate even with this restriction on confidentiality but the channels for doing so do not exist early in a transition. If confidentiality remains an issue in some areas of concern anonymous written comments sent directly to the commissioner in state A might be feasible.

The benefits of cross-state peer-consulting relationships flow to both parties. The host commissioner would get much more information on some issues than he or she is able to get directly. Possible misperceptions would surface as a result. The commissioner could then change strategies that the data suggested would have had counterproductive or other unanticipated consequences. The consulting commissioner would learn from the interviews in the other state by reflecting on the similarities and differences in his or her own department. Lastly, defensiveness greatly interferes with the ability to interpret new information. When the exploration is mediated by an external colleague, such defensiveness can be significantly lessened. Interagency peer consulting fosters an attitude of objectivity in evaluating staff attitudes and other factors that may inhibit or facilitate program information.

Internal Strategies

Within the new commissioner's own department, conscious efforts are needed to share information and aid in team building. Otherwise, the new executive may fall victim to accidentally shared, ambiguous information that is dysfunctional. A new leader's initial decisions, for example, have a double role; they resolve the matters at hand and they function as precedents via which employees build theories on how to relate to the new leader (Gabarro and Kotter 1980). Most executives are not as sensitive to this second function as are their subordinates, who are constantly trying to "read" the desired way of working. By responding to crises—or to other situations that seem narrow but have broader implications without adequate or accurate information—a new commissioner can become trapped into a pattern of managing that he or she would not choose, given sufficient time and background.

The first strategy offered—precedent-setting discussions—encourages information sharing in an informal, ad-hoc manner. Two other strategies, agenda-setting workshops and issue-focused workshops, are more formal, structured types of strategies.

Precedent-Setting Discussions. Informal discussions with one or more staff can be explicitly designed to set realistic expectations and facilitate staff learning. One useful strategy to enhance staff understanding of a new commissioner's values and goals is for the boss to comment explicitly about his or her motivations and beliefs about a pending issue or recent decision.

Group discussions about recent legal decisions, citizen-association critiques of past department performance, and the department's overall mission are also suggested. Since managers are reluctant to give feedback when performance criteria are unclear, as is the case in a transition, discussions can also be used to generate needed criteria. One approach is for the new leader at a staff meeting to outline some of the difficulties surrounding the transition and ask people to suggest criteria against which they think they should evaluate the transition. The leader then sets a date several months off for a day-long staff work session away from the office to reflect on progress and problems during these early months. Such a session has two effects. First, it provides a constructive channel for complaints about the way the transition has occurred. Second, it can prevent some misunderstandings from becoming chronic. Discussions about how any misunderstanding came about become critical opportunities for learning.

These group discussions need to be free of incessant interruptions. Also, unless scheduled and protected, these sessions are often deferred. They must be seen as important investments. The clearer staff are about the mission and guiding values, the better their own decisions can support those directions. In corrections at present, these discussions are particularly important because the public rhetoric rarely helps managers make the difficult decisions they face every day. When new leaders talk to their top staff using the same rhetoric that they use in public presentations, the staff often feel talked down to or mistrusted, as though their insider status has been slighted. When new leaders talk with outside groups they are often insensitive to how their staff will interpret the remarks. One new department head attacked the bureaucracy, which his staff took as criticism. Precedent-setting discussions are opportunities to discuss the issues fully, to clarify possible misunderstandings of positions, and to learn from one another.

Agenda-Setting Workshops. Only face-to-face interactions over long periods can build effective working relationships. Yet a new commissioner is dependent on many people with whom he or she may not have much contact. For example, a warden may see the commissioner during a visit to the institution, in monthly staff meetings, and on some ad-hoc critical issues. Months may pass before they have sufficient contact to assess each other's values and styles. In the absence of direct working experience, rumors tend to shape each individual's opinion of the other.

Formal off-site retreats early in a new leader's tenure can help build working relationships. When designed well, retreats and workshops are powerful means for building consensus about initial initiatives and for solving specific problems. When not designed well, such events can be damaging. For this reason, skilled third-party assistance is almost essential, at least until internal staff resources are better known.

To be sure, there is an artificiality to retreats and off-site workshops, but much can still be learned by staff and the new leader if observant. How a commissioner responds to two staff arguing about an issue in a workshop can reveal much about his or her conflict-resolution style on the job.

Either at the session or in presession interviews, the outside (third-party) consultants should explore staff priorities for departmental action. This probing helps ground in reality the many different expectations and hopes that people place on the new leader. If there is considerable agreement about priorities, the information helps focus the energy of the leader. If the information gathered covers a wide variety of issues and identifies conflicting views, staff can at least see the number and variety of their collective hopes and can then better place their own in context. Discussions of this type develop realistic expectations about priorities.

It is especially important to probe the so-called dark side of leadership transitions. New leaders often have too many dreams and too little appreciation of the true effort and time required. Much of the initial year can be spent simply coming to terms with constraints. In one workshop the following question was asked to help explore constraints: "What 3–5 issues do you regard as land mines or red herrings—issues that might consume considerable effort with little payoffs or have unanticipated risks—that commissioner X as an outsider might be tempted to work on but you think he should avoid?" Staff felt that their inside knowledge had been requested when this question was asked. There was considerable overlap in the advice given. Many spoke about the danger of certain new initiatives. Because the department had been through several leaders in a short period, many were weary and cynical of a new commissioner's pet agenda that would once again make them short-change their basic programs. The advice helped the new commissioner understand the culture he was entering.

When lists of what people want the commissioner to accomplish and to avoid are compared, contradictory pressures among existing staff are often revealed. Early on in a new leader's tenure, existing staff often imagine that they all want the same things from the new leader, and that he or she is not going to give it to them and is instead favoring some inner circle. By identifying their own priorities, staff often find differences among themselves. They cannot simply blame the new leader, but must work through their own differences.

Some time at the workshop is usually spent in clarifying and building consensus about the overall department mission. One approach that has proven effective is to ask division-level people to look at strategic-level issues through the eyes of the new leader to develop some appreciation of the difficulties inherent in trying to balance the different emphases among divisions. Asking staff to adopt a different role in a safe setting like a workshop proves helpful in changing their expectations. The experience can also produce new insights about the department's mission.

Workshops also allow the leader to try different combinations of people in task groups and learn about their productivity. In one recent workshop, the commissioner privately expressed a concern to the third-party consultant that the membership of one group seemed weak. The group was left intact, and the commissioner was pleasantly surprised when it produced the best work. In another situation, a subordinate of a bureau chief proved to be an extremely effective leader and presenter. Subsequent to the workshop, he was detailed to a special personnel assignment and later became the bureau chief of another unit. The workshop thus provides additional data for assessing the strengths and weaknesses of existing staff.

Individual staff members often view issues from a narrow lens. For example, a bureau chief may want action on a top-priority item that would seemingly take the commissioner only a few minutes work. But action on that item, may entail confronting several interrelated items that have also travelled upward to lodge on the boss' desk. An effective workshop can make these overall patterns more visible.

Informal time together at an off-site session can be as important as the formal time participants spend together. In the evening at one workshop, two groups had formed, one playing poker, the other charades. The commissioner wisely split his time between the two groups. It was striking how the two games revealed different aspects of the department and the people who chose one game or the other. In play, two major underlying issues surrounding the transition were addressed: power and image versus substance. Many phrases drawn from these games were germane to the transition: "upping the ante," "call their bluff," "it's a charade," and "what are the stakes." A well-designed and well-managed two-day workshop can greatly speed up agenda setting as well as learning, whether through formal or informal sessions.[4]

Issue-Focused Workshops. Workshops can also be designed to focus on a specific topic. For example, in one state a new secretary and his new commissioner of corrections joined with a local corrections association to sponsor a two-day workshop on state-local relationships. Past relationships between the state and localities had been strained. In this session, several dominant stereotypes surfaced: locals saw the state as unresponsive and ignorant of local problems, and the state saw locals as lacking professionalism and uncooperative. By working actively at the session for the full two days, the new state leaders were able to improve significantly working relationships with almost all the counties. The follow-up task groups that were created with state and local membership led to solid accomplishments in the area of standards, monitoring, and community corrections.

Issue-focused workshops help a new leader think through the consequences of initial choices in a structured, open manner before those choices must be made. Often the information gained in those sessions can be put to later use to facilitate the transition in completely unrelated ways. One new commissioner, for example, learned that many of his initial initiatives would elicit opposition from correctional officers. Therefore, he wanted to be particularly sensitive to opportunities for building support among the officers. Some of his strategies were to: (1) send letters of commendation for positive actions; (2) via a network of contacts at each institution, learn about personal events such as funerals and hospitalizations and send cards; (3) visit institutions and have informal conversations with officers; and (4) schedule meetings on evenings and night shifts and make holiday visits on all three shifts to maximize his contact time. The combined effects created good will that has significantly reduced opposition. Even when correctional officers disagree philosophically with the commissioner, they have at least had a sense of his caring for them as employees.

The benefits of issue-focused workshops tend to be the same as those occuring from agenda-setting workshops: working relationships are improved and expectations become tested and grounded in reality.

Conclusions

Other strategies to support a transition can be cited. Taskforces, for example, are a common device in most transitions to test staff abilities and gather information about critical issues. One recent appointee asked the governor to create a taskforce of outside experts on overcrowding, to provide a broader forum to help with this particularly difficult issue. Little is known, however, about the effectiveness of taskforces as part of a transition strategy.

Use of the strategies presented help balance the pressures created during the four transition phases cited earlier. The pressures and pitfalls are many. The stakes for early errors are high; and there often is too little discretion provided new leaders to let them learn from their mistakes.

An increased appreciation of the reasons for the increasing turnover in top corrections positions is essential. Research is also needed to build our understanding of the dynamics within a transition. The approach presented in this chapter needs refinement and testing. Other strategies that can build transition effectiveness need to be collected and formally evaluated.

Two directions for action are recommended. First, support networks of top corrections leaders across state lines must be strengthened. These networks are useful, immediate resources, available to new leaders through peer consulting, for example. Second, a series of structured sessions with both new and seasoned commissioners to explore transition issues is needed. Ideally, specific recommendations for research and future resource development would result. A formal body of knowledge can begin to emerge as learning is shared through active collaboration around transition issues.

Notes

1. John Isaacsson has some excellent unpublished materials on staffing and recruiting top-level appointees that he presented at the 1977 John F. Kennedy School of Government Conference of Newly Elected Mayors.

2. McCleery (1968) provides an account of the disruptions surrounding a change in administration. Jacobs (1977) offers a fascinating longitudinal account of successive wardens at one prison and shows how turnover can affect the maintenance of control in a volatile institution.

3. Golembiewski (1978, p. 44) offers some excellent advice on confidentiality, suggesting a flexible approach to prevent being hampered by a promise of confidentiality and thus forfeiting major opportunities to make a change.

4. Agenda-setting workshops would work equally well at the institution level. The U.S. Army has developed a one-day, structured-management-succession workshop that helps people get acquainted, clarifies expectations, sets priorities, and designs strategies to follow through on the priorities. Sometimes both the outgoing and incoming commanders participate. This model might be particularly appropriate given the paramilitary character of correctional institutions.

References

Ewing, David. 1979. "Canning Directions." *Harpers* 259, issue 1551(August): 16-22.

Gabarro, John. 1979. "Socialization at the Top." *Organizational Dynamics* 7, no. 3 (Winter):3-23.

Gabarro, John J. and John P. Kotter. 1980. "Managing Your Boss." *Harvard Business Review* 58(January–February):92–100.

Golembiewski, Robert T. 1978. "Managing the Tension between OD Principles and Political Dynamics." In *The Cutting Edge,* edited by Werner Burke, LeJolla, Calif.: University Associates, pp. 27–45.

Gouldner, Alvin. 1954. *Patterns of Industrial Democracy.* New York: Free Press.

Heclo, Hugh. 1977. *A Government of Strangers: Executive Politics in Washington.* Washington, D.C.: Brookings Institution.

Isaacson, John. 1977. Unpublished papers on staffing and recruiting. Presented at the 1977 John F. Kennedy School of Government Conference for Newly Elected Mayors, Cambridge, Mass.

Jacobs, James B. 1977. *Stateville.* Chicago: University of Chicago Press.

Levinson, Harry. 1974. "Don't Choose Your Own Successor." *Harvard Business Review* 52:53–62.

Louis, Meryl Reis. 1980. "Surprise and Sense Making: What Newcomers Experience in Entering Unfamiliar Organizational Settings." *Administrative Science Quarterly* 25:226–251.

McCleery, Richard. 1968. "Correctional Administration and Political Change." In *Prison within Society,* edited by L. Hazelrigg. New York: Doubleday.

McCormick, Richard T. 1970. "Some Thoughts for Newly Assigned Senior Political Appointees on the Management of the Bureaucracy." President's Advisory Council on Executive Organization. Mimeo.

National Governors' Conference. 1975. *The Critical Hundred Days.* Washington, D.C.: National Governors' Conference.

New Mexico, State of. 1980. *Report of the Attorney General on the February 2 and 3, 1980 Riot.*

Ohlin, Lloyd. 1974. "Organizational Reform in Correctional Agencies." In *Handbook of Criminology,* edited by Daniel Glaser. Chicago: Rand McNally, pp. 995–1021.

Peters, Charles. 1974. "How to Take over the Government." *Washington Monthly* 6, no. 7 (September):15–23.

Rumsfeld, Donald. 1979. "A Politician Turned Executive Surveys Both Worlds." *Fortune* (September):89–94.

Schein, Edgar. 1973. "Management Development as a Process of Influence." In *Managerial Insights,* edited by Robert H. Doktor and Michael Moses. Englewood Cliffs, N.J.: Prentice-Hall, pp. 283–301.

———. 1979. *Career Dynamics.* Reading, Mass.: Addison-Wesley.

Steele, Fritz. 1978. *The Open Organization: The Impact of Secrecy and Disclosure on People and Organizations.* Reading, Mass.: Addison-Wesley.

Yin, Robert K. 1976. "R and D Utilization by Local Services: Problems and Proposals for Further Research." Santa Monica, Calif.: Rand Institute.

10 Conflict Resolution and Social Change in Corrections

John R. Hepburn

Prisons represent a most rigidly structured and authoritarian pattern of social organization, one that diminishes the likelihood of social change. Prison administrators and staff have the formal authority to maintain and enhance the existing pattern of relationships between the "keeper" and the "kept"; that is, physical constraints, the threat of force, manipulation, fragmentation, and cooptation are traditional means by which the authorities attempt to preserve the existing disparities in power and resources that characterize the social and political order of the prison. Any attempt at *social change,* defined as the redistribution of power (the control over decisions) and resources (goods, services, privileges), is often resisted on the premise that it will exacerbate internal problems of custody and security. When change appears inevitable, the correctional system takes steps to limit the scope of the change. An examination of mechanisms to resolve inmate grievances provides an opportunity to assess the potential for social change within correctional institutions.

Traditional Grievance Resolution

Historically, correctional officers have been expected to deal with the majority of inmate complaints. Analyses of the relationship between inmates and staff have generally described a symbiotic relationship based on informal bargaining, which creates a tenuous, superficial social order in the prison. There exists in most correctional facilities, especially those oriented to custody rather than treatment, a strong, cohesive inmate culture, with its own antiadministration inmate code and informal inmate leaders. To control the inmate population, the staff is provided the tools of force (physical coercion and segregation) and incentive (custody grade and early release, for example). Yet a stable pattern of social control depends on an accommodation to the interests of inmate leaders, an accommodation developed by means of informal bargaining.[1]

On the one hand, inmate leaders want to maintain their position of leadership and privilege. To do this the inmate must demonstrate that he can secure favors from the staff. On the other hand, line staff want to maintain order as a

The author is indebted to the anonymous referees whose comments have improved this chapter.

means of protecting both their physical safety and their jobs. This accommo-
dative relationship provides the inmate leader with the necessary recognition of
leadership and scarce privileges by the staff in exchange for the leader's control
of the inmates.[2]

This form of inmate-staff bargaining has its advantages to the custodial
staff. First, it is always easier to bargain from the position of the superior with
one subordinate person rather than with either a subordinate group or the subordinate group's representative (who is then held accountable by the group for
his bargaining skills). Second, the unequal distribution of privileges allows the
custodian to bestow such favors on those inmates most effective in controlling
the other inmates. Finally, bargaining in this manner diminishes the likelihood
that the frustrations, inequities, complaints, and grievances of the inmates will
go beyond the level of the line officer. It is for these reasons that correctional
officers generally feel that, except in extreme cases, they should be the persons
to handle inmate complaints.[3]

Yet informal bargaining of this nature is not without its adverse consequences. It perpetuates and escalates a sense of powerlessness among the majority of inmates because of their inability to bargain effectively as individuals
with the administration and staff. It demonstrates that goals can be obtained by
illegitimate means. It allocates the scarce rewards to those inmates most skilled
at intimidation, physical coercion, and manipulation. It encourages internal
divisiveness and competition for positions of leadership. It promotes the exercise of routine disciplinary actions disproportionately and discriminately against
those inmates who are unpopular, weak, and members of minority groups. It
places the officers in a position of increased susceptibility to corruption. It
constrains social change.

Inmate or resident councils represent a more formal and more centralized
procedure for addressing inmate grievances. A small group of inmates, either
elected by the inmate population or appointed by the warden, is charged with
conveying the grievances of inmates to the warden either during regularly
scheduled (for example, monthly) meetings or on an as-needed basis. Individual
grievances are inappropriate within this forum, which is explicitly designed as a
vehicle for the resolution of collective or institutional grievances. Inmate-
administration negotiations typically result in administrative adjudication,
because the balance of power and legitimacy rests within the administration.
Hence the administration, even in meeting to negotiate with inmate representatives, retains the power to stipulate the outcome of the dispute. The administration aligns the facts of the case and the behavior of the grievant to the rules of
the facility to ascertain the correct resolution of the grievance. The sanctity of
the rules, seldom challenged, remains intact, and normative change is rarely
considered.[4]

To some extent, there is a structural inducement to social change within
this problem-solving model of grievance resolution. The inmates represent a

constituency to whom the inmate representatives must report their success and also one with whom they most clearly identify. Furthermore, the inclusion for discussion of only those grievances that affect a sizeable segment of the inmate population confronts the administration with issues about which there is some degree of unified inmate support. However, the potential for social change is sharply limited by the overwhelming power retained at the top of the prison bureaucracy. The warden retains administrative control, deciding whether the group shall meet, which of the issues on the proposed agenda are legitimate and worthy of discussion, and, of course, the nature of the resolution. How the issue is resolved will usually depend predominantly on the warden's interpretation of existing rules and regulations, budgetary restrictions, limitations of existing resources, and/or the likelihood of approval by those higher in the bureaucratic organization. Furthermore, the warden's decision is rarely subject to appeal or review. Whether the inmate negotiates with a single officer or inmate representatives meet with the warden, social change rarely occurs.

Threats to Administrative Control

It has been only recently that formalized and universalistic standards have been introduced to circumvent the arbitrary and particularistic decision making that has long characterized the treatment of inmate grievances. These new grievance-resolution mechanisms were viewed by wardens as an opportunity to undermine the informal leadership structure among inmates, but that desire is not sufficient to explain their adoption.[5] Nor can their implementation be attributed to a desire to make the resolution process explicit, uniform, and equally accessible to all inmates, although that may be a worthy goal. Rather, the movement toward alternative mechanisms of grievance resolution grew out of increased threats to administrative control.

Three events during the past fifteen years have seriously challenged the established patterns of prison management and threatened to remove control over the institution from traditional authorities. One series of events has been the public airing of inmate complaints by means of violent and nonviolent prison riots, disturbances, and/or confrontations. Although the causes of such acts are not isolated, there is agreement that both individual and collective violence in prisons is due in part to unresolved grievances.[6] A second factor has been the increasing bureaucratization of our prisons. Many states have established autonomous departments of corrections, transferred much of the authority from local wardens to central-office administrators, and imposed other bureaucratic characteristics throughout the staff organization.[7]

The third event is the transition by the courts from a so-called hands-off doctrine with regard to the internal affairs of prisons to a position of active involvement in the protection of the rights of inmates. The number of inmate petitions filed in federal courts has doubled since 1966, and the 23,001 petitions filed in 1979 represent about 14 percent of all civil cases filed in federal courts.[8] Greater judicial involvement in inmate grievances increases the likelihood that decisions affecting the policies and procedures of the correctional institution will be taken out of the hands of those most knowledgeable about and responsible for the operation of the institution. The autonomy of correctional administrators, traditionally protected from judicial interference by the separation of powers, the practical needs of managing a large facility, and the lack of judicial expertise in corrections, has been eroding. Correctional administrators have been faced with the possibility that the court might dictate changes even more sweeping than sought by the grievant. Rather than risk undesirable and unpredictable changes imposed by judicial decree or legislative bodies, prison administrators have turned to grievance-resolution alternatives, which promise controlled confrontation within the more predictable atmosphere of the correctional system.

Rational-Legal Grievance Resolution

The informal and discretionary handling of inmate grievances worked well for some persons and for some situations. Increasing bureaucratization and the encroachment of legal remedies, however, necessitated the addition (not necessarily a substitution) of a procedure with more universalistic and uniform decision making. The intervention model of formal negotiation, in which specially trained third parties are authorized to intervene in disputes between inmates and administration, is exemplified in two recently adopted grievance-redress mechanisms.

Ombudsman programs have been initiated in about thirty state or county correctional departments, and most of these have been adopted since 1975.[9] The ombudsman is authorized to investigate complaints, judge their merit, and recommend an appropriate institutional or departmental response. The redress of individual grievances is the primary objective of an ombudsman. In principle, however, the ombudsman should have the time and general perspective needed to identify and propose changes in those policies and procedures that generate individual grievances. This requires that the ombudsman's office be independent of the local institution or the state's department of corrections. Yet in only Iowa, Minnesota, and Connecticut is the ombudsman an independent agent; in some localities the ombudsman is employed by and reports to the commissioner, and in other states the ombudsman is directly accountable to a warden. In such situations, the impartiality of the ombudsman is compromised. Few ombudsman have unquestioned access to departmental records. Even fewer have the expertise to resolve grievances stemming from problems of law and administrative policy. A large number of grievances, in light of the resources allocated to the ombudsmen's office, result in lengthy delays, incomplete investigations, and a tendency to dismiss or ignore those grievances that are not deemed meritorious. Beseiged by individual grievances and lacking the necessary authority and autonomy to enforce resolutions, ombudsmen are rarely able to introduce social change.

The other approach to using third-party intervention entails formal grievance procedures. Variants of this approach have been implemented widely since 1970 and are present in nearly all prison systems and many jails.[10] All provide a multilevel mechanism wherein the grievant may appeal the initial decision to a higher level, although rarely do the levels exceed the control of the department of corrections. All are advisory, but there is great variation in the levels of appeal, the imposition of time limits, the openness of hearings, the requirement of written response, and the definition of grievable issues. Despite these variations, two unique types may be observed. Most typical is the nonparticipatory grievance procedure in which the inmate's grievance is processed internally by various levels of administration. Inmate participation and third-party intervention are absent. A more recent variation, similar to the typical union grievance system, is the participatory grievance procedure. Inmates and officers participate in the procedure's design and implementation, an inmate clerk serves at the point of entrance into the procedure to assist grievants either to resolve informally or to better prepare the written statement of the grievance, a committee of inmates and officers constitutes the first level of review and recommends a resolution, and review by some authorized agent outside the correctional system (for example, New York has used members of the American Arbitration Association) precedes final review by the highest administrative level.

These characteristics of the participatory grievance procedure, together with short, enforceable time limits for making and implementing decisions, guaranteed written responses for every grievance at every level of appeal, and a continuing system to monitor the procedure's operation, suggest that social change will occur. This procedure brings together and obtains input from inmates, officers, local administrators, top departmental administrators and civilians. The goal is to clarify policy matters, reduce arbitrary behavior, and provide a forum for cooperative experiences. Compared to other means of grievance resolution, this forum of cooperative exchange makes more likely the redistribution of power and resources and an increased openness and equity in decision making.

Yet the procedure also contains prospects for social control. The administration retains control over the definition of issues that are grievable; decisions pertaining to parole, furlough, work release, classification, and discipline—the decisions that most affect inmates—are not grievable. Furthermore, the administration retains control of the ultimate resolution, and the involvement of inmates, officers, and civilians may be viewed as palliative. Collective grievances are not permitted, and grievances (even those against departmental policy) are frequently *nol prossed* when the grievant is transferred or released.[11] Finally, the court's admonition to inmate appellants to exhaust all administrative remedies prior to litigation may well delay court review by six to twelve months.

Preliminary data obtained from California's Youth Authority and adult facilities in New York, South Carolina, and Kentucky indicate that the participatory grievance procedure generates substantially more grievances per inmate than either the nonparticipatory procedures (such as operate in the Federal Bureau of Prisons) or independent-ombudsman programs (such as in Connecticut and Minnesota). Furthermore, the available evidence suggests the inmate's request is more likely to be granted in whole or in part within the participatory procedure than within either the nonparticipatory procedure or the ombudsman program.[12] Although these results portray the participatory grievance procedures as more credible and more responsive to inmates than other grievance mechanisms, they do not address the issue of social change.

Social change is more likely during the first year of the procedure's operation, for it is then that the floodgates of the reservoir of untested policies and procedures are opened, and many time-honored rules must pass careful scrutiny. Shortly thereafter, however, it is unlikely that inmates will grieve successfully the policies and procedures that remain. It is at this point than the proportion of grievances pertaining to individual problems increases, and these grievances are least likely to produce social change.[13] Since the participatory procedure was introduced in California's Youth Authority, for example, individual grievances increased from 60 percent of the grievances filed in 1973-1974 to nearly 80 percent in 1976, while grievances against rules and procedures decreased from 30 percent in 1973-1974 to only slightly over 15 percent in 1976.[14]

Systematic data are not available to assess the relation between the type of grievance and the type of resolution. That a large proportion of grievances are upheld in whole or in part may reflect a large proportion of easily remedied individual grievances. Whether policy grievances are equally likely to be upheld and whether this probability remains relatively unchanged over long periods are yet to be determined. Perhaps some inference can be made from the fact that the central administration in New York resolved the grievance in favor of the grievant in whole or in part in 79 percent of those grievances sampled that were felt to be clearly justiciable and in only 26 percent of those grievances sampled that were without sufficient legal merit to bring to the attention of the courts.[15] These data suggest that the administration may be successfully utilizing the procedure to interrupt meritorious complaints likely to receive court attention, but the absence of information pertaining to the nature of the grievance and the nature of the remedy do not permit an assessment of the potential for social change.

Finally, it is noteworthy that the introduction of these rational-legal procedures has not displaced the arbitrary, particularistic, and control-oriented procedures. Rather, the value and utility of competing formal mechanisms, such as counselors and the inmate council, have become more limited.[16] Some inmates reject any form of administrative remedy and prefer the time-honored tactic of negotiating with a correctional officer directly or through an informal inmate leader. More relevant is the apparent differentiation between the inmate council and the rational-legal procedures. Since neither the ombudsman nor the grievance procedures are independent of the department of corrections, and since neither possess enforcement powers, their ability to create change may not be viewed by inmates as appreciably greater than that of the inmate council. What these rational-legal procedures do offer, however, is a technique for redressing individual complaints. Consequently, it appears that a bifurcation has emerged. Grievances against policies and procedures, in which the inmate may desire anonymity to avoid retaliatory staff actions, are presented by the inmate council. Grievances that pertain to only the individual inmate, which are of more immediate concern to inmates and are likely to be resolved quickly and informally, are presented to the ombudsman or grievance procedure.

Grievance Resolution and Social Change

Prisons will continue to serve society's demand for vengeance, and the need for security and custody have not been compromised. It is the type and disparity of power within the person that have been altered recently. The introduction of the ombudsman and the participatory grievance procedure represents a partial transformation from decentralized, traditional authority toward centralized, rational-legal authority. Equally significant, the participatory grievance procedure increases the potential for inmate involvement in policy decisions. If these structural changes in the means of grievance resolution are to result in meaningful social change in the conditions that affect inmates four fundamental questions need to be addressed.

1. Does the grievance procedure provide for and result in a redistribution of power within the institution? Formal power in prisons is centralized at the top, characterized by a rigid hierarchy and quasi-military structure. The power disparity between administration and inmates is great. Yet power may be redistributed if the structures and processes of the grievance mechinery move the system toward greater openness, more democratic and cooperative decision making, and greater accountability for those decisions. The mere presence of a mechanism for inmates to seek redress is insufficient to realign power unless it is responsive to inmate needs and curtails arbitrary behavior by the powerful. If inmate needs are to be addressed, the administration must relinquish its absolute control over the definition of which issues are grievable. To determine which issues, under what conditions, are legitimately subject to review and to assert that only a limited range of resolution alternatives are available is to minimize the likelihood that power will be redistributed. Therefore, the first step in the redistribution of power is to legitimate the inmates' voice in the design and implementation of such a procedure, including appropriate scope and available remedies.

2. Does the grievance procedure produce a change in the conditions under-lying the grievance? If each grievance is treated as an individual problem, each inmate may receive some measure of redress, and the procedure appears to be working effectively. Such a case-work approach, however, undermines the probability that the resolution will bring about a change in the procedure or policy that generated the grievance, especially when collective grievances are not permitted. The grievance itself may be easily resolved informally, as when an error occurs in an inmate's account or when a package for the inmate is unduly delayed in the package room, and the grievant is satisfied with the resolution (correct the error or deliver the package), but the existence of a large num-ber of such grievances suggests that case work be abandoned and that future grievances be prevented by systemic change. Case work is more attractive be-cause it provides immediate restitution to the grievant and little systemic change. Grievances should not be viewed only as discrete events. They must be closely monitored to determine the extent to which there are a sufficient number of grievances pertaining to a particular policy, procedure, or area of the institution to suggest that some form of structural change is warranted. Monitoring by an autonomous agent is also required, of course, to assure the resolutions involving systemic change are implemented quickly and completely.[17]

3. Does the grievance procedure affect all rights of the inmates? The rational-legal procedures have resulted in some broad changes in policy and pro-cedure. Successful challenges have revised policies pertaining to visitation, hair length, access to the canteen, dress codes, medical care, and telephone calls. In each case, the inmate has acquired greater privileges or services. These issues, together with such issues as equity of treatment and harrassment by staff, are the recipient rights of citizenship. The procedures have had the least impact in regard to participative rights of citizenship. The right to assemble, the right to vote, the right to collective bargaining, and other rights that would enable in-mates to exercise a direct voice in the policies and procedures of the institution and the state are largely unaffected by the grievance procedures. The rational-legal procedures aid the inmates' quest for recipient rights—services and priv-ileges—but fail to address the participation rights—control over decisions.[18] To the extent that social change includes a redistribution of both power and re-sources, then the rational-legal procedures cannot be viewed as implements of social change until all rights are addressed.[19]

4. When does conflict prevention and resolution become suppression of legitimate issues that often surface and are ameliorated only through conflict? Movement to rational-legal grievance resolution converts to factual-legal conflict what is fundamentally political conflict. Moreover, rational-legal conflict resolu-tion depends on normalizing what is otherwise abnormal, regularizing the ir-regular, and formalizing the informal. Individual emotions, mitigating and extenuating circumstances, and a sense of urgency are among those features that are ignored when a set of finite categories is created and grievances are examined

in terms of their most salient aspect. In doing so, there is the risk that grievance-resolution procedures become so normal, regular, and formal that they become repressive. That is, the bureaucratic response is to treat each grievance as routine, just like all others in that category, thus ignoring the unique aspects of the grievance and the importance to the inmate of this grievance. In addition, when the procedure fails to address adequately issues other than those that are routinized, deep-seated frustrations among inmates may arise. Frustration is especially likely if the inmates believe that even the routine grievances will not be resolved if they press for resolution of the nonroutine grievances. For example, inmates may feel that too many grievances against staff treatment or sacred procedures will result in a posture of unresponsiveness to their individual complaints. Conversely, the pacification of routine grievances may coopt the inmates to the point that nonroutine grievances are suppressed. Finally, are there not certain structural or policy changes that can only be fully brought to light by the emotional intensity and publicity that attend partisan and open conflict? Many policies cannot be redressed without legislative action, either to amend the policy or to provide the funding necessary to correct inadequate facilities. In some cases, public opinion must be enlisted to support desired changes. Also, open conflict may be the most effective means of acquiring a new warden or commissioner.

Conclusion

The transition from traditional to rational-legal mechanisms of inmate grievance resolution does not result necessarily in social change. This evolution may represent no more than movement toward a more efficient vehicle of monitoring inmates and institutional "hot spots" or as a strategem for delaying or aborting court intervention and coopting inmates; in short, the difference in grievance-resolution techniques may represent a difference in social-control techniques. All organizations are conservative, and correctional institutions, with a social-control mandate, are least likely to be the exception.

Even when the best of procedures is adopted, when inmate empowerment and systemic change are maximized, there is reason for concern. Inmate expectations for change may exceed the organization's ability to respond, thereby intensifying inmate frustration and fueling the conflict. The relationships between inmates and staff may become more impersonal and calculated, thereby undermining certain rehabilitative goals. In addition, the time and resources of the organization that must be devoted to rational-legal grievance resolution, when added to other rational-legal activities such as disciplinary hearings, classification hearings, and furlough hearings (each with levels of appeal and review), may force the correctional institution beyond the point of operational efficiency and responsiveness.[20] Those who would advocate the new procedures must take steps to ensure sufficient time, resources, and planning to prevent (or reduce) the occurrence of such unintended and counterproductive consequences.

It is axiomatic that prison organizations are based on coercive power, requiring compliance among inmates to organizational rules and procedures. Coercive power results in an alienative involvement with the prison by inmates and in a need among the administration for extensive order and control.[21] Grievance procedures serve the function of maintaining order and control while granting, even encouraging, the legitimate expression of that inmate alienation. Such procedures may be an invaluable safety-valve of the institution, but they are not inherently implements of social change. The ombudsman and the participatory grievance procedure, two rational-legal adaptations, may provide some redress to a large number of grievants, may create greater administrative accountability, and may produce changes in policies or procedures that affect recipient rights, but they will not be significant social-change agents unless they also can demonstrate a redistribution of power, a change in the grievance-producing prison conditions, and a responsiveness to all issues affecting the quality of prison life.

Notes

1. See, for example, Gresham Sykes and Sheldon Messinger, "The Inmate Social System," in *Theoretical Studies in Social Organization of the Prison,* ed. Richard Cloward, et al. (New York: Social Science Research Council, 1960), pp. 5-19, and Bernard Berk, "Organizational Goals and Inmate Organization," *American Journal of Sociology* 71(March 1966):522-534.

2. This accomodative relationship is discussed more fully in Clarence Schrag, "Some Foundations for Theory of Correction," in *The Prison: Studies in Institutional Organization and Change,* ed. Donald Cressey (New York: Holt, Rinehart and Winston, 1961), pp. 309-357, and Richard Cloward, "Social Control in the Prison," in *Prison within Society,* ed. Lawrence Hazelrigg (Garden City, N.Y.: Doubleday, 1968), pp. 78-112.

3. When correctional officers at Attica were asked to whom an inmate should go first when he had a problem, three-fourths of the respondents indicated that the inmate should go to an officer. Less than 5 percent considered a counselor as an appropriate choice, and only one officer replied that the inmate should take the matter to the warden. Correctional officers were not asked pointedly whether the inmate should drop the complaint if the officer does not resolve it or whether the inmate should appeal to a higher level. They were asked, however, what kinds of actions inmates had a right to take if inmates feel strongly that they are unfairly treated by the staff. Two-thirds of the officers responding indicated that the inmates have a right to write to the superintendent, and one-half of the officers responded that the inmates have a right to write to

the commissioner. Only one-fourth of the officers felt the inmates have a right to file a law suit, and less than 15 percent agreed that inmates have a right to write to a local newspaper. Should the inmate complaint go beyond the correctional officer, it is apparent that the officers feel the matter should remain intramural. See John R. Hepburn and James H. Laue, *To Do Justice: An Analysis of the Development of Inmate Grievance Resolution Procedures* (St. Louis: University of Missouri, 1978).

4. For a more detailed description of this form of grievance hearing, see J.E. Baker, "Inmate Self-Government," *Journal of Criminal Law, Criminology and Police Science* 55(March 1964):39-47; J. Michael Keating, Jr. et al., *Grievance Mechanisms in Correctional Institutions* (Washington, D.C.: U.S. Government Printing Office, 1975); William Felstiner, "Influence of Social Organization on Dispute Processing," *Law and Society Review* 9(Fall 1974):63-94.

5. Keating et al., *Grievance Mechanisms*, p. 14.

6. Among those linking inmate grievances to prison violence are Edith E. Flynn, "The Ecology of Prison Violence," in *Prison Violence,* ed. Albert Cohen, George Cole and Robert Bailey (Lexington, Mass.: Lexington Books, D.C. Heath, 1975), pp. 115-136, and Vernon Fox, "Why Prisoners Riot," *Federal Probation* 35(March 1971):9-14.

7. James B. Jacobs, *Stateville: The Penitentiary in Mass Society* (Chicago: University of Chicago Press, 1977).

8. According to the administrative office of the U.S. Supreme Court, there were 18,502 petitions filed by state prisoners and 4,499 petitions filed by federal prisoners in calendar 1979.

9. David D. Dillingham and Linda R. Singer, *Complaint Procedures in Prisons and Jails: An Examination of Recent Experience* (Washington, D.C.: Center for Community Justice, 1979).

10. Ibid., p. 18.

11. *Collective grievances* are those in which more than one inmate files the grievance. For example, a grievance at New York State's Auburn Correctional Facility against the mess hall, signed by over three hundred inmates, was disallowed. *Individual grievances* pertain to one inmate's complaint, such as missing one's rotation in the exercise yard or being denied a package in the mailroom, the resolution of which affects only the grievant. *Institutional grievances* are those against policy and procedure, the resolution of which affects the grievant and other inmates.

12. Dillingham and Singer, *Complaint Procedures.*

13. There appear to be several factors operating to reduce policy and procedure grievances. One restraint on grievances against policy and procedure in New York, for example, is a rule (yet to be grieved) that a policy or procedure cannot be the subject of a second grievance until six months after the resolution of the first grievance. In South Carolina, many grievances that could have resulted in change were treated as individual grievances and resolved informally.

Also, in one New York facility, the warden refused to respond to grievances against policy and procedure. This stance undermined the procedure's credibility to address those complaints, and, consequently, the inmates filed a disproportionately high rate of individual grievances.

14. See California Youth Authority, *Grievance Activity* (Sacramento: California Youth Authority, 1976).

15. John R. Hepburn and James H. Laue, "The Resolution of Inmate Grievances as an Alternative to the Courts," *The Arbitration Journal* 35(March 1980): 11-16.

16. Inmate responses obtained prior to and one year following the introduction of a participatory grievance procedure at New York's Auburn Correctional Facility indicate little change in inmate preference for the assistance of other inmates or an officer with complaints. Inmate preference for the grievance procedure (21 percent) reduced the preference for the alternatives of counselor, inmate council, and warden. Similarly, the preference for the inmate council in South Carolina's Kirkland Correctional Institution was reduced from 34 percent prior to the new grievance procedure to 11 percent one year after the procedure's implementation. See Hepburn and Laue, *To Do Justice*.

17. Such monitoring occurs on a monthly basis in and by the California Youth Authority. Grievances from each facility are monitored on the basis of issue grieved and status within the procedure. When the monthly data are compared against a norm derived from the data of the preceding three months, sudden changes can be detected and inquiries can be made.

18. See Jameson W. Doig, "Citizens and Serfs: The Changing Patterns of Authority in Complex Organizations", Woodrow Wilson School, Princeton University, 1975.

19. It is important to distinguish two issues relating to participation rights. One issue is the degree to which the inmates participate in decisions. Some degree of inmate input is structured into the participating grievance procedure, which differentiates it from the other procedures. This participation, however, is only at the lowest level of review. The second issue pertains to the extension of participation rights to all inmates in other decisions that affect their lives. Participation in disciplinary hearings or in reviewing furlough requests, for example, would extend inmate rights. So too would collective bargaining and unionization among inmates. These issues are beyond the bounds of most grievance procedures.

20. The impact of increasing bureaucratization within one prison is thoroughly developed in Jacobs, *Stateville*.

21. Lower-level participants in an organization that uses coercive power are characterized as having an alienative involvement with, or an intensely negative orientation to, the organization. In contrast, organizations such as churches and schools, which use normative power, elicit the moral involvement of the lower-level participants based on an internalization of norms. See Amitai Etzioni,

A Comparative Analysis of Complex Organizations (New York: Macmillan, 1975). It is of no small interest that greater participation of inmates in the decisions affecting their lives should increase their commitment to the institutional order. It is doubtful that this will result in a "shared culture" rather than the current physical constraints to maintain order in prisons, but the effort to explain and justify current policies and procedures to the inmates and to involve inmates in the resolution of grievances pertaining to policies and procedures is a move in that direction.

Part IV
The Role of the Courts

11 Judicial Strategies in Prison Litigation

Daryl R. Fair

American courts have become a major factor in prison reform and administration over the last two decades. The Supreme Court set the stage for this development in *Monroe* v. *Pape.*[1] In that case the Court held that Title 42 of the United States Code, section 1983, which imposes civil liability on persons depriving others of constitutional rights under color of state law, applied to police officers who were acting unlawfully. In *Robinson* v. *California,*[2] the Court made the cruel-and-unusual-punishment clause of the Eighth Amendment applicable to the states through the due-process clause of the Fourteenth Amendment; then, in *Cooper* v. *Pate,* the justices ruled that a state prisoner could sue the warden of a prison under section 1983 over alleged denials of constitutional rights.[3] Thus state prisoners could sue the wardens of their prisons, alleging denial of their right not to be subjected to cruel and unusual punishment. Federal prisoners had been able to bring such suits prior to the 1960s but had not been notably successful because of reluctance on the part of the courts to interfere in prison administration. State prisoners were quick to take advantage of their new opportunity, however, and they found the reticence of the federal courts decreasing.[4]

In ruling on early suits by individual state prisoners contending that they were being subjected to cruel and unusual punishment, the courts had to confront the hands-off doctrine that they had used for years to reserve decisions about prison conditions and the treatment of inmates entirely to prison administrators. The courts rejected this doctrine with amazing speed and unanimity, perhaps because of the extreme brutality disclosed by the facts in some early prisoners'-rights cases from the states. As the courts began to grapple with these cases, however, it became apparent that they were quite complex. The simple case in which a discrete event (for example, a beating) was alleged to constitute cruel and unusual punishment was a rarity. More typical were situations in which the purported unconstitutionality resulted from several ongoing conditions. In response to such circumstances, the courts ruled that the cumulative impact of several prison conditions can result in cruel and unusual punishment even though no one of those conditions, considered singly, would violate the Eighth Amendment.[5]

This chapter was written while I was a National Endowment for the Humanities Seminar Fellow at the University of Wisconsin during 1979–1980. The views expressed are mine, however, and reflect the official position of neither the endowment nor the university.

A related development found petitioners alleging that an entire prison or prison system could be so barbaric that merely incarcerating inmates there constituted cruel and unusual punishment. This approach came to be known as the "totality-of-circumstances" doctrine. It held that even where no single practice or condition within an institution was constitutionally void, a combination of conditions could produce an overall environment sufficiently inhumane to violate the Eighth Amendment. The first prison or prison system to be found as a whole to violate the cruel-and-unusual-punishment clause was the Arkansas Penitentiary System in 1969.[6] Since that time, numerous prisons and prison systems have been found constitutionally deficient. One study cites cases from thirty-one jurisdictions,[7] and a survey in 1980 by the National Prison Project of the American Civil Liberties Union found nineteen states under court order to improve the conditions of their penal institutions; prisons in eleven other states were under court challenge as of the same date.[8] Clearly the courts have been exceedingly active in the field of prison reform.

It is one thing to declare that prison conditions violate the Constitution; it is quite another, however, to restructure an entity as complex as a correctional institution, and that is essentially the task to which federal judges committed themselves when they held state prisons and local jails to violate the Eighth Amendment. For every right, there must be a remedy; and when the courts declare that inmates have the right to be free of cruel and unusual punishment caused by the totality of conditions in a prison, then the remedy must of necessity have far-reaching impact on the structure and functioning of that institution. This chapter examines several of the more prominent approaches used by federal judges in the remedial phase of prison-conditions litigation, with particular attention to the leading cases of *Holt* v. *Sarver*[9] and *Pugh* v. *Locke*.[10] The chapter also addresses whether some approaches lead to greater compliance and impact than do others, accomplishing this task by comparing the outcome of *Holt, Pugh,* and the additional case of *Alberti* v. *Sheriff of Harris County, Texas*.[11] These cases are studied by analyzing their decision paths. Finally, the chapter offers some recommendations as to how judges might fruitfully approach the remedial process.

Decision Paths and Judicial Choices

Courts remedy violations of prisoners' rights through a four-stage process that includes (1) determining whether there has been a constitutional violation, (2) formulating a decree or court order designed to remedy the violation, (3) monitoring compliance with the decree, and (4) enforcing the order if the defendants in the case do not comply to the satisfaction of the court. This process resembles in some respects incremental decision making as depicted by Charles E. Lindblom in his classic article, "The Science of Muddling Through."[12] That is, each stage of each case consists of a number of decision points at each of which the judge can select from among several alternatives. Each decision forecloses certain options at future decision points or at least makes it more difficult for the judge to select those options. Thus by incremental steps the judge works through the various decision points making up the four stages of the case, establishing in so doing a *decision path* for that case.

Table 11-1 presents a summary of the decision points that are most prominent in prison-conditions litigation. The table includes eleven such decision points within the four major stages of a prison-condition case. At each decision point the judge has from two to seven options (or more—the lists are not necessarily exhaustive). Some of the options are mutually exclusive (for instance, the court either retains jurisdiction or does not), but others are not (for instance, reports may be required and inspections held at decision point eight).

Table 11-1 may be used to trace decision paths in actual or hypothetical cases. For instance, one simple decision path might be (1.2, 2.2). That is, the judge decides that no constitutional violation exists and therefore relinquishes jurisdiction, or dismisses the case. A more complex decision path would be (1.1, 2.1, 3.1, 4.1, 5.2, 6.1, 7.1, 8.1, 9.2). In this example the judge would find a constitutional violation (1.1), retain jurisdiction (2.1), and formulate the decree (3.1) through the use of hearings (4.1). The decree would be general in nature (5.2), and the judge would retain jurisdiction (6.1), using the plaintiffs' attorneys to monitor compliance (7.1). The judge would also require reports on compliance (8.1), and, having been satisfied that the decree was being complied with, would relinquish jurisdiction (9.2).

Holt v. Sarver: The Use of Traditional Remedies

Decision-path analysis of this sort can be used to compare the methods used by judges to handle the remedial process in different prison suits. Two cases that have been held out as contrasting models of the remedial process are *Holt* v. *Sarver,* the Arkansas lawsuit previously mentioned, and *Pugh* v. *Locke,* the celebrated case involving the Alabama prison system. Decision-path analysis of the two cases will allow us to see how different they really are. The decision path in *Holt* v. *Sarver* may be described as (1.1, 2.1, 3.2, 4.1, 5.2, 6.1, 7.1/7.3, 8.1/8.2/8.4, 9.1, 10.1, 11.1). That is, a constitutional violation was found (1.1), and jurisdiction was retained (2.1). Judge J. Smith Henley relied heavily on the defendants to formulate the decree (3.1) and used hearings on their proposed decrees (4.1) to arrive at an order that was general in nature (5.2). The court then retained jurisdiction (6.1) and monitored compliance, joined during this phase by the plaintiffs' attorneys (7.1/7.3). The monitoring process employed written reports, deadlines, and inmate complaints extensively (8.1/8.2/8.4). The court retained jurisdiction throughout this process (9.1) and awarded attorneys'

Table 11-1
Decision Points in Possible Decision Paths in Prison-Condition Cases

Constitutional Decision	Decree Formulation	Monitoring	Enforcement
1.1 Violation exists	3.1 Court formulates	7.1 By plaintiffs' attorneys	10.1 Attorneys' fees awarded
1.2 No violation exists	3.2 Defendants formulate	7.2 By master	102. Money damages awarded
	3.3 Master formulates	7.3 By judge	10.3 Contempt citations given
		7.4 By citizens' committee	10.4 Prisoners released
2.1 Retain jurisdiction	4.1 Hearings used		10.5 Prison closed
2.2 Relinquish jurisdiction	4.2 Inspections used	8.1 Reports required	10.6 Receiver appointed
	4.3 Negotiations used	8.2 Deadlines set	10.7 Some of above threatened
	4.4 Conferences used	8.3 Inspections held	
		8.4 Inmate complaints heard	11.1 Retain jurisdiction
	5.1 Decree is specific	8.5 Hearings held	11.2 Relinquish jurisdiction
	5.2 Decree is general		
		9.1 Retain jurisdiction	
	6.1 Retain jurisdiction	9.2 Relinquish jurisdiction	
	6.2 Relinquish jurisdiction		

fees (10.1) to be paid by defendants because of their lack of cooperation with the court during the course of the litigation.[13] The court retained jurisdiction (11.1) even after the award of attorneys' fees and eventually appointed a special master in an attempt to induce greater compliance with its decree.[14] Appointment of the special master could be added to the end of the decision path (7.2), but I arbitrarily decided to exclude such feedback loops for purposes of this analysis.

As this summary suggests, the *Holt* decision path is distinguished by its reliance on traditional remedies and procedures from the law of equity.[15] For instance, in equity the judge traditionally relies on the defendants to prepare a proposed decree for the judge to use as a basis for the eventual order. The plaintiffs are allowed to raise objections to the proposed decree, and the court fashions a final order out of these proposals and counterproposals. This procedure is essentially what Judge Henley used in *Holt*. He also relied on plaintiffs' attorneys and the plaintiffs themselves through the device of inmate complaints in monitoring compliance with his decree. This, too, is consistent with traditional equitable procedure. In addition to reliance on equity as a model, the *Holt* decision path is characterized by the use of hearings in decree formulation and by a decree that is general in nature. These characteristics seem to be more a reflection of the judge's personal style than a result of his following a model such as traditional equitable procedure.[16]

Some commentators have advocated the use of *Holt*-type relief in contrast to what they see as the more intrusive procedure used in cases such as *Jones* v. *Wittenberg*[17] and *Pugh* v. *Locke*. Thomas A. Young, for example, argues that allowing the defendants to formulate the decree makes possible the inclusion of innovative forms of relief that go beyond constitutional minima and that would, in his view, therefore be inappropriate if mandated on the court's initiative. He also contends that *Holt*-type relief has the advantage of placing responsibility for prison reform on public officials in the executive branch, where it rightfully belongs and where ability to secure needed funding is likely to be located.[18]

The Alabama Cases: The Court as Administrative Officer

The best known of the prison-conditions cases is undoubtedly *Pugh* v. *Locke*. This is in part because of the far-reaching nature of the decision itself, but it is also due in part to its context as one of several cases in which Judge Frank M. Johnson, Jr. held institutions of the state of Alabama to be unconstitutional, thereby incurring the wrath of Governor George Wallace, among others. The remedy in *Pugh* is often contrasted with that in *Holt,* and decision-path analysis confirms that there are indeed differences, although there are many similarities as well. The decision path in *Pugh* was (1.1, 2.1, 3.1, 4.1, 5.1, 6.1, 7.4, 8.1/8.2, 9.1, 10.6, 11.1). Table 11-2 compares the decisions paths of the two cases.

Table 11-2
Comparison of *Holt*, *Pugh*, and *Alberti* Decision Paths

Holt	Pugh	Alberti
1.1	1.1	1.1
2.1	2.1	2.1
3.2[a]	3.1[a]	3.1
4.1	4.1	4.1/4.2
5.2[a]	5.1[a]	5.1
6.1	6.1	6.1
7.1/7.3[a]	7.4[a]	7.1/7.4
8.1/8.2/8.4[a]	8.1/8.2[a]	8.1/8.5
9.1	9.1	9.1
10.1[a]	10.6[a]	10.7
11.1	11.1	11.1

[a]indicates different routes, comparing *Holt* and *Pugh*.

There are five points of difference between the decision paths, as will be summarized. In *Pugh,* Judge Johnson formulated the decree himself; in *Holt,* Judge Henley relied on the defendants. The *Pugh* decree was specific, whereas the *Holt* decree was general in nature. Judge Johnson appointed a citizens' committee to monitor compliance,[19] whereas Judge Henley relied on the plaintiffs and their attorneys. Both judges used reports and deadlines to monitor compliance, but Judge Henley also reviewed inmate complaints. Judge Henley awarded attorneys' fees in an attempt to enforce his decree; Judge Johnson eventually appointed a receiver for the Alabama prison system.[20]

Commentators such as Young would view Judge Johnson's role in *Pugh* as involving undue judicial interference with administrative decision making. Ira P. Robbins and Michael B. Buser, however, defend Judge Johnson's actions. They note that, after all, it is the totality of prison conditions that are called into question in such cases as *Holt* and *Pugh*; they suggest that there are eleven conditions that go to make up the totality that the court must judge: physical facilities, overcrowding, classification system, isolation cells, medical program, food service, sanitation/hygiene, personal security, prison personnel, rehabilitation, and miscellaneous matters such as racial segregation, search and seizure, First Amendment claims, and due process in disciplinary proceedings.[21] Robbins and Buser argue that a court order must specifically address each of these considerations in a significant way because modest, piecemeal improvements are not likely to lead to overall improvement; because broad and vague statements are likely to be evaded, ignored, or misinterpreted; and because in totality-of-conditions cases, courts must be assumed to have the authority to issue totality-of-conditions decrees.[22] Robbins and Buser are not concerned about the activist posture assumed by the court in *Pugh,* justifying it in terms of necessity. They argue that *Pugh*-type relief is the least-interventionist technique for achieving effectively a modicum of improvement in prison living conditions.[23] Furthermore, they suggest that this approach saves courts time and energy and actually encourages legislators and administrators to take action to solve problems on their own initiative.[24]

The Broader Context of Reform

Much, therefore, has been made of the differences between the *Holt* and *Pugh* approaches. However, as indicated in table 11-2, the two cases have several decision points in common. Moreover, when one looks at the outcomes of the two cases, one finds that the entire prison system of each state is still under court order, as of this date, dealing with inadequacies in the total conditions of the system. A receiver was appointed in 1979 for the Alabama prison system, a special master for the Arkansas penitentiary system in 1978. Thus despite the different choices made by the two judges at five points in the decision path—differences considered crucial by some commentators—each case has wound up as somewhat of a standoff between the courts and the prison administrators, at least for the time being.

Chapter 12 in this book examines the handling of the *Alberti* case, involving the Harris County Jail in Texas, by Judge Carl O. Bue, Jr.[25] The author concludes that Judge Bue achieved a great deal of success in reforming the jail. The decision path in that case was (1.1, 2.1, 3.1, 4.1/4.2, 5.1, 6.1, 7.1/7.4, 8.1/8.5, 9.1, 10.7, 11.1). This decision path is summarized and compared with *Holt* and *Pugh* in table 11-2. Scrutiny of the table indicates that *Alberti* was more like *Pugh* than *Holt.*[26] Yet it seems clear that Judge Bue was more successful in achieving reform in *Alberti* than Judge Johnson has been in *Pugh.* Why? One suspects that the method used by the judge in the remedial stages of the litigation is less important than other factors in determining the degree of compliance and impact achieved. The variables of (1) willingness and ability to comply on the part of one or more necessary actors, and (2) judicial determination to compel compliance have been suggested as especially important.[27] If these are indeed the most salient variables, then compliance is substantially a political problem, but it can still be aided by the judge's understanding of the range of choices available at each stage. It may not matter very much what sort of decision path a judge follows in a prison-conditions case so long as that path does not foreclose too early certain options that the judge may need to exercise later.

A recent *Harvard Law Review* note recommend a procedure for the remedial phase of prison-conditions litigation that is quite consistent with these realities.[28] The suggested procedure is flexible and is intended to allow judges to apply the amount of pressure they believe is needed to induce prison administrators and local officials to comply with court orders. According to this scenario, the court should first issue a declaratory injunction if constitutional violations are found, specifying what those violations are.[29] If necessary, the court should also issue a prohibitory decree to protect the plaintiffs. The court should retain jurisdiction and require the public officials to take corrective action. After determining what action has been taken, the court should then either relinquish jurisdiction or require the officials to submit a plan for additional remedial action. If the plan is not acceptable, the court should then fashion its own. In doing so, or in reviewing plans submitted by public officials, the court may seek input from the plaintiffs, other affected parties, or expert witnesses. The court should try to arrive at its own decree by requiring negotiations between the affected parties; if that should fail, the court would then have to develop the decree itself or through a special master.

This suggested procedure recognizes what the use of decision-path analysis makes clear: a prison-conditions case consists of a number of decision points; at each the judge has several options. It adds the notion that the judge should choose with an eye toward the larger context of the case, in some circumstances selecting one option, in others another—perhaps returning to a decision point and selecting a second or even a third option if initial choices are not effective. It seeks to put substantial responsibility for the decree on the parties by recommending that the judge require that they attempt to arrive at a negotiated decree. In other words, the remedial process is viewed as a tool for maximizing compliance and impact. This is an essential perspective if the court's intervention is to be anything but an exercise in frustration.

What the *Harvard Law Review's* recommended procedure fails to recognize, however, is that broader political conditions will often place constraints on the judge's ability to influence the results achieved through choices of procedures alone. Yet choices of procedures are not totally without effect; although they are not the only, or necessarily the most important, factor in the compliance/impact phase of a case, they are a factor. Such choices, for instance, can be used to signal to others that the judge is determined to compel compliance. Therefore, they may increase the willingness of prison administrators to alter policies, allocate more funds, and otherwise act to comply with court orders. Used in this way, the remedial process can be designed to fit optimally into the political context within which judges attempt to secure compliance with their orders in institutional-reform litigation.[30]

If the remedial process is viewed in this way, then the *Harvard Law Review's* recommended procedure makes good sense. It is flexible and can be custom designed for each case. Judges are not locked into a pattern of heavy reliance on the plaintiffs as in *Holt* or minimal use as in *Pugh*. They can adjust their procedures to fit the situation in each suit rather than using a predetermined procedure and hoping that it fits the circumstances in the case. Adopting either *Holt*-type or *Pugh*-type relief as the standard would be accepting this kind of straightjacket.[31] The *Harvard Law Review's* recommended procedure allows the judge to use the remedial process as a resource in the political struggle to secure compliance with court orders and make some impact on the jails and prisons of the country. For this reason it promises to be a more effective model for the remedial process in prison litigation than any of those used to date by members of the federal judiciary.

Notes

1. 365 U.S. 167 (1961).
2. 370 U.S. 660 (1962).
3. 378 U.S. 546 (1964).
4. Prisoners also based section-1983 suits on constitutional provisions other than the cruel-and-unusual-punishment clause: free exercise of religion, freedom of speech, freedom of the press, equal protection of the laws, due process of law, and access to the courts. The totality-of-conditions cases with which I will be dealing, however, are essentially Eighth Amendment cases.
5. William H. Danne, Jr., "Prison Conditions as Amounting to Cruel and Unusual Punishment," *American Law Review* 51(1973):126.
6. Holt v. Sarver, 300 F.Supp. 825 (E.D.Ark. 1969).
7. Daryl R. Fair, "The Lower Federal Courts as Constitution-Makers: The Case of Prison Conditions," *American Journal of Criminal Law* 7(1979):137-140.
8. National Prison Project, *Status Report—The Courts and Prisons,* mimeo. (Washington, D.C.: ACLU National Prison Project, 1 April 1980), pp. 1-6.
9. 300 F.Supp. 825 (E.D.Ark. 1969); 309 F.Supp. 362 (E.D.Ark. 1970); 442 F.2d 304 (8th. Cir. 1971); Holt v. Hutto, 363 F.Supp. 194 (E.D.Ark. 1973); Finney v. Arkansas Board of Correction, 505 F.2d 194 (8th Cir. 1974); Finney v. Hutto, 410 F.Supp. 251 (E.D.Ark. 1976); 548 F.2d 740 (8th Cir. 1977); Hutto v. Finney, 437 U.S. 678 (1978); Finney v. Mabry, 458 F.Supp. 720 (E.D.Ark. 1978).
10. 406 F.Supp. 318 (M.D.Ala. 1976); Newman v. Alabama, 559 F.2d 283 (5th Cir. 1977); *cert. denied,* 438 U.S. 915 (1978); 466 F.Supp. 628 (M.D.Ala. 1979).
11. 406 F.Supp. 649 (S.D.Tex. 1975).
12. *Public Administration Review* 19(1959):79-88.
13. Attorneys' fees may be awarded by the federal courts under the Civil Rights Attorney's Fees Awards Act of 1976, Title 42, U.S. Code, section 1988 (1976 ed.), to the prevailing parties in suits under certain civil-rights laws as part of the reasonable costs of litigation. An equity court may also award attorneys' fees, generally against a party who acts in bad faith by delaying or disrupting proceedings or by obstructing enforcement of a judicial decree. Hutto v. Finney, 437 U.S. 678 (1978).

14. Finney v. Mabry, 458 F.Supp. 720 (E.D.Ark. 1978). Special masters may be appointed by the federal courts under rule 53 of the Federal Rules of Civil Procedure. They normally receive evidence and file a report containing findings of fact and conclusions of law for the judges to consider. In the prison cases, masters have been used to assist in formulating standards and monitoring compliance with judicial decress.

15. *Equity* refers to the power of courts to deal with legal problems not covered by specific, existing laws applicable to situations in which one person's rights are violated by another; see Daniel Oran, *Law Dictionary for Non-Lawyers* (St. Paul, Minn.: West, 1975), p. 120.

16. M. Kay Harris and Dudley P. Spiller, Jr., *After Decision: Implementation of Judicial Decrees in Correctional Settings* (Washington, D.C. National Institute of Law Enforcement and Criminal Justice, Law Enforcement Assistance Administration, U.S. Department of Justice, 1977), pp. 96-99.

17. 323 F.Supp. 93 (N.D.Ohio 1971); 330 F.Supp. 707 (N.D.Ohio 1971); Jones v. Metzger, 456 F.2d 854 (6th Cir. 1972).

18. Thomas A. Young, "Equitable Remedies Available to a Federal Court after Declaring an Entire Prison System Violates the Eighth Amendment," *Capital University Law Review* 1(1972):115.

19. The Fifth Circuit Court of Appeals struck down this device and substituted a single monitor for each prison, supervised by a master or magistrate. It did so, however, because of the broad, vague grant of authority that Judge Johnson had given the citizens' committee rather than because of any objections to the device of a citizens' committee per se. Judge Johnson had said the committee was to have authority to take any action necessary to accomplish its purpose; the Court of Appeals thought this too imprecise and too prone to produce conflict and confusion in the administration of the prisons. Newman v. Alabama, 559 F.2d 283, 288-290 (5th Cir. 1977).

20. Newman v. Alabama, 466 F.Supp. 628 (M.D.Ala. 1979).

21. Ira P. Robbins and Michael B. Buser, "Punitive Conditions of Prison Confinement: An Analysis of *Pugh* v. *Locke* and Federal Court Supervision of State Penal Administration under the Eighth Amendment," *Stanford Law Review* 29(1977):909-914.

22. Ibid., pp. 917-920.

23. Ibid., p. 926 (italics added). Thus although *Holt*-type relief is admittedly less intrusive, Robbins and Buser regard it as also ineffective. Therefore *Pugh*-type relief is, to them, the least intrusive effective form of relief.

24. Ibid., pp. 925-926.

25. Thomas S. Ostrowski, "Judicial Intervention and Jail Reform."

26. *Holt* and *Alberti* are completely different at three decision points (3, 5, 10) and partially different at three more (4, 7, 8). *Pugh* and *Alberti* are completely different at only one decision point (10), and they are also partially different at three (4, 7, 8).

27. Harris and Spiller, *After Decision,* p. 5.

28. "Developments in the Law—Section 1983 and Federalism," *Harvard Law Review* 90(1977):1243-1249. These recommendations are similar in many respects to the procedures for implementation of court orders in prison cases recommended by the Joint Committee on the Legal Status of Prisoners of the American Bar Association in "Criminal Justice Section Project on Standards Relating to the Legal Status of Prisoners," *American Criminal Law Review* 14 (1977):584-588.

29. This is the usual procedure in a prison-conditions case; it is not unique to the *Harvard Law Review's* recommendations.

30. See Colin S. Diver, "The Judge as Political Powerbroker: Superintending Structural Change in Public Institutions," *Virginia Law Review* 65(1979): 43-106, for a discussion of institutional-reform litigation as a political-bargaining game. Diver is generally unsympathetic to this sort of litigation, however.

31. Judges Johnson and Henley, it can be argued, foreclosed their options by committing themselves to particular courses of action at crucial decision points (see table 11-1). Judge Johnson chose to use a specific decree at decision point 5, thus locking himself in for the duration of the case with respect to that aspect of the remedial process. Judge Henley decided to use hearings to formulate the decree (decision point 4) thus setting a pattern of interaction between himself and the parties to the case, and among the parties themselves, which affected the development of the litigation.

12 Judicial Intervention and Jail Reform

Thomas S. Ostrowski

Traditionally jail policymaking in the United States has been the domain of local public officials. Such was the case in Harris County, Texas, where the local officials, however, had only a minimal interest in jail problems. That situation changed in the 1970s as the result of a class-action suit, *Alberti v. Sheriff and Commissioners Court of Harris County,* filed in 1972 by the Houston chapter of the American Civil Liberties Union (ACLU). This suit, filed on behalf of the prisoners in the Harris County jails, in time made U.S. District Judge Carl O. Bue, Jr. a central participant in jail reform and compelled reluctant local officials to alter their jail policies.

This chapter analyzes the impact that Judge Bue had on the jails and the approach that he used to achieve that impact. The focus will be on two facets of Judge Bue's activities: his strategy in dealing with the other actors in the policy process and his approach to defining and solving the jail problems.

The principal other actors with whom Judge Bue had to work were the Sheriff of Harris County and the Harris County commissioners.[1] The sheriff, who is an elected official, is the "keeper of the jails."[2] Five individually elected county commissioners are responsible for appropriating funds for the jails as well as for other county institutions and services.[3]

This analysis of Judge Bue's participation in the jail-policy process should be of general interest because, for the most part, the jail problems in Houston were typical of jail problems throughout the nation. Inmate living conditions were clearly inhumane; the majority of prisoners were pretrial detainees; the jails were components of a badly fractured criminal-justice system; and the jails were funded and operated by local public officials.

The analysis should be of further interest because it allows for comparisons with three jail studies published by the American Bar Association in 1976: *Hamilton v. Schiro, Collins v. Schoonfield,* and *Holland v. Donelson.*[4] Each study examined the participation of a U.S. district court judge in a local jail-policy process, and each involved jail settings and jail conditions that were similar to those in Harris County. Furthermore, the methodology used in each case was sufficiently similar to that used here to allow for comparison.

The kinds of data considered, classified by source, are documents and records, interviews, court testimony, and observations.[5] A sequential framework for policy analysis is used to analyze Judge Bue's strategy for jail reform.[6] In brief, the framework posits the following sequence of behavior in the policy process: Problems are identified; possible alternative solutions are formulated, each with associated costs and benefits; a preferred solution is adopted and funds appropriated; the solution is applied to the problem; and the impact of the solution or policy is evaluated.

Although the evaluation phase is the final step in the policy sequence, it ordinarily does not terminate the policy process. Thus in the Harris County case the evaluation phase of each sequence marked the end of that sequence and signaled the beginning of a new one. In this study we are concerned with four policy sequences: 1972-1975, 1975-1976, 1976-1977, 1978-1980. An examination of Judge Bue's behavior in each of the sequences will enable us to understand his approach to jail reform.

Round I: 1972-1975

For all practical purposes, Judge Bue had no impact on the jails during this period. In August 1972, the ACLU formulated a list of jail problems, and in February 1975 the defendants agreed to a set of solutions when they signed a consent judgement. However, the county commissioners were unwilling to appropriate the funds needed to implement the solutions. Therefore, at the request of the ACLU, Judge Bue called a hearing for September 1975, to allow the court "to assess existing conditions at the county detention facilities and the causes for those conditions."[7]

Round II: 1975-1976

In his efforts to define the jail problems, Judge Bue relied heavily on the ACLU attorneys, James Oitzinger and Gerald Birnberg. It is important to emphasize that reliance does not mean blind dependence or anything close to it. The ACLU did present most of the evidence, but all the principal actors in the September hearing agreed that Judge Bue retained an air of independence and impartiality throughout the hearing.[8] My observations of Judge Bue's behavior led me to the same conclusion.

Judge Bue obviously appreciated the quantity and quality of the work done by Oitzinger and Birnberg.[9] However, he also recognized the important contributions of the defense attorney, Edward Landry, and, especially, of Sheriff Jack Heard.[10]

Sheriff Heard had been elected as a reform candidate after the ACLU filed suit, but he agreed to become a defendant because he was committed to jail reform. Although he was a defendant, Sheriff Heard behaved more like a plaintiff. He and his staff not only responded affirmatively to the ACLU's requests for information but also frequently advised Birnberg and Oitzinger about courthouse politics and about the operations of the criminal-justice system. And, on at least two occasions, the sheriff ordered members of his staff to spend the night collecting data for the ACLU's case.

Although Judge Bue recognized the contributions of the other participants in the hearing, the quality of his orders made it evident that he too worked diligently. In fact, he made it very clear that he and his law clerks spent considerable time and effort on the case. "We did an awful lot of homework. Collectively, over a three-month period, we spent many sessions at night studying the problems."[11]

Analyzing the Evidence

To organize the voluminous evidence presented by the ACLU, Judge Bue used a systems approach introduced to Harris County by the National Clearinghouse for Criminal Justice Planning and Architecture.[12] This approach treats the jails as a subsystem of the criminal-justice system, which, in turn, is viewed as a component of the political system. By using such an approach, Judge Bue was able to devise a more comprehensive definition of the jail problems than had been formulated in the past, when the jails were treated as if they existed in a vacuum.

As part of his efforts to better understand the situation, Judge Bue took time out from the hearings to tour the jails. This tour had a profound impact. Sheriff's-department personnel who toured the jails with him said, "He was visibly shaken."[13] Judge Bue's description of the experience indicates that he was. In his December 1975 order, he said, " . . . the many and varied conditions at the detention facilities degrade and dehumanize even those persons who voluntarily tour the facilities briefly as did this Court."[14]

The following were some of the conditions that distressed Judge Bue:

> Average living space per inmate is 20 square feet. . . . More than 500 inmates had no bed on which to sleep. . . . An intolerable stench pervades the atmosphere. . . . Adequate medical treatment is not available. . . . The mentally ill are incarcerated without access to any special facilities or treatment or even to dayrooms. . . . Inmates who are in withdrawal from narcotics or alcohol also lack proper care and treatment. . . . An insufficient number of guards and staff work in the jails. . . . Violent attacks consistently occur between inmates. . . . Inmates are required to eat in their cells, or wherever they sleep, and the introduction of food into the living quarters enhances introduction of bacteria and other unsanitary elements such as roaches and rats into such quarters."[15]

Judge Bue's visit better enabled him to empathize with the prisoners than if he had simply listed to testimony about the conditions in the comfort of his courtroom. Certainly his experience made him more determined to achieve jail reform than if he had not taken the tour.

Once the hearings were concluded, Judge Bue and his law clerks began the process of drafting an order, which was issued 16 December 1975. The ninety-two-page order concluded that: ". . . the *Clearinghouse Report* accurately analyzed the problem of corrections in Harris County as one which exists on three levels: 1) physical conditions at the jails, 2) movement of an inmate through the criminal justice system; and 3) fiscal resources of the criminal justice system."[16]

Judge Bue went beyond simply describing the problems to analyzing their causes. For example, he maintained that overcrowding was the central problem in the jails and that this was caused primarily by the following conditions: (1) On the average, indigent pretrial detainees do not have counsel appointed for them until they have been in jail for fifty days. This means that during the first fifty days of a person's incarceration no one is processing his case. So nothing happens except that the person takes up jail space. This situation resulted from the county commissioners' reluctance to fund the criminal-justice system adequately. (2) Also, ". . . commissioners have done little more than provide a brittle skeletal framework for the one agency (Pretrial Release) which was intended to possess sufficient strength to blunt the force of a rapidly expanding jail population."[17] Judge Bue recognized that the professional bail bondsmen were an important political force in Harris County, and he thought that the commissioners were keeping the Pretrial Release Agency weak and ineffective to retain the support of the bondsmen. (3) The county had an insufficient number of criminal courts. This deficiency resulted in a tremendous backlog of cases, and it too was caused by the commissioners' neglect of the criminal-justice system.

The commissioners did not consider their own attitudes to be crucial to the jail problem. On the contrary, they felt that Judge Bue was being unreasonable because he would not recognize that the county's limited financial resources were the main reason why jail conditions could not be significantly improved quickly. Furthermore, they thought that his systems approach to analyzing jail problems would result in the formulation of some very expensive and complex solutions. Commissioners preferred to isolate the jail problems from other criminal-justice concerns, supposedly making those problems more manageable and less costly to solve. Moreover, financial concerns were not the only ones felt by these local officials. Some of the commissioners, for example, were worried that the Pretrial Release Agency would set free persons who were a threat to the community.

One other point about the commissioners' definition of the jail problems is worth mentioning. E.E. Schattschneider has observed that when the scope of a local conflict is expanded to include federal actors, the local officials frequently define the expansion as a part of the problem.[18] These officials claim that the right of local self-government has been violated. After federal Judge Bue entered the case, the county commissioners did just that, defining Bue's involvement as a part of the jail problem. County commissioner Jon Lindsay spoke of "the federal intrusion into local government."[19] And he, as well as other commissioners and their supporters, frequently argued that Judge Bue "overstepped his authority."[20] Judge Bue did not respond to these criticisms because he had decided to "let (his) orders stand on their own."[21] But there were responses by the local news media. For example, *The Houston Post* commented in an editorial, "Local officials complain—often with justification—about federal interference in local affairs. But Harris County jail is an instance of local government asking for it." According to the editorial, "the county has forfeited a measure of local control by default."[22]

The Search for Remedies

Just as the problem-definition activity in this policy sequence occurred primarily in the context of the September 1975 hearings, so too did the policy-formulation effort. Thus, the process of formulating solutions to the jail problems was closely interrelated with the process of defining problems. In this phase, the ACLU held the lead role in outlining possible remedial actions, and again, the *Report of the National Clearinghouse* was a primary resource.

Among the solutions set forth by Judge Bue in his December order were the following: (1) The county commissioners must surrender their operational control of the Pretrial Release Agency to the state district judges of Harris County. The agency's staff was to be expanded and upgraded. Furthermore, the agency was to adopt a mode of operations similar to that employed by the Manhattan Bail Project.[23] (2) The commissioners were to establish two courts that would hear only jail cases, that is, those cases involving pretrial detainees. (3) The county must provide a computerized list of all qualified attorneys available to represent indigents so that magistrates can systematically appoint counsel on a rotating basis. Judge Bue felt that this was particularly important "because it is axiomatic that a criminal case moves towards disposition more rapidly once counsel is retained or appointed."[24] (4) Commissioners must establish a preliminary-hearing system so that each person charged with a crime will be brought before a magistrate within twenty-four hours of his arrest. (5) The classification of prisoners must be done twenty-four hours per day, seven days per week. Judge Bue emphasized that the classification criteria must not allow pretrial detainees to be housed in the same cell block with convicted and sentenced prisoners. (6) Those prisoners who are mentally ill must be removed from the jail and housed elsewhere. (7) Health, education, and social services were to be established or improved. The jails were to be cleaned and vermin exterminated.

Judge Bue attempted to convince county officials, particularly the commissioners, of the merits of his solutions. For example, he demonstrated that reducing the jail population before constructing a new jail made good sense in economic terms. He did this, in part, by citing the experiences of similar jurisdictions. Judge Bue estimated that if Harris County would adopt his pretrial-release proposal, "the county would save the taxpayers $225,000 a year on detention costs alone."[25]

Although he used persuasion in his order, Judge Bue expressed clearly that even if the commissioners did not accept his reasoning, compliance was expected: "Should the jails be found to be operated in continued violation of state and federal law and the Consent Judgement, the Court will not hesitate to give serious consideration to adopting an entirely different course of action previously employed by other federal district courts whereby local jails have been ordered closed as of a fixed future date."[26] This warning was reinforced by the establishment of an Office of Ombudsman to be staffed by the ACLU attorneys. Strictly speaking, the attorneys were not ombudsmen; their responsibility was to monitor county criminal-justice operations to determine whether the county was complying with Judge Bue's order.

In his December 1975 report, Judge Bue also required that commissioners submit to him a variety of weekly and monthly reports so that he could follow the policy developments personally. Furthermore, Judge Bue scheduled an evaluation hearing for June 1976.

Sheriff Heard reacted to Judge Bue's order with enthusiasm. "These are the things I've wanted all along," he said.[27] But the commissioners expressed antagonism.

> "It might be cheaper, when a man robs a bank, to put him on a pension and let him live out at a home somewhere," Commissioner Bob Eckels said during the budget session.
>
> "Yes, but it has to be next to a golf course somewhere," said Commissioner E.A. "Squatty" Lyons.
>
> "I would like to put him by the judge (meaning Bue)," said Eckels.[28]

During another budget session, Commissioner Jim Fonteno said, "I don't remember Judge Bue calling me and asking if we had the money. He said do it. That comes first. Everything else is secondary because a federal judge is God."[29] Fonteno went on to say that he would refuse to take actions that would put the county in the same type of financial crisis as that experienced by New York City.

Commissioners appropriated some funds to comply with Judge Bue's order, but these funds were far short of the amount needed to achieve the reforms required. Also, during this policy sequence the voters of Harris County approved a $15-million bond proposal for jail construction. The commissioners were pleased with the outcome of the bond election, but Judge Bue tempered their joy by informing them that the $15 million was only a down payment on what was needed.

As of 1 April 1976, the county had made some minor progress in implementing Judge Bue's order, but much remained to be done. In fact, I concluded from my observations that the jails were in essentially the same "degrading and dehumanizing" condition on 1 April 1976, as they were when Judge Bue toured them on 24 September 1975.[30]

The feedback that Judge Bue received from the ombudsmen and from the county led him to the same conclusion. Thus, on 1 April 1976, he unexpectedly called a hearing for 20 April so that he could evaluate the county's efforts to implement his order. The April 1 date marked a turning point in this case because, through his action, Judge Bue finally convinced the commissioners that he was determined to obtain compliance. The 20 April hearing was somewhat anti-climactic, for the commissioners had already begun to make a greater effort to comply. Beginning in early April, they were less parsimonious in appropriating money, and they were far less strident in their comments about Judge Bue and the financial burdens of jail reform.

Round III: 1976–1977

In his 2 July 1976 order, Judge Bue adjusted his definition of the jail problems to fit current circumstances. Many of the problems that he had defined in December 1975 had been solved or were being solved as of 2 July. In addition, he had decided that some of the remaining problems were more critical than others. It was these critical problems that he chose to stress in his July 1976 definition of the jail problems. These were the excessive jail population and the continued failure of the Pretrial Release Agency to reduce the size of that population, the continued incarceration in the jail of persons with mental problems, and the inadequate medical-screening program.

Just as Judge Bue's definition of the jail problems was modified in mid-1976, so too were his proposed solutions. The policy statements in the 2 July 1976 order conveyed a greater sense of urgency than past pronouncements. The judge's heightened concern is illustrated in his comments about inadequate medical and psychological programs:

> . . . the Court cannot countenance any further delay on the part of the Commissioners Court to formulate and implement an appropriate medical and psychological screening program and alternative housing plan for persons suspected of mental instability in accordance with the law of this State. . . . If, at the end of ninety (90) days, the Commissioners Court has not commenced implementation of a definitive plan which satisfies fully the mandates of paragraph three of Article 5115 V.A.T.S. and the December 16 Order Nos. 27, 28, and 29, this Court will take appropriate steps to order a plan and impose the necessary sanctions, financial and otherwise. . . .[31]

Less than two weeks after Judge Bue issued his July order, the commisioners appropriated funds for a thirty-bed psychiatric unit at a county hostpial.

Moreover, they continued to appropriate funds for other aspects of jail reform, so that by the end of 1977, the county was in compliance with most of Judge Bue's directives. However, it was not in total compliance. For example, the thirty-bed unit was not adequate for housing all the inmates with psychiatric problems; and the jails remained somewhat overcrowded. But Judge Bue was satisfied that good progress was being made. Furthermore, he expected that the construction of a new jail would bring the county into total compliance.

Round IV: 1978-1980

The major issue during this sequence was the design of the new jail. The county presented a plan to Judge Bue that called for a fourteen-story facility with one floor used as a gymnasium and another used for a psychiatric unit. Four of the floors were to be left in shell form. Without the shell floors, the jail will house slightly more than 2,000 prisoners. Upon completion of the shells, the jail could hold in excess of 3,500 prisoners.

Judge Bue and the ACLU thought that the county was making a mistake in planning to house only 37 percent of the prisoners in single cells. He concluded:

> ... it is apparent from documentary evidence and testimony presented at the hearing that a more humane, efficacious and practical structure than the one contemplated might be planned and constructed by the defendants. Nevertheless it is not initially the province of the Court to redesign the facility in a fashion that comports with its personal opinion or those of plaintiffs' expert witnesses advocating jail design, but only to pass on the question of whether the proposed plan contravenes minimum standards.[32]

Judge Bue approved the plans conditionally. He told county officials, "At such time as the defendants seek the Court's approval for the completion of the additional four floors and the closing of the [old jails], the Court will re-evaluate the facility and the single cell situation to determine if the then-existing law is satisfied."[33] Thus, Judge Bue assured himself a role in the Harris County jail-policy process at least through 1982, when construction is expected to be complete.

Conclusion

My observations and interviews as well as county records indicate that the improvements achieved by Judge Bue have been sustained, at least through March 1980. Living conditions in the jails remain dramatically improved; human services are still being provided at a decent level; the criminal-justice system continues to operate fairly effectively as a system, at least as it affects the jail population; and the jail population is still down. Perhaps Judge Bue's most basic achievement was the gradual but steady reduction in the jail population, from a high of 2,511 in 1975 to a daily average of 1,901 prisoners in 1979. This 24-percent reduction reversed a long-standing trend of an expanding jail population.[34] It proved to be a crucial accomplishment, because many of the other reforms that are associated with Judge Bue's efforts hinged on a reduced jail population.

It should be noted that Judge Bue's impact has not been assessed on the basis of how close he has come to developing an ideal jail in Harris County. Rather, the assessment has been based on how far he has moved Harris County from the jail situation that existed prior to his involvement in the case. From this perspective, Judge Bue has had a very significant positive impact on the jails. Furthermore, it is obvious that the longer Judge Bue remained active in the policy process, the greater his impact became.

Judge Bue's accomplishments occurred, of course, in a political context. In this regard, the American Bar Association (ABA) studies concluded that "non-compliance with judicial decrees seems to be a function of two variables: 1) unwillingness or inability to comply on the part of one or more necessary actors, and 2) lack of judicial determination to compel compliance."[35] For the most part, all those to whom Judge Bue addressed his decrees were able to comply in some reasonable manner. The sheriff and the ACLU were not only able but were willing and anxious to ensure compliance. The commissioners, on the other hand, were unwilling to comply initially because their priorities did not call for increased appropriations for the jails. However, Judge Bue, at times quietly persuasive and at other times forceful and demanding, was able to move them toward compliance.

Judge Bue's handling of the case, that is, his systematic and comprehensive definition of the problems and formulation of solutions, his persistence in getting the commissioners to appropriate funds, his attention to compliance reports and his willingness to hold compliance hearings, all served notice to the other actors in the policy process that he was determined to achieve results. Thus, as in the ABA studies, compliance reports and hearings were most useful in convincing others of the judge's determination.[36]

Just as judicial determination is essential to securing adherence to judicial orders, so too is a comprehensive understanding of jail problems and their causes essential to achieving reform. Judge Bue's success in Harris County was not just a matter of being determined to move the commissioners to improve jail conditions. The substance of those orders themselves was an integral part of his success. He used the systems approach to analyze the jail problems and their causes and to develop solutions. He was proud that his orders were "accurate, thorough, and [that] they withstood the scrutiny of people who know more about jails than I do."[37] Judge Bue thought that it was essential to "do things right the first time because I knew that we would get another suit if we didn't."[38]

Indeed, that was what happened in one of the cases studied by the ABA. In *Collins* v. *Schoonfield,* although the judge was determined to gain compliance with his decrees, he did not recognize overcrowding as a key element of the Baltimore city-jail problems. Thus, two years after *Collins* ended, a civil suit, *Duvall* v. *Mandel,* was filed on behalf of the prisoners in the Baltimore jail to end the overcrowding.[39]

It appears that such suits will be avoided in Harris County in the foreseeable future. But we can only speculate about what will happen when Judge Bue removes himself from the policy process and the jails are again entirely in the hands of local public officials. Recall that this case, like those studied by the ABA, began with the losers from the past jail-policy processes—namely the prisoners—petitioning the federal judiciary to join their side against local officials.[40] In Harris County, as in two of the three ABA cases, the change in the scope of conflict worked well for the prisoners. But what will happen when the jails revert to a strictly local issue, and the advantage of having Judge Bue is gone?

It seems unrealistic to expect the commissioners to finance additional fundamental reforms. But it does seem likely that, because of the vigilence of Judge Bue and others, the reforms achieved in this case have had sufficient time to become firmly established in the Harris County criminal-justice system. Thus, they probably will be maintained for some time to come.

Notes

1. The county-commissioners court is the principal government body in Texas county government. A county judge serves as the presiding officer of the court, but despite the use of the terms *court* and *judge,* it is not a judicial body. To avoid confusion with the judiciary, this chapter will refer to the Harris County Commissioners Court as the Harris County commissioners.

2. Texas, *Vernon's Annotated Revised Civil Statutes of the State of Texas,* 15, article 5116 (St. Paul, Minn.: West, 1971), p. 281.

3. Ibid., article 5115, p. 279.

4. M. Kay Harris and Dudley P. Spiller, Jr., *After Decision: Implementation of Judicial Decrees in Correctional Settings* (Washington, D.C.: American Bar Association Commission on Correctional Facilities and Services, 1976).

5. I spent four months observing jail policy processes and policy outputs prior to the issuance of Judge Bue's order to the county officials to bring the jails up to constitutional and statutory standards. On issuance of the order, I spent seven months observing Judge Bue's impact on the jails. My observations were conducted in the jails during all hours of the day and night. Since conducting the initial eleven months of observations in 1975 and 1976, I have periodically returned to the jails to monitor the progress and the permanence of

Judge Bue's reform efforts. This monitoring has taken the form of observing in the jails, conducting interviews, and studying documents and records.

6. This framework is developed in depth by James E. Anderson, *Public Policy-Making* (New York: Praeger, 1975) and Charles O. Jones, *An Introduction to the Study of Public Policy* (North Scituate, Mass.: Duxbury, 1977).

7. Alberti v. Sheriff and Commissioners Court of Harris County (Judge Carl Bue's ruling, p. 4, December 1975), 406 F.Supp. 649 (S.D.Texas 1975).

8. The county attorney, Ed Landry, who represented the county commissioners, held this view. Likewise, the ACLU attorneys, Sheriff Heard, and other county officials stated in interviews that Judge Bue remained impartial throughout the hearings.

9. Judge Carl O. Bue, Jr., interview held at the U.S. Court House, Houston, Texas, March 1980.

10. Ibid.

11. Ibid.

12. U.S., Department of Justice, Law Enforcement Assistance Administration, National Clearinghouse for Criminal Justice Planning and Architecture, *Harris County Corrections Plan* (Washington, D.C., 1975).

13. Major Robert Breckenridge, interview held at Harris County Rehabilitation Center, Houston, Texas, July 1976.

14. Alberti v. Sheriff, p. 13.

15. Ibid., pp. 10–13.

16. Ibid., p. 9.

17. Ibid., p. 25.

18. E.E. Schattschneider, *The Semisovereign People* (New York: Holt, Rinehart, and Winston, 1960), p. 11.

19. *Houston Post,* 6 January 1976.

20. Ibid.

21. Judge Carl O. Bue, Jr., interview held at the U.S. Court House, Houston, Texas, March 1980.

22. *Houston Post,* 6 January 1976. Reprinted with permission.

23. Alberti v. Sheriff, p. 43.

24. Ibid., p. 48.

25. Ibid., p. 31.

26. Ibid., p. 8.

27. Sheriff Jack Heard, interview held at Harris County Court House, Houston, Texas, January 1976.

28. *Houston Post,* 21 January 1976. Reprinted with permission.

29. *Houston Post,* 24 January 1976. Reprinted with permission.

30. Alberti v. Sheriff, p. 13.

31. Alberti v. Sheriff and Commissioners Court of Harris County (Judge Carl Bue's Interim Order, p. 7, 2 July 1976).

32. Alberti v. Sheriff and Commissioners Court of Harris County (Judge Carl Bue's order, p. 7, 14 September 1978(.

33. Ibid., p. 16.

34. Judge Bue achieved this through the combined reforms in the court system and the pretrial-release program.

35. Harris and Spiller, *After Decision,* p. 3.

36. Ibid., p. 13.

37. Judge Carl O. Bue, Jr., interview held at the U.S. Court House, Houston, Texas, March 1980.

38. Ibid.

39. M. Kay Harris, *After Decision: Implementation of Judicial Decrees in Correctional Settings—A Case Study of Collins v. Schoonfield* (Washington, D.C.: American Bar Association Commission on Correctional Facilities and Services, 1976), p. 7.

40. This is consistent with Schattschneider's thesis that those who lose at one stage will seek to expand the scope to include additional political actors who might favor their side in the conflict. See Schattschneider, *Semisovereign People,* p. 16.

13 Developing Legal Remedies for Unconstitutional Incarceration

Candace McCoy

Even the noblest of experiments must be subjected to the careful scrutiny of evaluators, who decide whether the hypothesis has been proven or the goal attained. In the field of correctional reform, the sociolegal experiment of the past two decades—whereby the Warren Court dramatically expanded the constitutional rights of the convicted, and federal district courts undertook the difficult task of enforcing those rights—now is being evaluated by the Burger Court. That Court apparently deems one part of the experiment a success: the substantive rights of prisoners will not be cut back, at least in theory.[1]

But the Burger Court is traditionalist, not activist. If it relies on *stare decisis* and will not retract rights accorded prisoners by the Warren Court, neither will it expand them. Furthermore, it has definitely signaled the lower federal courts to discontinue use of the equitable remedy for prison abuse. That remedy was developed in the Warren era and is used so extensively that in 1980 nineteen states were operating prison systems under court orders, and an additional twelve were facing court challenges.[2]

Alarmists view these trends as proof that the Burger Court is reactionary and legally conservative, but this is not necessarily the case. Recent case law shows that the Court is willing to work toward new and innovative resolutions of correctional problems, but not in the activist style of the Warren Court. Accordingly, corrections policy in the future will be strongly influenced by traditional lawsuits, in which aggrieved prisoners demand money from their jailers. Lawsuits that result in court orders designed to monitor institutions until they comply with constitutional guidelines will be deemphasized.

In short, the Burger Court finds many disadvantages in the equity-model remedy for unconstitutional incarceration. Dissatisfied with experimental results in this procedural area, the Court proposes a solution of its own: expansion of the traditional money remedy. The void created by deemphasizing the familiar equitable remedy can be filled—although not completely—by the money model. The king is dead! Long live the king!

Case Law: From the Hands-off to the Hands-on Doctrine, and Beyond

Traditional American legal wisdom holds that it is not the function of courts to administer prisons or any executive agency, just as it is not the function of courts to write legislation. Of course, the Warren Court was willing to disregard traditionalism if abuses of the administrative process clearly violated that Court's vision of the Constitution. The many cases of the 1960s and 1970s, in which the constitutional rights of the incarcerated were held to have been violated by administrative policies and in which specific changes were ordered, destroyed the old hands-off doctrine.[3]

These Warren Court decisions emphasized the role of courts as enforcers of the rights of prisoners, instead of leaving protection of constitutional rights to the discretion of correctional administrators.[4] This judicial-activist role represents a hands-on doctrine.

The decisions were activist not only in their expansion of the substantive rights of prisoners but also in the procedural remedies devised by district courts to enforce those rights. Few remedies could be more hands-on than a court retaining jurisdiction over a case once its legal issues had been decided in order to guide administrators and politicians in detailed clean-up programs. Under this model, which is still being used, the local federal district court would declare correctional policies unconstitutional and would then fashion complex injunctive decrees as the appropriate remedy. Implementation of the clean-up decrees would be monitored by the same court.[5]

Obviously, this thrust on the district courts the Herculean task of "running the prison" until it met constitutional guidelines. Certainly, such an approach is reasonable when constitutional abuse is widespread. The familiar thesis that judges are not trained or constitutionally permitted to administer prisons is often an excuse, no doubt, to allow administrators to continue the abuse. Nevertheless, it seems reasonable to conclude that:

> The cases have produced ringing judicial rhetoric and "stunning paper victories," but less impressive results in the real world. In large part these disappointments may be traced to the traditionally limited concept of the judicial role as one of passive dispute resolution removed from public political realities. This role implies a model of institutional change through litigation which is incomplete in its attention to the implementation process.[6]

Why had the Warren-era decisions originally fixed on this type of response as the proper remedy for unconstitutional incarceration? It is an equitable remedy, not a remedy at law. A remedy "at law" is so called because it is the most traditional legal action. In earliest common law, judges usually ordered that money be paid to recompense the wrong that had been proven in court. The concept of equity developed in the Middle Ages in England only as a response to those suits in which this traditional legal remedy was deemed inadequate—that is, where specific actions or inactions were required to right the wrong and money was not the object.

Thus, "compelling the performance of certain affirmative acts is nothing new in principle, but [in recent prison case law] it is new in degree."[7] Obviously, the hands-on approach in prison-reform litigation uses equity as a model, requiring of prison administrators changes in correctional policies rather than change from their pockets.

Surely the equity model was intended by the Warren-era district courts to have the most direct effect possible on the behavior of government officials. The courts themselves would mandate specified reforms. The current Supreme Court, however, has considered several disadvantages of the remedy, and for reasons of policy and tradition, reflecting its vision of acceptable judicial functioning, the Court is now downplaying the equity model and expanding the money model.

Comparison: The Use of Two Enforcement Models

If a prisoner wishes to go to court to right the wrongs against him, basically two legal avenues are available. He may sue the wrongdoers personally in tort, the traditional civil action against another person who has negligently or intentionally harmed him. Or he may sue under the comparatively new body of law that has developed to protect civil rights, a field known in the vernacular as "constitutional torts." The majority of prison suits today charge violation of civil rights by administrators, their staffs, and various institutional policies and conditions in general. The ability to bring these charges to court was given to citizens by Congress in the Civil Rights Act of 1866. Section 1983 of that statute is the most widely used device for gaining access to courts to challenge unconstitutional policies.

The majority of the senators who voted for passage of the Civil Rights Act of 1866 believed that they were enacting enabling legislation for the Thirteenth and Fourteenth amendments. Blacks were to be free and equal citizens, and federal courts were to be the watchdogs enforcing the new equality. "As the face of the Act discloses, the framers little trusted the State courts to enforce Negro rights."[8] Therefore, they provided in section 1983 that "any person who, under color of state law, subjects . . . any citizen of the United States . . . to the deprivation of any rights . . . secured by the Constitution and laws, shall be liable to the party injured in an action at law, suit in equity, or other proper proceeding for redress."[9] Just as the majority of the senators would have been amazed that the Fourteenth Amendment would later be used to apply virtually the entire federal Bill of Rights to the states, they would probably be surprised to find that section 1983 now serves as the major statutory vehicle for lawsuits against a wide variety of state and local governmental defendants, including administrators of jails and prisons.[10]

But the language of the act is sweeping, and section 1983 is to be given a liberal construction, since it is remedial legislation enforcing one of the most dearly cherished of American rights—the right to be free of unwarranted governmental intrusions.[11] Accordingly, the persons subject to suit can include cities[12]; and "acting under color of state law" means that the workers for the state or city were acting in pursuance of governmental policy, not personal ends.[13] The entire body of constitutional rights is protected, and of course courts may fashion whatever remedies they desire to vindicate these rights.

What interests us here is this fashioning of the remedy for constitutional violations, because the effect of litigation on administrative policymaking is most keenly felt when the court announces not only who won and why but also what the loser must do in recompense.

The Warren Court's Equity Model

The language of section 1983 permits remedies in law, equity, or both, but the remedies may influence public policy quite differently. The equity model would remedy constitutional violations with court-ordered clean-ups of prisons and jails. Goals and timetables for taking prescribed administrative actions are written. Courts monitor the progress of the improvements.

There may be several advantages to this approach. Certainly, it exercises a clearcut effect on policy. Administrators know exactly what they must do and when they must do it. In theory, there is little room for evasion. Furthermore, this forceful demand from the judiciary makes legislatures aware of the monetary needs of correctional institutions and forces funds into providing correctional improvements that certainly would not be made otherwise.[14]

The equity model can be quite sweeping. It attempts to remedy systematic bureaucratic abuse by mandating wide-ranging and detailed changes. It is often used in cases where plaintiffs have joined together in class actions, underscoring the need for systematic change rather than mollification of individual inmate plaintiffs. (Note, however, that class actions are also possible under a money model.) These cases are often pursued by plaintiffs' attorneys, who are public-interest lawyers paid by legal-aid programs or by correctional-reform groups. Public-policy considerations are paramount for them, in contrast with the narrower aim of winning a civil-rights case and simply collecting the attorney's fees included as part of the damages by the provisions of the Civil Rights Act.

The role of the judge is a major strength of the equity model. He or she is objective insofar as he or she is not involved in prison administration or in the legislative and executive politics that affect it. The judge is not as likely to be affected by lobbyists and interest groups as are administrators of jails and prisons. Yet the court can call on the expertise of a wide variety of professionals for advice as to the proper content of a clean-up decree. The objective-umpire role is a traditional one for a judge, also, and although the information gathering in which he engages prior to formulating a decree is not obtained through the traditional adversarial courtroom approach, the many experts who provide a wide variety of opinions and information should allow him to move with confidence into decree formulation and implementation. Finally, a major advantage of this model is that courts act rapidly once a remedy is required, compared to other actors in the correctional arena.[15]

Interviews with administrators of correctional facilities indicate that these injunctions and clean-up decrees indeed have the effect of encouraging more careful attention to protection of prisoners' constitutional rights.[16] But one may ask whether other models that also mandate change would not achieve the same effect, and even a stronger one. This is a necessary inquiry when the disadvantages of the equity model are considered.

The major objection recalls the underlying problem of separation of powers, on which the old hands-off doctrine was based. The judiciary simply is not part of the executive branch or its administrative agencies. When it extends its power to include not only definition of rights but detailed executive action to protect them, it may be overstepping its constitutional boundaries.[17] Surely judicial review of other branches of government has been a revered concept ever since Hamilton wrote *The Federalist No. 78* and Marshall wrote *Marbury* v. *Madison.* However, critics of the courts contend, the goal of judicial review is to declare actions of other governmental branches unconstitutional or constitutional. It is not to prescribe affirmative remedies designed to erase the unconstitutionality. That must be left to the chastised agencies themselves.

This argument emphasizes that courts lack managerial and administrative expertise. One result of judicial policymaking is that

> ... such proceedings give weight to *theoretical* knowledge as against *practical* or *clinical* knowledge ... [T]he effect is to reduce the responsibility and authority of the worker at the face of social policy, but also to reduce the weight of the insight and experience he can provide in the formulation of policy.[18]

In the equity model, judges, lawyers for all parties, policymakers, and social scientists attempt to weigh the myriad factors that block change and that must be removed to reform correctional institutions. The effect on administrators themselves may be ambiguous. Although they change policies to comply with court orders, undoubtedly they resent encroachment on their turf. The encroachment would never have occurred, say the lawyers, if the turf had not been allowed to deteriorate so badly. This may be true, retort the administrators, but our professional judgment as to how to repair it has been usurped. Resentment and evasion of court orders may result.[19]

Furthermore, assuming that sweeping equitable action is legally or even morally necessary to reform prisons, it may still be accurate to say that the judiciary is ill-equipped to be a policymaker. The equity model relies on negotiations, political give-and-take, and long-term implementation. A judge and his or her advisors may wade into the unfamiliar waters willingly, because the situation demands it. But the method of decree formulation is foreign to a judge. The equity model is characterized by:

> (1) a careful decree formulation process that generates fairly detailed, often consensual policy objectives, typically based on professional norms; (2) monitoring mechanisms that elicit from adversarial sources information which is only occasionally useful in promoting enforcement; (3) enforcement mechanisms that are not only triggered infrequently and erratically, leaving much of the initiative to actors over whom the judge exercises only moderate control, but also are insuffiently sensitive both to information gathered in the course of compliance and to bureaucratic obstacles to change; and (4) a recognition of the need for something called an implementation plan without a clear sense of its contents or role.[20]

The method of court decision making is ill-suited to a policymaking role. Judges hear cases that are presented in a winner-take-all adversary fashion. If both litigants neglect to represent the interests of third parties—institutional staff or outside groups, for example—there are few provisions to include consideration of these problems in the court's deliberations.

Furthermore, judges are trained to consider only the cases before them. The legal system assumes that the eventual outcome of individual conflict resolutions in thousands of cases will result in a common thread of justice and wise policy, but by no means is overall social policy to be a major consideration in any particular case at hand. The judicial mind is unaccustomed to weighing information and theory to formulate long-range policies.[21]

Current Case Law: Return to Traditionalism

Whether the Burger Court has weighed these advantages and disadvantages of the equity model is a matter of speculation. It is clear, however, that the Court believes that running prisons is a job for administrators, not courts. On this point, at least, the Burger Court is adamant. Chief Justice Burger, writing for a 5-4 majority in *Bell* v. *Wolfish,* says:

> The deplorable conditions and draconian restrictions of some of our Nation's prisons are too well known to require recounting here, and the federal courts have rightly condemned these sordid aspects of our prison systems. But many of these same courts have, in the name of the Constitution, become increasingly enmeshed in the minutiae of prison operations. Judges, after all, are human. They, no less than others in our society, have a natural tendency to believe that their individual solutions to often intractable problems are better and more workable than those of the persons trained in the running of the particular

institution under examination. But under the Constitution, the first
question to be answered is not whose plan is best, but in what branch
of the Government is lodged the authority to initially devise the plan.
This does not mean that constitutional rights are not to be scrupulously
observed. It does mean, however, that the inquiry of federal courts into
prison management must be limited to the issue of whether a particular system violates any prohibition of the Constitution, or in the case
of a federal prison, a statute. The wide range of "judgement calls" that
meet constitutional and statutory requirements are confided to officials
outside of the Judicial Branch.[22]

The return to an emphasis on expertise of administrators is not exclusively
used for analysis of correctional problems, either. The Burger Court seems to
have accepted it as a common starting point for court review of any public institution. In *Parham* v. *J.L. and J.R.*, the Court held that superintendents of mental
hospitals may make the decision whether to commit a child to the hospital on
his parents' request, and that due process does not require a precommittment
hearing before a court or objective administrative factfinder.[23] Burger stated
that superintendents would of course rely on a wide range of reports, medical
exams, and interviews to reach their decisions, but no court need review them.

In corrections, *Bell* v. *Wolfish* and *Greenholtz* v. *Inmates of Nebraska
Penal and Correctional Complex* show the Supreme Court directing lower
courts to abandon the equity model. *Bell* upheld security measures used against
pretrial jail inmates, such as strip searches, double bunking, and limits on receiving publications by mail, because "administrators . . . should be accorded wide-
ranging deference in the adoption and execution of policies and practices that
in their judgement are needed to preserve order."[24] *Greenholtz* overturned an
Eighth Circuit order that a state parole board institute new procedures affording
more due-process protection in parole granting.[25] The Supreme Court refused to
expand due process at this stage of the correctional process and stated that it
was within the parole board's discretion to deny inmates hearings.

Clearly, then, this Court will not expand the substantive constitutional
rights of the convicted. Just as clearly, the Court is signaling the lower courts
to discontinue use of the activist equity model for enforcement of existing
rights. But as any law student will say, a right without a remedy is no right at
all. It is conceivable that the Burger Court, by cutting the remedy for constitutional violations, intends to cut the rights, too. In this backhanded manner,
the Court would not have to state baldly that it is trimming the rights of the
convicted, but the same effect would be achieved.

This is a plausible analysis, but it ignores two facts concerning recent
court decisions. First, the Burger Court wishes to return the U.S. Supreme
Court to the traditional mainstream of American judicial functioning, and this
traditionalism abhors activist tools such as equitable decrees. Second, the Court
has indeed provided a remedy for the rights in its emphasis on the traditional
private legal remedy.

Traditionalism is the foil to judicial activism. By scrupulously following traditional forms of judicial decision making, a judge avoids the criticism that he has overstepped the boundaries of his particular governmental branch. He can claim that his purpose is not to form social policy but merely to decide "cases and controversies." Judicial realists, of course, declare that the result is still political—that the machinations of judicial functioning might be different from those of the legislature or executive but that the result is still policymaking. Whether this is true or not, courts are designed to operate in a manner that signals to the world that they are apolitical or at least committed to solutions that are somehow objectively achieved.

Thus, there are familiar institutional checks on activism. Courts must hear only actual "cases and controversies"[26] brought to them (not sought by them) by two individual litigants; they may not decide "political questions;"[27] they must rely on the rule of precedent; and no case may be heard if it is moot, not ripe, or if its petitioner lacks proper standing.[28] Furthermore, lawyers and the judges they become are trained into a value system which attempts to achieve the apolitical. Whether this truly is a government of laws and not of men, judges wish to believe it is, and thus they are generally uncomfortable with overt judicial policymaking.

The Burger Court, if it is anything, is traditional. Clearly it is uncomfortable with activist reform in prison cases and, indeed, in any type of case for which policy guidelines are prescribed as a remedy.[29] However,

> Judges who recoil at innovation in constitutional lawmaking may not see the same dangers at all in the interpretation of statues . . . judges concerned to avoid the excesses that are believed to have characterized the Supreme Court of the 1930's and 1960's may still embark on ambitious ventures of judicial reform in the name of statutory construction.[30]

A traditionalist court can cling to the perception of staying within proper boundaries for lawmaking when it merely interprets policy choices already made by other branches—where those branches are free to redefine the choices if the court definition is unacceptable to them. The Burger Court's expansion of section 1983 of the Civil Rights Act of 1866 shows its traditionalist stripes and also a reformist approach.

The Burger Court's Money Model

How does one convince administrators to run correctional institutions in conformity with the dictates of the Eighth Amendment? If consent decrees are distasteful, one can instead extract compensatory damages.[31] Money damages may come from city coffers or directly from the pockets of prison personnel.

Using both routes, this traditional remedy has been expanded by recent case law to be used against nontraditional defendants. Again, for prison policymakers and reformers, the use of a private money remedy for unconstitutional conduct carries distinct advantages and disadvantages vis à vis the equity model.

Compensatory damages as a major remedy in section-1983 cases has been embraced by the Court for reasons of traditionalism and, in addition, perhaps out of a desire to encourage ongoing reform of governmental bureaucracies. The Court is willing to hold administrators personally liable for "willful" (not merely negligent) violations and to hold cities liable for continuance of unconstitutional "customs, policies, or practices." Never before have these defendants been placed in as vulnerable a position.

Personal liability in tort or for civil-rights violations is directed, of course, toward reform motivated by the self-interest of administrators. Recently, the Court has abandoned the absolute immunity to suit previously enjoyed by government officials.[32] In general, the expanded scope of liability for administrators is that "supervisory officials are not liable for civil rights violations comitted by their subordinates [simply because they are employers of those subordinates;] personal involvement of the supervisor is the touchstone of liability ... if the constitutional violation takes place at the direction of the supervisory official or with his knowledge and consent, or if [he] is deliberately and recklessly indifferent to constitutional violations by his subordinates," he may be sued.[33]

In abolishing absolute immunity and holding supervisors responsible for intentional or reckless violation of rights, courts are demanding more attention by administrators to the problems of brutal incarceration, but they are accomplishing it without detailed clean-up decrees. The money model says "do it right or pay your victims for your callousness." Essentially, prison administrators are now being charged successfully for professional malpractice, when intentional conduct occurs.

Such a development should affect the most flagrant examples of official abuse. However, it does not address the problem of the prisons and jails with administrators who are conscientiously trying to perform adequately, but in which a systematic overhaul of the entire system is the only way to confront institutionalized abuse. This root problem of systematic accountability was addressed by the Warren Court equity model. The Burger Court counterpart demands money from municipalities as a prod for policy reform.

In 1961, *Monroe* v. *Pape* held that a city was not a "person" under section 1983 and therefore was immune from civil-rights suits.[34] In a rare move, the Court recently acknowledged that it is overruling the earlier case, and in 1979 held that municipalities may be sued under section 1983.[35] The city is liable if it allowed a systematic denial of rights under a city "custom, policy, or practice." Quite consistently, the Court later decided that the city could not claim a good-faith defense to the civil-rights violations, either.[36] Thus, "the knowledge that a municipality will be liable for all of its injurious conduct, whether committed in good faith or not, should create an incentive for officials who may harbor doubts about the lawfulness of their intended actions to err on the side of protecting constitutional rights."[37]

The thrust of this new case law is to force cities to reassess their institutional administration and to achieve constitutionality as best they can without court monitoring. If they fail, city money that would have been spent elsewhere must instead be paid directly to aggrieved inmates. These inmates are usually represented by private attorneys, who receive fees from the city as part of the damage award if they win the case.

The goal, of course, is to persuade elected officials to ensure that jails meet constitutional standards. Unless jail officials are intentionally brutal, they need not fear direct personal liability—although they may feel chastised indirectly, when the wrath of their superiors who have just paid large judgments descends on them. This policy is designed to keep them working without fear of losing their paychecks but to encourage their constant vigilance as they avoid the displeasure of higher city officials.

In another case, the Court has expanded potential liability of the federal government for civil-rights violations. Expanding *Bivens* v. *Six Unnamed Agents,* the Court held that the mother of a deceased federal-prison inmate could sue officials for denial of proper medical care and would not be required to delay the suit by pursuing all possible tort remedies first.[38]

States, however, are immune to all such suits. The Eleventh Amendment shields states from suit in tort or under section 1983, and this sovereign immunity is a major stumbling block to prison reform under the money model. Federal prisons and local city jails are affected by *Monell* and *Owens,* the policy cases, but the Eleventh Amendment blocks money actions against states. Thus, courts must proceed under the disfavored equity model in attempting to achieve state correctional reform.

Because of this gaping hole in the scope of the new money model, the Burger Court may indeed be trimming prisoners' rights. If the Court in the future holds an equity-type decree to be impermissible (a move foreshadowed by *Bell* v. *Wolfish,*) state prisoners will not be able to substitute the money remedy. A serious deterioration of state institutions could result.

This major flaw in the money model has not been directly addressed by the Court. In *Hutto* v. *Finney,* however, it sidestepped the Eleventh Amendment and ordered the state of Arkansas to pay $22,500 in attorney's fees to the plaintiff's lawyers, who, under the equity model, litigated the famous *Holt* v. *Sarver* case.[39] The award was indirectly against the state, the Court reasoned, since the direct remedy was the equitable clean-up decree. Whether the Court will ever take the dramatic step of allowing direct damage suits against states is a matter of speculation. In this writer's opinion, a narrow reading of the amendment as prohibiting traditional tort suits against states—but not constitutional tort suits—is needed to mend the flaw in the present money model.[40]

Will such a model achieve institutional reform where the equity model failed? Money is a powerful thing, perhaps as powerful as negotiated planning. The money model seems more straightforward. Government and its officials may disregard the declared rights of the incarcerated, but they will do so at considerable expense. No court is involved in "the minutiae of administration," returning this function to the hands of experts, but by no means are courts keeping hands-off, either. Because cities are liable for continuing unconstitutional policies, systemwide policy review is mandated, and "the threat of monetary judgments against governmental units may spur officials to design their training and hiring programs, disciplinary procedures, and internal rules so as to curb misconduct."[41]

There seems to be something missing, though. Simply put, the money model lacks style. Gone is the excitement of the class action resulting in a sweeping declaration of rights, written in consultation with correctional experts, civil-rights groups, and public policymakers. Once more prisoners seek redress from courts that make no pretense at long-range policymaking.

In its stodgy traditionalist way, however, the Burger Court mandates compliance with the constitutional minima prescribed by the 1960s explosion of prisoners' rights, and it will strictly review actions of municipalities and their employees in protecting those rights. It has given the tasks of administration back to the experts. But it has told these officials that, if they believe that they can reform institutions better than courts can, they had better live up to their promises.

Notes

1. There are very few reported cases in which the Burger Court has stated it would carve away major cornerstone prisoners' rights laid down by the Warren Court. This Court even strengthened the right to receive proper medical care in prison in Estelle v. Gamble, 429 U.S. 97 (1976). However, that the Court will not expand those rights, and will interpret them narrowly, is illustrated by Bell v. Wolfish, 441 U.S. 520 (1979). There, due-process rights of pretrial detainees were not expanded, despite a district court trend to do so.

2. "31 States Involved in Prison Litigation," *Criminal Justice Newsletter* 5 (1980).

3. That earlier doctrine is well described in "Beyond the Ken of the Courts: A Critique of Judicial Refusal to Review the Complaints of Convicts," 72 *Yale L.J.* 506 (1963).

4. Good examples of the Warren Court activist approach are cases such as Washington v. Lee, 390 U.S. 333 (1968); Cooper v. Pate, 378 U.S. 666

(1962); or Muniz v. U.S., 305 F.2d 285 (2d Cir. 1962) *aff'd* 374 U.S. 150 (1963). It was the federal district courts, however, that devised the equitable remedy. School desegregation and busing plans are the same sort of detailed court-ordered institutional clean-ups as are prison decrees. Prison cases illustrative of the model are Holt v. Sarver, 309 F.Supp. 362 (E.D. Ark. 1970) or Cluchette v. Procunier, 328 F.Suppl. 767 (N.D.Cal. 1971).

5. Chapter 11, by Daryl Fair, admirably describes and catalogs the process of fashioning and enforcing these equitable remedies. See also "Implementation Problems in Institutional Reform Litigation," 91 *Harvard Law Review* 428 (1977).

6. 91 *Harvard Law Review* 428, *Supra*, at 456. Copyright © 1977 by the Harvard Law Review Association. Reprinted with permission.

7. Donald L. Horowitz, *The Courts and Social Policy* (Washington, D.C.: Brookings Institution, 1977), p. 7.

8. Raoul Berger, *Government by Judiciary* (Cambridge, Mass.: Harvard University Press, 1977), p. 224.

9. Title 42, U.S. Code, section 1983.

10. Although section 1983 actions are taken against state defendants, federal officers are also liable for civil-rights violations under Bivens v. Six Unnamed Agents, 430 U.S. 388 (1971). Also the federal government may be liable in tort under the Federal Tort Claims Act, which waives federal sovereign immunity. States as governmental units are immune from suit under the Eleventh Amendment.

11. Basista v. Weir, 340 F.2d 74 (3rd Circ.1965).

12. Monell vs. Department of Social Services, 436 U.S. 56 (1979).

13. Shemaitis v. Froemke, 189 F.2d 963 (7th Cir.1951).

14. 91 *Harvard Law Review* 428, *supra* at 454.

15. Chayes, "The Role of the Judge in Public Law Litigation," 89 *Harvard Law Review* 1281 (May 1976).

16. Turner, "When Prisoners Sue: A Study of Section 1983 in the Federal Courts," 92 *Harvard Law Review* 610 (1979).

17. Several books and articles on judicial activism have raised this criticism. See, for example, Lino P. Graglia, *Disaster by Decree* (Ithaca, N.Y.: Cornell University Press, 1976), and Berger, *Government by Judiciary, supra*. An excellent comparison of judicial policymaking compared to legislative or executive policymaking is found in Horowitz, *Courts and Social Policy, supra* at 23–67.

18. Glazer, "Should Judges Administer Social Services?" 50 *The Public Interest* 78 (Winter 1978).

19. "Prisoners, Section 1983, and the Federal Judge as Warden," 9 *Toledo Law Review* 873 at 885 (Summer 1978).

20. 91 *Harvard Law Review* 428, *supra* at 456. Copyright © 1977 by The Harvard Law Review Association. Reprinted with permission.

21. Glazer, "Should Judges Administer?" *supra* at 79.

22. Bell v. Wolfish, 441 U.S. 520 (1979).

23. Parham v. J.L. and J.R., 442 U.S. 584 (1979).

24. Bell v. Wolfish, *supra* at 474.

25. Greenholtz v. Inmates of the Nebraska Penal and Correctional Complex, 442 U.S. 1 (1979).

26. U.S. Constitution, Article III, section 2, clause 1.

27. Philippa Strum, *The Supreme Court and Political Questions: A Study in Evasion* (University, Ala.: University of Alabama Press, 1974) critiques the doctrine.

28. The Warren Court was willing to circumvent these restrictive requirements in many cases, as would be expected of an activist court. Thus, Douglas in the *Scenic Hudson* case thought a river should have standing as a plaintiff, and "the mootness doctrine is so riddled with exceptions that it is almost a matter of discretion whether to hear a moot case." Horowitz, *Courts and Social Policy, supra* at 8.

29. The obvious parallel to the prison case law is equal rights for blacks. Although the Burger Court loudly reaffirms the principle of equal rights, the remedies are often traditional. Where the Warren Court had ordered a solution such as desegregation "with all deliberate speed" and encouraged desegregation plans to achieve it, the Burger Court is bound by *stare decisis* to the right but not the remedy. The difference between equity and traditional models becomes important here, too. In Milliken v. Bradley, 418 U.S. 717 (1974) a Burger concurrence foreshadowed such current cases as Weber v. Kaiser Aluminum. In *Milliken,* Burger wrote that where blacks were illegally denied job advancement, the proper remedy is not to force the employer to place them in the jobs they would have had but for the discrimination. Rather, it is to pay them the money they would have earned and have them work their way up the now presumably discrimination-free job ladder.

30. Horowitz, *Courts and Social Policy, supra* at 13. Professor Owen Fiss, in "Foreword: The Forms of Justice," 93 *Harvard Law Review* 1 (1979) maintains that the highest constitutional values should be pursued through the means of the monitoring model. Given the slide toward the money model, it becomes important to protect those values in the traditionalist context. The demise of the monitoring model need not mean the decline of valid constitutional values if they can be vigorously defended in the traditional model.

31. City of Newport v. Fact Concerts, Inc., U.S. ___ , 69 L.Ed. 2d 616, 101 S.Ct. ___ (1981), held that plaintiffs who prevail in Monell-type suits against municipalities (which often challenge conditions in city jails) must be limited to recovery of compensatory damages. Both compensatory and punitive damages, however, may still be assessed against individual correctional personnel, both on the state and local levels.

32. Scheuer v. Rhodes, 416 U.S. 232 (1974) (governor of state may be personally sued for reckless action resulting in wrongful death, done while

performing official duties), Procunier v. Navarette, 434 U.S. 555 (1978) (prison officials immune from negligence suit but not immune from suit charging intentional or malicious denial of rights), O'Connor v. Donaldson, 422 U.S. 563 (1975) (same "malicious or intentional" standard for superintendent of state hospital), Butz v. Economou, 438 U.S. 478 (1978) (federal officials are not absolutely immune from suit even where the challenged action was discretionary).

33. Perry v. Elrod, 436 F.Supp. 299 (D.C. Ill. 1977).

34. Monroe v. Pape, 365 U.S. 167 (1961).

35. Monell, *supra.*

36. Owen v. City of Independence, Missouri, 445 U.S. 622, 100 S.Ct. 1398 (1980).

37. Ibid. at 1516.

38. Carlson v. Green, 446 U.S. ___ , 64 L.Ed. 2d 15 (1980); following Bivens v. Six Unnamed Agents, 403 U.S. 388 (1971).

39. Hutto v. Finney, 98 S.Ct. 2565 (1978).

40. Lehmann, *"Bivens* and Its Progeny: The Scope of a Constitutional Cause of Action for Torts Committed by Government Officials," 4 *Hastings Const. Law Q.* 531 (1977), explains the concept of a "constitutional tort." The phrase is often used as legal shorthand, distinguishing wrongs against constitutional principles from wrongs against common-law principles.

41. "Damage Remedies against Municipalities for Constitutional Violations," 89 *Harvard Law Review* 927 (1976).

**Part V
Further Perspectives on Reform**

14 Codifying Sentencing Experience

Stuart S. Nagel

A key problem in the recent movement to lessen judicial sentencing discretion is the problem of determining the sentences that judges shall be required to impose on convicted defendants in view of their crimes, prior records, and possible aggravating or mitigating circumstances.[1]

Various researchers have proposed that determinate sentences should be scientifically determined by first calculating the benefits and costs for alternative sentences for a given crime and prior record and then picking the sentence that provides the most benefits minus costs. Such sentences may, however, not be politically feasible with regard to being acceptable by state legislatures, whose values may not be the same as those included in such a benefit-cost analysis.[2]

This chapter will discuss the methodological feasibility of such a sentencing scheme. There may not be a need to get to the political-feasibility problem if the benefit-cost analysis cannot be performed because social-science research cannot determine the relevant effects of alternative sentences. After showing the lack of meaningfulness of a rational inductive-reasoning approach to arriving at optimum sentences via benefit-cost analysis, the chapter will show that an incremental deductive-reasoning approach—involving the averaging of existing sentences—may make more sense, provided that one is willing to accept certain reasonable premises.[3]

The Lack of Meaningfulness of a Benefit-Cost Approach to Criminal Sentencing

The Relations Graphed

Figure 14-1 shows in theory how one should arrive at an optimum sentence length through benefit-cost analysis. The figure shows the assumed relation between sentence length and holding cost, releasing cost, and total cost. As sentence length increases, the holding cost goes up at a roughly constant rate if we adjust for inflation. In other words, it costs about twice as much to hold a person in jail for 10 years as it does for 5 years. As sentence length increases, the releasing cost supposedly goes down, in the sense that the longer a convict is held in prison the less damage he or she is likely to do when released. The releasing cost goes down because of an increase in maturity, deterrence, and rehabilitation with each passing year, although those effects tend to plateau

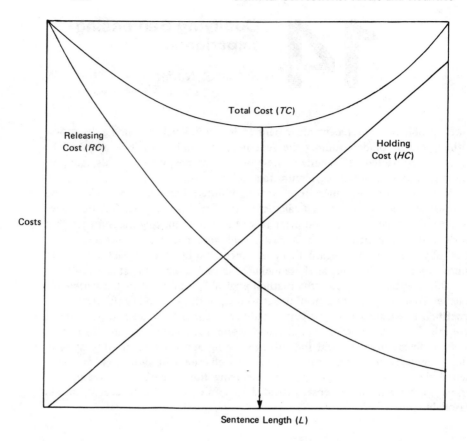

Figure 14-1. Optimum Sentence Length in Light of Holding and Releasing
Costs

with time. The releasing cost also goes down as a result of delaying the post-release criminal behavior, since that decreases the total amount of subsequent crime the defendant can commit by decreasing the remainder of his or her criminal career.

The total-cost curve simply represents the sum of the holding cost and the releasing cost at each sentence length. The total-cost curve goes down at first and then goes up, as a result of (1) the positively sloped linear relation between length and holding cost, and (2) the negatively-sloped nonlinear relation between length and releasing cost. Where the total-cost curve bottoms out is the optimum sentence length. That point is semantically the same as the point where one maximizes holding benefits minus holding costs, or releasing benefits minus releasing costs. (Holding benefits are simply the releasing costs saved by holding a defendant, and releasing benefits are the holding costs saved by releasing a defendant.) In theory, that kind of curve drawing makes sense. When one analyzes actual data, however, the results may not be so sensible.[4]

Numerical Values

Table 14-1 shows the results of analyzing approximately one thousand federal criminal cases in which we know for each case:

1. The crime for which the defendant was convicted, including the eight crimes analyzed

Table 14-1
Empirical Relations and Optimum Sentences

Crime	N	a	b_1	b_2	r
Vehicle theft	313	9.49	− .20	.02	.03
Narcotics offense	125	213.75	−1.05	−.35	.26
Burglary or larceny	130	2.17	− .13	.18	.08
Robbery or kidnap	28	.17	.82	.01	.27
Fraud check or counterfeiting	63	.26	.50	.35	.18
Income tax or embezzlement	25	2.80	.57	−.38	.33
Nonrobbery assault	37	19.82	− .58	.24	.21
Moonshine	104	6.85	− .24	.06	.04

	L^*	$L^* (R=10)$	$L^* (R=100)$	Comments
Vehicle theft	$1.91 (R)^{.01}$	2	2+	b_2 is almost zero
Narcotics offense	$53.85(R)^{-.26}$	51	30	b_2 is negative
Burglary or larceny	$.21(R)^{.21}$	0	1	b_1 is almost zero
Robbery or kidnap	$-.14(R)^{.01}$	0	0	b_1 is positive
Fraud check or counterfeiting	$-.02(R)^{.55}$	0	0	ditto
Income tax or embezzlement	$-.17(R)^{.28}$	0	0	ditto
Nonrobbery assault	$24.67(R)^{.31}$	50	103	b_1 and b_2 are high
Moonshine	$1.68(R)^{.06}$	2	2+	b_1 and b_2 are low

Note: b_1 shows the relation between releasing costs (S^2/D) and length of sentence (L); b_2 shows the relation between releasing costs and prior record (R) in the equation, $S^2/D = a(L)^{b_1}(R)^{b_2}$; N is the number of cases; r is the multiple-correlation coefficient between S^2/D and both L and R together; L^* is the optimum sentence in light of those relations and the specified prior record: $L^* = -1/(b_1 a(R)^{b_2})$ raised to the power $1/(b_1-1)$.

2. the number of months that the defendant actually served in prison (L)
3. the number of months the defendant previously served in prison as a measure of the severity of his prior record (R)
4. the number of months the defendant subsequently served in prison for a felonious conviction after being released, as part of the data gathering of a twenty year followup study (S)
5. the number of months the defendant delayed committing the felony for which he was subsequently convicted (D)[5]

With that information one can determine the relation between a measure of releasing cost and length of sentence while statistically holding constant prior record. Prior record must be held constant because otherwise there is likely to be a positive relation between sentence length and severity of subsequent criminality. This is so because defendants with bad prior records tend to get longer sentences, and defendants with bad prior records tend to have worse subsequent records. Thus, prior record causes sentence length and subsequent criminality to go up together, rather than inversely, unless prior record is held constant.

For an appropriate measure of releasing cost, one could simply use S/D as a function of L and R in the form $S/D = a + b_1L + b_2R$. In doing so, we are simply saying that the releasing cost goes up as the subsequent crime severity goes up, and it goes down to the extent the subsequent crime is delayed. We can, however, recognize that severity is more important than delay by tentatively squaring severity. Later we can see if exponents other than 2 can produce more meaningful results. Likewise, we can also recognize that the functional relation between releasing cost (that is, S^2/D) and both L and R is probably nonlinear (as is shown in figure 14-1), rather than linear (as in the previous equation). That means changing the equation to the form $S^2/D = a(L)^{b_1}(R)^{b_2}$.

We would now like to determine numerical values for the three coefficients of a, b_1, and b_2. Given the data, we should be able to do so for vehicle-theft cases by feeding into a computer information on S, D, L. and R for each of the 313 vehicle-theft cases in the data set along with a command asking for a non-linear-regression analysis. The result (as indicated on row 1 of table 14-1), is: $a = 9.49$, $b_1 = .20$, and $b_2 = .02$. The 9.49 tells us that if $L = 1$ and $R = 1$, the releasing cost is 9.49, with all the variables expressed in the common unit of months. The .20 tells us that if sentence length goes up by 1 percent, then releasing cost comes down by 1/5 of 1 percent. Likewise, the .02 tells us that if prior record goes up 1 percent, then releasing cost goes up 2/100 of 1 percent. The last number in the row, .03, tells us that L and R together explain less than 1 percent of the variation on releasing cost across the vehicle-theft cases (that is, the square of .03). A similar interpretation can be given to the other seven rows in the top of table 14-1.[6]

With that information, one can now determine the numerical value of the optimum sentence for vehicle-theft cases as a function of prior record. Doing so involves recognizing that total cost is the sum of releasing cost plus holding cost. Algebraically, that means $TC = a(L)^{b_1}(R)^{b_2} + L$. The expression to the left of the plus sign is releasing cost, as defined. The expression to the right of the plus sign is holding cost given the perfect linear relation between holding cost and sentence length, as shown in figure 14-1. To determine the numerical value of L when TC reaches bottom, we need to determine the slope of TC relative to L, set that slope equal to 0, and solve for L. By the elementary rules of the slopes of curves,[7] the slope is $b_1 a(L)^{b_1-1}(R)^{b_2} + 1$. If we insert the numerical values from row 1 of table 14-1, set that slope equal to 0, and solve for L, we get $1.91(R)^{.01}$, as is shown in the first row of the bottom half of table 14-1. The optimum value of L for a given prior record is symbolized L^*. If we insert 10 months in place of R, the optimum sentence comes out 2 months. If we insert 100 months, the optimum sentence comes out slightly more than 2 months. A similar interpretation can be given to the other seven rows in the bottom of table 14-1. In theory, that kind of quantitative analysis makes sense. When one seeks to interpret the results, however, the analysis might not be so sensible.

Interpreting the Meaning

The results do not make sense for at least three general reasons, namely, b_1 is not sufficiently negative, b_2 is not sufficiently positive, and no adjustments will sufficiently improve b_1 and b_2 to make this approach meaningful. In more verbal, less quantitative terms, the relation between sentence length and releasing cost should be negative, as shown in figure 14-1. That relation, however, is positive for robbery/kidnap, checks/counterfeiting, and taxes/embezzlement. It is almost positive in burglary/larceny and moonshine. The explanation may be that bad defendants get longer sentences and commit the worse subsequent crimes even when we hold prior record constant, because prior record is not sufficient for separating out the relatively bad defendants. Even if we also hold constant job record and age, however, we still do not obtain consistently negative relations between sentence length and subsequent crime severity. In other words, the longer the sentence the worse the subsequent record—either because we are not sufficiently controlling for "badness," or because long prison sentences increase rather than decrease subsequent criminal behavior.

One would likewise expect the relation between prior record and subsequent crime severity to be a positive relation, in the sense that defendants with the worse prior records should have the worse subsequent records. That relation, however, is negative for narcotics offenses and taxes/embezzlement, and it is almost negative for robbery/kidnap and moonshine. When the relation is negative, the optimizing analysis in effect says to give shorter sentences to the defendants with the worse prior records. The explanation for the negative relations between prior and subsequent record may be that defendants with the worse prior records are older, and for certain crimes older defendants are not so likely to recommit their crimes or other crimes. That may be true of narcotics offenses. Another explanation may be that for certain crimes, longer prison sentences are more deterrent, and the defendants with the worse prior records get those longer, more-deterrent sentences. That may be true of taxes/embezzlement, where middle-class jobs are more jeopardized. Holding constant age and job record as well as prior record, however, does not consistently generate positive b_2 relations. In other words, the worse the prior record is, the better the subsequent record will be, either because we are not sufficiently controlling for other variables or because prison time has virtually no predictive power for predicting S and D, regardless of whether the prison time is R or L. Those largely meaningless relations stay meaningless even when a variety of variations are tried on the basic data analysis, such as varying the weight of S relative to D, using other kinds of nonlinear relations to relate S and D to L and R, and controlling for additional variables.

The Greater Meaningfulness of an Averaging Approach to Criminal Sentencing

The Averaging Approach

A possibly more meaningful approach to arriving at determinate sentences for each of the same eight crime categories (or any set of crime categories) is simply to calculate the average actual time served by defendants who have been convicted of those crimes. The actual time served by convicted defendants reflects the collective wisdom of numerous (1) legislators who have written the traditional sentencing laws, (2) judges who have imposed sentences within those statutory ranges, and (3) parole-board members and prison administrators who have the power to reduce judicially imposed sentences through early release. One could argue that the collective wisdom of all those decision makers may arrive at optimum decisions in the sense of maximizing societal benefits minus costs when one averages across all the cases involving a given crime. In any given case, any one of those decision makers can be quite wrong, but by averaging across both the decision makers and the cases, the errors may balance out so that the averages make sense from a benefit-cost perspective.

If, however, we simply average the actual time served for a given crime, we will not be taking into consideration the prior records of the convicted defendants. A simple way to do that is to divide the cases for each crime into those cases in which the defendant had no prior record and those in which the defendant had some prior record. That approach is used in the top half of table 14-2. The table uses the same cases as table 14-1, but the sample sizes are larger on

Table 14-2
Average Sentence by Crime and by Prior Record

Crime Category	No Prior Record		Some Prior Record	
	M_0	N_0	M_1	N_1
Vehicle theft	15	(80)	21	(261)
Narcotics offense	20	(43)	27	(89)
Burglary or larceny	16	(41)	21	(99)
Robbery or kidnapping	37	(17)	71	(15)
Fraudulent checks or counterfeiting	16	(13)	22	(55)
Income-tax evasion or embezzlement	10	(19)	30	(6)
Nonrobbery assault	38	(28)	46	(12)
Moonshine	10	(33)	13	(73)

	L^*	$L^* (R=10)$	$L^*(R=100)$	r
Vehicle theft	$14(R)^{.11}$	18	23	.33
Narcotics offense	$18(R)^{.20}$	23	29	.36
Burglary or larceny	$13(R)^{.09}$	16	20	.28
Robbery or kidnapping	$22(R)^{.26}$	41	74	.53
Fraudulent checks or counterfeiting	$15(R)^{.07}$	17	20	.21
Income-tax evasion or embezzlement	$9(R)^{.24}$	16	28	.52
Nonrobbery assault	$32(R)^{.03}$	34	36	.07
Moonshine	$8(R)^{.13}$	11	15	.46

Note: Prior record is expressed in terms of months of previous imprisonment; the numbers in parentheses indicate the number of cases on which those averages are based.

each row of table 14-2, since a case must have information on $S, D, L,$ and R to be useable in table 14-1, but it only needs information on L and R to be useable in table 14-2. The first row, for example, involves 80 vehicle-theft cases in which there was no prior record and 261 in which there was some prior record. The 80 cases averaged 15 months per case, and the 261 cases averaged 21 months per case, meaning the overall weighted average was 19.5 months.

The trouble with that approach to arriving at average sentences per prior record is that all convicted defendants with some prior record are lumped together, regardless of prior-record severity. The bottom half of table 14-2 involves the use of regression analysis to predict sentence length from prior record; the sentence length and the exact prior record for each case within a given crime category are fed into a computer, which is then asked to provide the numerical parameters for a predictive formula. From that analysis, row 1 in the bottom of the table shows that sentence length in vehicle-theft cases is equal to $14(R)^{11}$. The 14 means that if the defendant's prior record is 1 month, then a good prediction would be a sentence of 14 months. The .11 means that if prior record goes up by 1 percent, then the predicted sentence length goes up by 11/100 of a percent, indicating diminishing returns between prior record and sentence length. Thus, if the prior record were 10 months, the predicted sentence would be 18 months; and if the prior record were 100 months, the predicted sentence would be 23 months, as determined by inserting those prior records into the basic formula for predicting sentence length in vehicle-theft cases. If the defendant has no prior record, then one uses the left side of the top of table 14-2. The .33 at the end of the first row indicates that 11 percent of the variation in sentence length can be accounted for by prior record (that is, the square root of .33), and 89 percent by other variables.

To use this kind of table in determinate sentencing, a sentencing judge (or a probation officer preparing a presentence report) would calculate a predicted sentence for the crime for which the defendant was convicted, taking into consideration the defendant's prior record. The calculation would be made by using formulas like those shown in the L^* column in the bottom of table 14-2. The decision maker would then add as much as about 25 percent to that base figure for aggravating circumstances or deduct for mitigating circumstances. The adjusted figure might then be doubled to take into consideration that under some determinate-sentencing laws, the defendant gets one day off for every day of good behavior. Thus, by doubling the sentence, the defendant who behaves well serves the average amount of time, and other defendants serve more than the average. A more complicated system could be developed whereby the sentence is not quite doubled so that defendants who misbehave the average amount will serve the average time, and defendants who behave well will serve less than the average. That complication, however, may not be worth inserting to make the future averages the same as the past averages, because not doing so provides (1) simplicity in predicting one's sentence, and (2) a way of increasing the severity of the average sentence to satisfy legislators who will not endorse determinate sentencing unless the average severity is increased.[8]

Common-Sense Justifications

The main justification for an averaging approach to criminal sentencing is that it represents the collective wisdom of a lot of decision makers across a lot of cases. Those decisions are based on factual perceptions and normative values. One implication in the averaging approach is that those decision makers have reasonably accurate factual perceptions, at least relative to alternative predictive methods such as the kind of statistical analysis on which table 14-1 is based. A second implication in the averaging approach is that those decision makers apply values that roughly reflect what society wants and that such a democratic reflection is desirable. This does not mean that criminal-justice decision makers or other governmental decision makers are generally perceptive or are usually likely to apply representative values. It only means that, in the criminal-sentencing context, they seem to be operating in line with those implications, at least collectively and relatively speaking.

In other decisional contexts, one may find a very different situation. In pretrial release, for example, judges may consistently misperceive the likelihood of defendants appearing in court, such that a statistical-prediction method may be substantially more accurate there than relying on judicial perceptions. More important, in the pretrial-release context, an individual judge may be seeking to maximize personal benefits minus costs, more so than in the sentencing context. Personal values manifest themselves in pretrial release when judges hold defendants in jail prior to trial because the judge would personally suffer a greater embarrassment cost by a releasing error than by a holding error. Society, however, may suffer more by wrongly holding people who would appear in court than by wrongly releasing people who would fail to appear. That is less of a problem in reaching a decision on length of sentence, although it may be a problem in the preliminary decision to incarcerate rather than grant probation.

The matter of general deterrence is an important factor that an averaging approach implicitly considers, but that is not considered by the statistical benefit-cost analysis of table 14-1. *General deterrence* means the effect of sentences on deterring the general public from crime committing, as contrasted to *specific deterrence,* which refers to the effect of sentences on deterring future wrongdoing by the specific defendant being sentenced. The statistical analysis only looks to the effect on the convicted defendants. The averaging analysis implicitly includes the effect on the public in the perceptions and values of the decision makers. One could do a statistical analysis relating average-sentence levels to crime rates (using states or time periods as the sampling units). Those kinds of analyses are even less conclusive than relating individual sentences to subsequent crimes (using individual cases as the sampling units) because of the greater confounding influence of other variables and because of reciprocal relations between crime rates and sentence levels.

Another important factor that an averaging approach may implicitly consider more so than the statistical approach is the incapacitation factor. *Incapacitation* is the elimination of crime committing against the outside world by a defendant while he is in prison. The statistical approach is only concerned with the subsequent crime committing. The averaging approach involves decision makers who (when sentencing defendants) are likely to have incapacitation in mind, and incapacitation thus tends to be built into those averages. An averaging approach also has the additional common-sense justification of being more politically feasible because it represents less deviation from the status quo. On the average, it represents no deviation at all, although in individual cases some defendants will be receiving longer sentences than they otherwise would, and other defendants will be receiving shorter sentences. Still another advantage of an averaging approach over a benefit-cost approach is that it is much simpler to develop, explain, and apply. That, perhaps, should be a more important criterion in policy analysis than it normally is, if policy analysts are going to communicate effectively with policymakers and policy appliers.[9]

A Deductive Mathematical Justification

Although simplicity of analysis is something to be valued, one might also seek to justify recommended policies in optimizing terms. Doing so helps convince the more technically oriented policy analysts, and it may provide some additional insights that are not so well perceived by a nontechnical or common-sense approach. In this context, an optimizing approach might involve defining holding costs and releasing costs in a mathematical way rather than a statistical way and then deducing that the average-sentence length is the optimum length in the sense of minimizing the sum of the holding and releasing costs.

Holding cost is a positive linear function of sentence length, as previously mentioned. The simplest way to express that mathematically is an equation of the form $HC = a + b(L)$. Since there are no holding costs for an individual defendant when sentence length is 0, the value of a is 0. The value of b can be considered equal to 1, in the sense that one month of sentence length produces one unit of holding cost. The equation can thus be simplified to $HC = L$.

Releasing cost is a negative nonlinear function of sentence length, as previously mentioned. The simplest way to express that mathematically is an equation of the form, $RC = A/L$, where A is the average sentence for the crime for which the defendant was convicted. In other words, when the criminal-justice system gives a crime a 24-month sentence on the average, the system is in effect saying that crime has damaged society to the extent of 24 releasing-cost units. The average sentence for a crime thus represents the likely harm that is prevented mainly by way of incapacitation and general deterrence. The L represents the specific sentence given to a certain defendant. As L increases from one month on up, that potential harm is decreased. Saying $RC = A/L$, however, has the defect that it implies the releasing cost from lost incapacitation and general deterrence is equal in importance to the amount of delay from being incarcerated. One might consider severity to be worth about twice the value of delay, as previously mentioned. That would mean expressing releasing cost as $RC = A_2/L$.

With those mathematical expressions for holding cost and releasing cost, one can now express total cost as $TC = L + A^2/L$. With that expression for total cost, we can then apply the elementary slope rules to arrive at the slope of TC

relative to L. That slope or ratio between a change in TC and a change in L is equal to $1-(A^2/L^2)$. We can now set that slope equal to 0 and solve for L to find the value of L when TC bottoms out.[10] Doing so yields:

$$1-(A^2/L^2) = 0 \quad \text{(setting the slope of } TC \text{ equal to 0)}$$
$$-A^2/L^2 = -1 \quad \text{(subtracting 1 from both sides)}$$
$$A^2/L^2 = 1 \quad \text{(multiplying both sides by } -1)$$
$$L^2/A^2 = 1 \quad \text{(inverting both sides)}$$
$$L^2 = A^2 \quad \text{(multiplying both sides by } A^2)$$
$$L^* = A \quad \text{(taking the square root of both sides)}$$

In other words, by mathematically defining HC as L and RC as A^2/L, we can deduce that the optimum value of L to minimize TC is the average sentence or A for each crime. Doing so provides an additional justification for the average as the tentative optimum in terms of minimizing the sum of the holding and releasing costs. There are more complicated mathematical approaches to this same problem that take into consideration the probability that a released convict will commit a crime with a severity equal to the average sentence of the previous crime or that take into consideration that the subsequent crime severity may not be equal to the average sentence of the previous crime but only a close approximation to it. Those mathematical approaches, however, also tend to arrive at A (or the average sentence) as an approximation of L^* (or the optimum sentence length).[11]

Some Conclusions

The more specific conclusion of this chapter is that the previous average sentences per crime represent relatively good approximations to optimizing sentences for determinate-sentencing legislation. This does not mean that the previous average sentences are optimum as known by an omniscient being, who can accurately predict the behavior of each individual defendant and the average defendant. They may also not be optimum as known by an omnibenevolent being who has perfect values, since optimum sentencing is a combination of facts and values. Nevertheless, the previous averages can be considered to be about as optimum as we can humanly get at the present time. One might, however, reasonably argue that we can humanly improve on those previous averages. One form of research that would be helpful is to clarify the relations between stentence served and such predictors as prior record, job record, and age. Another form of research that would be helpful is to clarify the relations between sentence served and such alleged effects as subsequent individual behavior, general deterrence, and incapacitation, so that a data-based benefit-cost analysis might some day replace or supplement an averaging approach.

The more general conclusion of this chapter is that there are a variety of approaches or justifications for arriving at policy recommendations. Some may be better than others depending on the circumstances. One justification dimension is concerned with inductive reasoning from many instances (as shown in table 14-1), as contrasted to deductive reasoning from premises that are taken as givens (as for example in the mathematical justification of the averaging approach), although the premises could be inductively arrived at. Another justification dimension is concerned with the rationalism of benefit-cost analysis as contrasted to the incrementalism of the averaging approach. The classification of disaggregated or explicit evaluation versus aggregated, holistic, gestalt, or implicit evaluation is similar to rationalist versus incrementalist. Still another dimension is concerned with common-sense justification or being understandable to the general public (as in the common-sense justification of the averaging approach), as contrasted to technical justifications (as in either table 14-1 or the mathematical justification). Since there are two categories on each of these three dimensions, a justification for a policy recommendation could fit into any one of eight types.

The problem of arriving at optimum determinate sentences seems to be the type of problem in which a deductive, incrementalist, common-sense approach outweighs an inductive, rationalist, technical approach, unlike other problems that are more meaningfully resolved by other approaches. In other words, the controversies between inductive-deductive, rationalist-incrementalist, lay-technical approaches to policy analysis may be meaningless out of the context of specific problems. In that context, all approaches may be applicable. What may be needed is not more of any one of these approaches, but just more good policy analysis that draws conclusions that are convincing in that effectiveness, efficiency, equity, and other goals rather than in the methods used to justify the conclusions.

Notes

1. On determinate sentencing in general, see Alan Dershowitz and the Twentieth Century Fund Task Force on Criminal Sentencing, *Fair and Certain Punishment* (New York: McGraw-Hill, 1976); Pierce O'Donnell, Michael Churgin, and Dennis Curtis, *Toward a Just and Effective Sentencing System: Agenda for Legislative Reform* (New York: Praeger, 1977); and Richard Singer, *Just Deserts: Sentencing Based on Equality and Desert* (Cambridge, Mass.: Ballinger, 1979).

2. On a benefit-cost approach to determining sentences, see Brian Forst, William Rhodes, and Charles Wellford, "Sentencing and Social Science Research for the Formulation of Federal Sentencing Guidelines," 7 *Hofstra Law Review* 355-378 (1979); Peter Aranson, "The Simple Analytics of Sentencing," in *Policy Analysis and Deductive Reasoning,* ed. Gordon Tullock and Richard

Wagner (Lexington, Mass.: Lexington Books, D.C. Heath, 1978); and S. Nagel, Marian Neef, and Thomas Weiman, "A Rational Method for Determining Prison Sentences," 61 *Judicature* 371-375 (1978).

3. For further details concerning the points made in this chapter, see the much longer version entitled "The Average May Be the Optimum in Determinate Sentencing," available on request from the author.

4. On optimizing in a legal-policy context, see Gary Becker and William Landes (eds.), *Essays in the Economics of Crime and Punishment* (New York: Columbia University Press, 1974); and S. Nagel and Marian Neef, *Legal Policy Analysis: Finding an Optimum Level of Mix* (Lexington, Mass.: Lexington Books, D.C. Heath, 1977), especially 1-158. On optimizing in a public-policy context, see Michael White et al., *Managing Public Systems: Analytic Techniques for Public Administration* (Scituate, Mass.: Duxbury, 1980), especially 245-259 and 278-290; and Edith Stokey and Richard Zeckhauser, *A Primer for Policy Analysis* (New York: W.W. Norton, 1978), especially 139-142. On optimizing in general, see Samuel Richmond, *Operations Research for Management Decisions* (New York: Ronald, 1968), especially 3-126; and Michael Brennan, *Preface to Econometrics: An Introduction to Quantitative Methods in Economics* (Cincinnati, Ohio: South-Western, 1973), especially 1-192 and 308-352.

5. The authors acknowledge the helpfulness of Anne Schmidt of the National Institute of Justice and Daniel Glaser of the University of Southern California in providing them with the Federal Bureau of Prisons data referred to in this chapter. Previous studies that have used that data include Howard Kitchener, Anne Schmidt, and Daniel Glaser, "How Persistent Is Post-Prison Success?" 41 *Federal Probation* 9-15 (March 1977); and Daniel Glaser, *The Effectiveness of a Prison and Parol System* (Indianapolis, Ind.: Bobbs-Merrill, 1964).

6. On the use of computerized regression analysis to determine the nonlinear relation between (1) a dependent variable like releasing costs and (2) a pair of independent variables like sentence length and prior record, see Norman Nie et al., *Statistical Package for the Social Sciences* (New York: McGraw-Hill, 1975), especially 320-397; Hubert Blalock, *Social Statistics* (New York: McGraw-Hill, 1972), especially 361-472; and William Rich, Michael Saks, Paul Sutton, and Todd Clear, "Modeling the Sentencing Process: An Examination of Empirically Based Sentencing Guidelines" (paper presented at Law and Society Association Annual Meeting, June 1980, Madison, Wisconsin).

7. Two slope rules can generally handle most optimizing situations. One rule is that if $Y = a + bX$, then the slope of Y relative to X is b. The other rule is that if $Y = aX^b$, then the slope of Y relative to X is baX^{b-1}. The first rule relates to the holding-cost part of the total cost, since it involves a linear relation, and the second rule relates to the releasing-cost part, since it involves a nonlinear relation. The holding-cost part could be expressed as $Y = a + bX$, where $Y = TC$, $a = 0$, $b = 1$, $X = L$, and thus the slope equals 1. The releasing

cost part could be expressed as $Y = aX^b$, where $Y = TC$, $a = a(R)^{b_2}$, $X = L$, $b = b_1$, and thus the slope equals $b_1 a(R)^{b_2}(L)^{b_1-1}$.

8. Research related to the averaging approach is currently being conducted as part of the development of sentencing guidelines. Leslie Wilkins, *Sentencing Guidelines: Structuring Judicial Discretion* (Washington, D.C.: Law Enforcement Assistance Administration, 1978); and Don Gottfredson et al., *Guidelines for Parole and Sentencing* (Lexington, Mass.: Lexington Books, D.C. Heath, 1978). Sentencing guidelines, however, usually are not classified as a form of determinate sentencing, because the legislature or sentencing commission does not specify specific sentences but rather specifies sentencing criteria that are partly subjective and generally nonmandatory. The criteria may, though, involve working with charts that score the characteristics of the defendant and the crime to arrive at specific sentences.

9. These common-sense justifications tend to fit well into the incrementalist approach to policy analysis, which emphasizes building on existing policies. See David Braybrooke and Charles Lindblom, *A Strategy for Decision* (New York: Free Press, 1963); and Aaron Wildavsky, *Speaking Truth to Power: The Art and Craft of Policy Analysis* (Boston: Little, Brown, 1979). The contrary perspective that emphasizes benefit-cost and optimizing analysis is represented by the books cited in note 4. On a more philosophical level, that perspective is represented by Yehezkel Dror, *Public Policymaking Reexamined* (San Francisco: Chandler, 1968).

10. The same two slope rules mentioned in note 7 apply here. Thus the holding-cost part of the total cost still generates a slope of 1. The releasing-cost part could be expressed as $A^2(L)^{-1}$, which is algebraically the equivalent of A^2/L. The releasing-cost part can thus be expressed in the form, $Y = aX^b$, where $Y = TC$, $a = A^2$, $X = L$, $b = -1$, and thus the slope equals $-1A^2(L)^{-1-1}$, which is algebraically the equivalent of $-A^2/L^2$.

11. On deductive mathematical modeling in policy and economic analysis, see Martin Greenberger, Matthew Crenson, and Brian Crissey, *Models in the Policy Process: Public Decision Making in the Computer Era* (New York: Russell Sage, 1976); and Caroline Dinwiddy, *Elementary Mathematics for Economists* (New York: Oxford, 1967). Such an approach can be contrasted with that of statistical induction, as represented by the literature cited in note 6, although deductive premises can be based on inductive findings.

15 Restitution and Compensation: A Market Model for Corrections

Charles M. Gray

Introduction

The criminal-justice system has responded to the persistent growth of crime over the last several years by developing innovative—but not always effective—means of dealing with criminals and potential criminals. Law enforcement has undergone extensive experimentation and change; alternative corrections activities have arisen; the courts have sought more efficient means of handling a burgeoning caseload; and victims and witnesses have become more active participants in the criminal-justice process. Success has been less than heartening.

The focus here is on restitution to the victim as the social response to a crime. Restitution—which even a cursory inquiry reveals to be deeply rooted in history—has caught the fancy of many criminologists, criminal-justice practitioners, and the public. The National Institute of Justice and numerous state criminal-justice-planning agencies have funded many such programs in an effort to determine their effectiveness, and national evaluations are now underway. But the evaluations—and the programs themselves—suffer from the lack of a consistent theoretical model. Although efforts are underway to remedy this, the result in the meantime is a diverse, often contradictory, and noncomparable set of activities purporting to be restitution that in practice are difficult both to evaluate and to emulate.[1]

This chapter takes an economic perspective in exploring a hypothetical alternative to traditional criminal-justice policies.[2] We will use this approach to inquire into pertinent features of restitution, asking—and sometimes answering—selected questions: Is restitution equitable? Is restitution efficient? How, if at all, does restitution serve the goals of corrections?

This inquiry requires a statement of assumptions and a few preliminary definitions; the next two sections address these requirements. Then we present the example for scrutiny and explore selected implications. Finally, since additional research is virtually obligatory, a bit of guidance is provided.

This inquiry was funded in part by grants from the National Institute of Justice and the Minnesota Crime Control Planning Board. Among those making helpful comments and critiques at various stages were Joe Hudson, Steve Chesney, Sue Sanger, Ann Witte, and numerous others who have willingly or unwillingly entered into relevant conversations with the author. The author bears full responsibility for all opinions and conclusions.

The Institutional Setting

Restitution must of course be presented in the context of a larger socioeconomic milieu. This includes, in our society, a system of property rights accepted by the populace at large and enforced by the powers of the state. Although both the system and the enforcement enable the economic system to operate more effectively, they also are the preconditions for many types of crime (perhaps nearly all crimes, if the concept of property is extended to ownership of one's own human capital). The state is empowered to determine violations of property rights as well as liability in such cases.

Property ownership can be exchanged in a system of well-defined markets. These markets do not work perfectly for a variety of reasons, including price rigidities, the occurrence of externalities, costly and imperfect information available to participants, imperfect access to markets by different participants, and, no doubt, other reasons as well. The relative valuation of property to be exchanged in markets is denominated in terms of the prevailing currency. Money is used as a standard of value or unit of account; it has no value other than the resources it will command. By thus eliminating a barter system, the economy works more smoothly still.

Finally, individuals are viewed as rational utility maximizers, in keeping with the economic approach. Everyone is constantly weighing the relative net benefits of alternative courses of action, ultimately choosing that set of activities that are compatible with personal resources and hold forth the likelihood of greatest total satisfaction.

Economic Criteria

We will pose two criteria by which to judge the efficacy of restitution. The first, and perhaps most obvious, is efficiency. This is, of course, a natural concern of economists, who persist in inquiring whether any human activity is "technically efficient": Do we get maximum output from a given set of inputs? If the answer is no, it would follow that the process that transforms inputs into outputs must be altered in pursuit of greater efficiency.

The desired output (or outcome) of the criminal-justice system (CJS) has been defined by most economists as something like "minimization of the social costs of crime."[3] The corrections subsystem, the repository of those adjudicated guilty and the focus of our attention here, should contribute to this cost minimization. In contrast, most criminologists identify four goals of the corrections subsystem. One is general deterrence, the punishment of one offender to deter others (Klein, Forst, and Filatov, 1978; Nagin, 1978). A second is rehabilitation, whereby the punished offender has been altered so that he (or she) is unlikely to recidivate. The third is incapacitation, or simple constraint, which has the apparent benefit of protecting those who are outside prison walls from those who are inside (Cohen 1978). And punishment as a goal is often argued to be justifiable in its own right. Whether much progress has been made toward achieving these goals, especially the first two, is far from clear (Martinson 1974). Efficiency in the pursuit of these goals does not seem to have attracted much scholarly attention.[4] A policy of restitution does not require achieving any of these goals, however, although it may be consistent with all. (Restitution is consistent with economic efficiency at least to the following extent. If the private market is efficient in the absence of imperfections and such externalities as those generated by crime, then restitution, designed to restore the "status quo ante" [Becker's usage (1968)], restores efficiency to the degree that it existed previously.

Economists are also cognizant of the equity principle, by which outcomes are adjudged to be just or fair. Further definitional difficulties are finessed through use of a pair of policy guidelines. The concepts of vertical equity—those who do not share common characteristics along a relevant dimension should be treated differently—and horizontal equity—those who are similar should be treated similarly—provide some policy guidance. Simply stated, the seriousness of a transgression should determine the severity of the response.[5] Each of these criteria underlies the discussion that follows.

The Restitution Model

Restitution has in practice taken many forms (Barnett 1977). Direct repayment to the victim by the offender is perhaps the most widespread, but other restitution programs feature community service in lieu of incarceration (perhaps really in lieu of probation). Some encourage a face-to-face encounter between victim and offender, with a restitution agreement arising out of some negotiation by the principals. But these entail such shortcomings as failure to deal with costs incurred by the public sector, the needs of the victim, or other relevant aspects. Perhaps one could safely argue that the perfect restitution program does not exist, either in practice or in theory (Hudson and Chesney 1978).

What is suggested here is a means of confronting many of these shortcomings—although, to be sure, many new ones will surface in their stead. The approximation to an ideal restitution program may be embodied in a state—or perhaps local or national—crime-victim compensation bank (CVCB), a financial intermediary operating as the primary activity of a corrections authority.

Upon an adjudication of guilty and determination of liability by the judiciary, the CVCB compensates those parties deemed to have been harmed by the offense in question. Direct victims receive appropriate compensation, and some portion of the costs incurred by the CJS is reimbursed by the bank. Figure 15–1 illustrates this process. By these actions, the offender has in effect taken out a

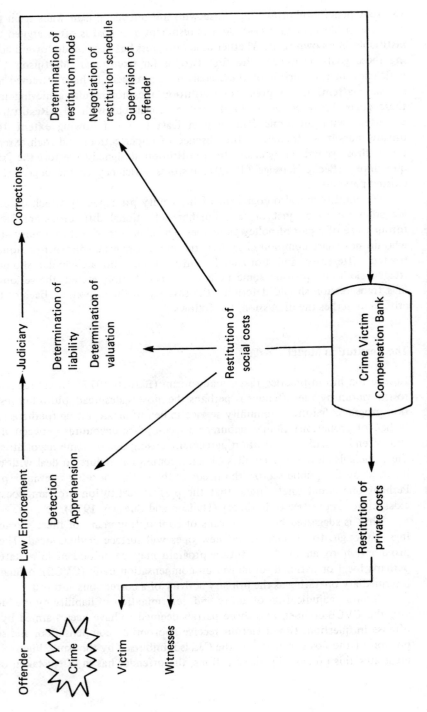

Figure 15-1. A Restitution-Based Criminal-Justice System

loan from the bank, and the corrections authority enters into negotiations with the offender and the counsel to determine a repayment (restitution) schedule. The amount of the loan would be determined by evaluation of such items as the following:

1. Value of any property taken, for example, replacement cost of market value of goods stolen
2. value of property damaged, that is, repair or replacement costs
3. compensation for deprivation of property use—for example, an auto theft deprives the owner of a mode of transportation, and additional costs are incurred.
4. hospitalization and other medical costs
5. compensation for physical discomfort and mental anguish of victimization
6. reimbursement for a pro-rata share of CJS expenditures—some (but perhaps not all, as will be explained later) of the CJS costs are directly attributable to criminal behavior and presumably any offender is liable for some share

Table 15-1 presents hypothetical data that might make this a bit more concrete. In this case, the loan for which the offender is liable amounts to $7,600. Determination of a repayment schedule hinges on consideration of several factors. If the offender is currently employed, restitution can be paid out of current income. Market interest rates and concurrent financial obligations of the

Table 15-1
Case Study: Burglary with Injury

Category	Valuation
Property stolen	$2,000
Property damaged	1,200
Compensation, property deprivation[a]	300
Medical expenses	600
Discomfort compensation[a]	$X > 0$
Compensation, lost income, and other opportunity costs of time	500
CJS reimbursement	3,000
law enforcement	
judiciary/prosecution	
witnesses	
corrections	
Total[b]	$7,600 + X$

[a]Absence of a market-determined value.

[b]This total obligation might be reduced for low-income offenders as part of a redistributive scheme.

offender will be partial determinants of monthly restitution payments. Further, recovery of all or part of any loot may reduce the size of the loan. Offenders may also choose to liquidate assets to reduce or retire the loan.

Many offenders are unemployed, which may be a factor contributing to commission of the crime in the first place. But if the offender has a marketable skill, the corrections authority may assist him or her in securing a job; an unskilled offender may qualify for some skills-acquisitions program.

If an offender is deemed unlikely to be cooperative in a community setting, he or she may be placed in a secure facility and employed in a free-venture type of correctional industry, earning a market wage and making restitution—including room and board payments. We will employ these concepts in creating a brief example.

The High-Income Offender

We might find, at one extreme, that the offender who generates the costs described in table 15-1 is in fact quite well-to-do.[6] Assuming this individual has already disposed of the loot and received street value of $800, the loan can be reduced by this amount—a down payment of sorts. This leaves a total restitution obligation of $6,800. With a market interest rate of 12 percent, the high-income offender may elect a repayment schedule of, say, $350 per month for some twenty-two months. This relatively speedy restitution would relieve the offender of further obligation.

The Disadvantaged Offender

At the other extreme we might find the offender who does not have a high current income, and who chooses an alternate restitution schedule. We may also suppose this offender to be highly mobile and subject to temptations to relocate with no prior notice. Hence the offender is placed in a prison industry and earns journeyman's wages—perhaps $4.00 per hour—dictating a longer repayment period. With the same market interest rate of 12 percent, manageable monthly payments of $75 would require 239 months, or about 19 years.

Selected Implications

Our example raises some obvious questions, a few of which are considered briefly here. Others are developed later as areas for further research.

The Question of Equity

The high-income offender's liability lasts less than two years; the low-income offender's obligation extends into nineteen years. Is this equitable? Certainly one is struck by the differential. In a correctional system where sentences are denominated by time, and offenders place identical values on time, the sentences would be inequitable. But when the sentence is denominated in dollars, the restitution obligation is identical, and total dollar payment differs only by the effect of interest over a time period; the sentences are in effect precisely the same. Horizontal equity is served by having offenders who have committed an identical crime receive exactly the same sentence—expressed in currency rather than time.

One might reasonably argue that determinate-sentencing schemes, such as those now in vogue around the country, are inequitable to the extent that high-income offenders, or those who value time highly, may receive and serve the same sentence as those who value time less highly. The direct and opportunity costs for the former may be much higher (Becker 1965).

Buying the Right to Commit a Crime?

Some who have been exposed to these ideas have argued that a sentence expressed in dollar terms amounts to permitting an offender to buy the right to commit a crime. The wealthy could purchase more such rights to commit a crime. In point of fact, if one insists on adopting this perspective, sentences denominated in time already permit such purchase. An individual who is willing to risk punishment is free to commit an offense. Since punishment in years of incarceration is less costly perhaps to the disadvantaged, these individuals enjoy something of a relative benefit. The concept does not alter, but the currency used and the endowment of currency do change when substituting restitution for more traditional incaraceration.

Is Restitution Racist?

It would seem likely that members of minority groups, who may have been denied access to education and/or income because of discrimination, would in general have longer repayment periods under restitution. Further, they may be placed in secure facilities more frequently, utilizing correctional industries to obtain restitution funds. Clearly this would be an outcome of discriminatory practices engendered by racism. Although unfortunate, it would not be a consequence of a restitution-based CJS; minorities may in fact be better off than under current practices, which lead to minorities comprising almost half of prison populations. The opportunity to gain an income—part of which, to be sure, finances restitution payments—may also facilitate skills acquisition and enhanced employability on release.

Questions Deserving Further Study

Restitution remains out of the mainstream of correctional research, and this specific set of ideas may be further out still. The questions raised are numerous, and most are quite challenging. For example, how serious might moral hazard be in a restitution-based CJS? Moral hazard refers to the greater risk that a potential victim may take because he or she perceives some chance of reimbursement (Pauly 1968). Private insurors resort to coinsurance or a deductible quantity to encourage the insured to bear some of the risk. The same might be employed in a restitution scheme, with the judiciary apportioning liability between offender and victim.

In the event of homicide or manslaughter, what restitution would be appropriate, and to whom is restitution made? These are particularly sticky issues, as economists remain stumped in attempting to fix a monetary value on life (Mishan 1971; Broome 1978; Linnerooth 1979). Further, the victim can in no way benefit directly from restitution in such an event.

Certain crimes are said to have no victims. To whom is restitution made in the event of gambling, prostitution, pornography, and other so-called victimless crimes? Indeed, implementing a restitution system may force one to reconsider whether these should be classified as crimes.

How much of CJS costs should be borne by offenders? Even in the absence of crime, the populace may exercise its option demand and maintain at least some minimal contribution. Presumably general tax revenues would finance some CJS activities, with offenders, via the CVCB, paying the balance.

Answering these and other questions raised by this exercise in fancy could be the focus of meaningful research. The payoff may be much higher than, for example, endless and—to date—fruitless inquiries into such topics as whether punishment deters (Martinson 1974) or whether criminals can be rehabilitated.

Notes

1. The topic of restitution is well summarized in the volumes edited by Hudson and Galaway (1975; 1978). On evaluations of restitution programs, see other volumes by these two authors listed in the references.

2. The economic approach, developed by Becker (1968) and his intellectual progeny (Erlich, 1973), is by now pretty well known and at least grudgingly accepted by most criminal-justice scholars.

3. The best statements perhaps are those by Rottenberg (1970).

4. Some exceptions are found in Gray (1979).

5. Obviously, this is not news to anyone; see Rothbard (1977).

6. One might well wonder why such an individual is committing this crime in the first place. The reader is free to choose among any of several theories of criminogenesis; the writer prefers to claim artistic license.

References

Barnett, Randy E. 1977. "Restitution: A New Paradigm of Criminal Justice." *Assessing the Criminal: Restitution, Retribution, and the Legal Process*, edited by R. Barnett and J. Hogel. Cambridge, MA: Ballinger.

Becker, Gary S. 1965. "A Theory of the Allocation of Time." *The Economic Journal* 74:493-517.

———. 1968. "Crime and Punishment: An Economic Approach." *Journal of Political Economy* 76:169-217. Reprinted with revisions in G. Becker and W. Landes, eds. *Essays in the Economics of Crime and Punishment.* New York: National Bureau of Economic Research, 1974.

Blumstein, Alfred; Jacqueline Cohen; and Daniel Nagin, eds. 1978. *Deterrence and Incapacitation: Estimating the Effects of Criminal Sanctions on Crime Rates.* Washington, D.C.: National Academy of Sciences.

Broome, John. 1978. "Trying to Value a Life." *Journal of Public Economies* 9:91-100

Cohen, Jacqueline. 1978. "The Incapacitative Effect of Imprisonment: A Critical Review of the Literature." In *Deterrence and Incapacitation: Estimating the Effects of Criminal Sanctions on Crime Rates,* edited by Alfred Blumstein; Jacqueline Cohen; and Daniel Nagin. Washington, D.C.: National Academy of Sciences, pp. 187-243.

Ehrlich, Isaac. 1973. "Participation in Illegitimate Activities: An Economic Analysis." *Journal of Political Economy* 81:521-565. Reprinted with revisions in G. Becker and W. Landes, eds. *Essays in the Economics of Crime and Punishment.* New York: National Bureau of Economic Research, 1974, pp. 68-134.

Galaway, Burt, and Joe Hudson, eds. 1978. *Offender Restitution in Theory and Action.* Lexington, Mass.: Lexington Books, D.C. Heath.

Gray, Charles M., ed. 1979. *The Costs of Crime,* Beverly Hills, Calif.: Sage.

Hudson, Joe, and Burt Galaway, eds. 1975. *Considering the Victim: Readings in Restitution and Victim Compensation.* Springfield, Ill.: Charles C. Thomas.

Hudson, Joe, and Burt Galaway. (n.d.) *Proposal for a National Assessment of Adult Restitution Programs.* Duluth, Minn.: School of Social Development, University of Minnesota.

Hudson, Joe, and Burt Galaway. (n.d.) *National Assessment of Adult Restitution Programs, Preliminary Report 1: Overview of Restitution Programming and Project Selection.* Duluth, Minn.: School of Social Development, University of Minnesota.

Hudson, Joe, and Steven Chesney. 1978. "Research on Restitution: A Review and Assessment." In *Offender Restitution in Theory and Action,* edited by Joe Hudson and Burt Galaway. Lexington, Mass.: Lexington Books, D.C. Heath.

Klein, L.; B. Forst; and V. Filatov. 1978. "The Deterrent Effect of Capital Punishment: An Assessment of the Estimates." *In Deterrence and Incapacitation: Estimating the Effects of Criminal Sanctions on Crime Rates.* edited by A. Blumstein, J. Cohen, and D. Nagin, Washington, D.C.: National Academy of Sciences, pp. 336-360.

Linnerooth, Joanne. 1979. "The Value of Human Life: A Review of the Models. *Economic Inquiry* 17:52-74.

Martinson, Robert. 1974. "What Works?—Questions and Answers about Prison Reform." *The Public Interest* 35:22-54.

Mishan, E.J. 1971. "Evaluation of Life and Limb: A Theoretical Approach." *Journal of Political Economy* 79:687-705.

Nagin, Daniel. 1978. "General Deterrence: A Review of the Empirical Evidence." In *Deterrence and Incapacitation: Estimating the Effects of Criminal Sanctions on Crime Rates.* edited by A. Blumstein, J. Cohen, and D. Nagin, Washington, D.C.: National Academy of Sciences, pp. 95-139.

Nakell, Barry. 1978. "The Cost of the Death Penalty." *Criminal Law Bulletin* 14:69-80.

Packer, Herbert L. 1968. *The Limits of the Criminal Sanction.* Stanford, Calif.: Stanford University Press.

Pauly, Mark V. 1968. "The Economics of Moral Hazard: Comment." *American Economic Review* 58:531-537.

Rothbard, Murray N. 1977. "Punishment and Proportionality." In *Assessing the Criminal: Restitution, Retribution and the Legal Process,* edited by R. Barnett and J. Hogel. Cambridge, Mass.: Ballinger, 259-272.

Rottenberg, Simon. 1970. "The Social Cost of Crime and Crime Prevention." In *Crime in Urban Society,* edited by B. McLennan. New York: Dunellen.

Index

Acton, H.B., 40
Aikman, Alexander, 95, 104
Alabama, 10, 157, 159-160, 161
Alberti v. Sheriff of Harris County, Texas, 156, 161, 164, 167, 177, 178
Alderson prison, 111-112, 117
Allen, Francis A., 59, 70
Allenwood prison, 119
Allinson, Richard S., 98, 103
Altshuler, Alan A., 10
American Arbitration Association, 143
American Bar Association, 165, 167, 175, 176
American Civil Liberties Union, 10, 156, 167, 168-171, 172, 174, 175, 177
American Correctional Association, 7, 8, 99, 125
American Medical Association, 99, 103
American Public Health Association, 99, 103
Americans for Democratic Action, 53
Anderson, C. Wilson, 69-70, 70
Anderson, Gerard, 43
Anderson, James E., 177
Anderson et al. v. Redman et al., 29
Anno, B. Jaye, 100, 103
Aranson, Peter, 206-207
Arizona, 10, 49
Arkansas, 101, 156, 157, 161, 188
Association of Directors of Social Services, 88
Attica prison, 110, 148
Attorney General's Task Force on Violent Crime, 10
Auburn Correctional Facility, 149

Bailey, Walter C., 39
Baker, J.E., 149
Baltimore, 176
Barnett, Randy E., 211, 217
Barrows, I., 120
Basista v. Weir, 190
Bayh, Senator Birch, 59
Bayh Act, 60-61
Bazelon, Judge David L., 7, 8, 11
Becker, Gary, 207, 211, 215, 217
Becker, T.L., 61, 70
Bedford Hills prison, 111, 117
Bell v. Wolfish, 184-185, 188, 189, 191
Bengur, Osmar, 66, 72
Bentham, Jeremy, 32
Berger, Raoul, 190
Bergsmann, I., 121

Beyer, Peter B., 96, 105
Birnberg, Gerald, 168
Bish, Frances, 103
Bivens v. Six Unnamed Agents, 188, 190, 192
Black, H., 78, 89
Blake, Gerald F., 66, 70
Blalock, Hubert, 207
Blizek, William, 40
Block, Michael, 101, 103
Blomberg, Thomas, 67, 70
Blumstein, Alfred, 122, 217
Boardman, Anthony, 43
Boland, Barbara, 40, 50
Bohnstedt, Marvin, 64, 71
Bottoms, A.E., 75, 84, 89
Bottoms, Tony, 73
Bouza, Anthony V., 8, 11
Bowker, L., 123
Braly, Malcolm, 15-16, 28
Braybrooke, David, 208
Breckenridge, Robert, 177
Brennan, Michael, 207
Brenner, M.H., 49, 50
Broome, John, 216, 217
Bue, Judge Carl O., 161, 167, 168-176, 177, 178
Bullington, Bruce, 59
Bullock, R., 85, 90
Bureau of Justice Statistics, 9, 105, 121
Bureau of Prisons, 29, 99, 111, 112, 120, 122, 144, 207
Bureau of the Census, 53, 96, 97
Burger, Chief Justice Warren, 184-185
Burger Court, 179, 184-186, 187, 188, 189, 191
Buser, Michael B., 160, 164
Butz v. Economou, 192
Byrne, John, 3, 4, 5, 15, 28

California, 64, 101, 112, 122, 144
California Youth Authority, 144, 150
Callaghan, James, 87
Cantrell, Chancellor Ben H., 9
Carlson, Norman A., 28, 122
Carlson v. Green, 192
Carriere, C., 123
Carter, Robert M., 30
Cawson, P., 85, 89
Cedarblom, J.B., 40
Chambliss, William J., 29, 39
Chayes, Abram, 190
Chesney, Steven, 211, 218

Chief Probation Officers' Conference, 88
Christian Science Monitor, 59
Churgin, Michael, 206
City of Newport v. Fact Concerts, Inc., 191
Civil Rights Act of 1866, 181, 182, 186
Clear, Todd, 207
Cloward, Richard, 148
Cluchette v. Procunier, 190
Coates, Robert B., 64, 71, 85, 90
Cohen, Jacqueline, 122, 210-211, 217
Cole, George F., 43
Collins v. Schoonfield, 167, 176
Colorado, 10
Commonwealth v. Butler, 122
Community-based corrections, 16-22, 24-
    25, 25-26, 27, 65
Comptroller General of the United States,
    100, 103, 110
Connecticut, 10, 32, 34, 37, 40, 121, 142,
    144
Cooper v. Pate, 155, 189-190
Correctional Economics Center, 98
Correctional institutions: crowding, 1, 6, 8,
    9, 16-17, 18-21; history, 1-2, 16, 28;
    and the judiciary, 4, 9-10, 29, 121-122;
    leadership, 125-126, 126-137; ombuds-
    men, 142-143; staff, 129-130, 132-136;
    for women, 109-123. *See also* Correc-
    tional reform; Jails; Juvenile facilities;
    Prisons
Correctional reform, 3-5, 15, 18, 20-21,
    27, 112, 202-204; through bureaucratic
    standards, 4-5, 98-100; through discre-
    tion of professionals, 5; failure of, 16,
    24, 64, 66-68, 75, 83-84, 98-99;
    through grievance resolution, 145-146,
    148; through judicial intervention, 156,
    161-163, 167-176, 179-181, 182;
    through market approach, 5-6, 10, 102;
    through reorganization, 5, 10, 125-137.
    See also Community-based corrections;
    Bayh Act; Juvenile justice systems;
    Great Britain, juvenile justice system;
    Jails; Correctional policy and the judici-
    ary; Restitution programs
Corrections, cost of, 26, 64, 101, 116-117,
    172, 195, 204-205
Corrections, purposes of, 3, 16, 22-23, 32,
    36-37, 39, 113-116. *See also* Punish-
    ment; Incapacitation; Deterrence; Re-
    habilitation; Retribution
Corrections policy, 3-6, 16; conflicts in,
    33-34, 37-39; decarceration ideology,
    25-26, 26-27; incarceration ideology,
    16-17, 21-25; and the judiciary, 60, 68-
    69, 156-163, 167-176, 179-189. *See
    also* Correctional reform; Corrections,
    purposes of; Decentralized correctional
    programs

Courts, 23, 141-142. *See also* U.S. Supreme
    Court, Correctional institutions and the
    judiciary; Correctional reform through
    judicial intervention; Federal courts;
    Jails, judicial intervention; Prisons,
    judicial intervention
Crago, T.G., 49, 51
Crenson, Matthew, 208
Cressey, Donald, 62, 70
Crime, 7-8, 10-11, 11; causes of, 43-49;
    and elected officials, 1, 7; statistics,
    43-49, 53, 197-198, 206-207; white-
    collar, 9, 10
Crissey, Brian, 208
Crossman, Richard, 87-88, 89
Curtis, Dennis, 206

Danielson, Michael N., 9
Danne, William H., Jr., 163
Danziger, S., 50
Davis, Edward M., 28
Davis, Kenneth Culp, 5, 10
De Beaumont, Gustave, 10
Decentralized correctional programs, 18;
    community resistance, 20, 21, 25. *See
    also* Community-based corrections;
    Furlough; Half-way house; Work release;
    Parole
Delaware, 10, 16-22, 24, 25, 27
Department of Commerce (U.S.), 96, 105
Department of Health, Education and
    Welfare (U.S.), 88
Department of Justice (U.S.), 62, 88, 96,
    105, 121, 177
Department of Labor (U.S.), 53
Department of Youth Services, 81, 87
Dershowitz, Alan, 206
Deterrence, 32, 33, 35-37, 114, 203, 210
De Tocqueville, Alexis, 10
Dillingham, David D., 149
Dinwiddy, Caroline, 208
District of Columbia, 4, 11
Ditchfield, J., 87, 89
Diver, Colin S., 165
Dodge, C.R., 28
Doig, Jameson W., 1, 9, 39, 43, 150
Donnison, D., 84, 89
Dothard v. Rawlinson, 122
Dror, Yehezkel, 208
Duvall v. Mandel, 176

Eckels, Bob, 172
Edwards, S., 76, 89
Ehrlich, Isaac, 217
Eighth Amendment, 155-156, 163, 186
Eleventh Amendment, 188-189, 190
Erikson, Kai, 1, 9
Ermann, M. David, 9
Estelle v. Gamble, 121, 189

Etzioni, Amitai, 150–151
Ewing, David, 129, 137

Fair, Daryl, 3, 4, 155, 163, 190
Fairchild, Erika S., 39
Familton, Sally F., 96, 105
Farrington, D., 87, 89
Fears, F., 87, 90
Federal Bureau of Investigation, 48, 53
Federal courts: cases, 19, 29, 85, 111, 117,
   120, 121, 122, 123, 156, 167, 176. *See
   also* Supreme Court
Feeley, Malcolm M., 61, 70
Felstiner, William, 149
Filatov, V., 50, 51, 210, 218
Finer, Herman, 5, 10
Finney v. Arkansas Board of Correction,
   163
Finney v. Hutto, 163
Finney v. Mabry, 163, 164
Fisher, F.M., 50
Fiss, Owen, 191
Florida, 10
Flynn, Edith E., 149
Fogel, David, 40
Fonteno, Jim, 172
Forst, Brian, 50, 51, 206, 210, 218
Fort Worth prison, 112, 120
Forts v. Ward, 122
Foucault, Michel, 84, 122
Fourteenth Amendment, 155, 181
Fox, Vernon, 149
Franceski, David, 43
Freedman, Estelle, 120
Friedman, L.M., 61, 70
Friedman, Milton, 10
Friedrich, Carl J., 5, 10
Fuller, R., 87, 90
Funke, Gail S., 96, 105
Furloughs, 18, 19, 20, 143

Gabarro, John J., 130, 133, 137, 138
Galaway, Burt, 216, 217, 218
Geis, Gilbert, 40
Georgia, 10, 47
Gibbons, Don C., 66, 70
Gillespie, R.W., 47, 50
Gilmore, Thomas, 2, 5, 125
Glaser, Daniel, 207
Glazer, Nathan, 40, 190
Glover v. Johnson, 111, 117, 121, 122
Goffman, Erving, 23, 30, 70
Goldfarb, Ronald, 96, 103
Golembiewski, Robert, 137, 138
Gordon, Diana, 11
Gordon, R.A., 50
Gorham, William, 40
Gornick, V., 122
Gottfredson, Don M., 104, 208

Gouldner, Alvin, 127, 129, 138
Graglia, Lino P., 190
Graham-Harrison, F.L.T., 88
Gray, Charles, 6, 209, 217
Great Britain (juvenile justice system),
   73–91; alternatives to remand in custody, 81–82, 87; corporal punishment,
   77, 86; courts, 73–74, 84; diversionary
   and decarceration, 77–78, 80; history
   of, 73–84; intermediate treatment, 80–
   81; juvenile facilities, 73, 75–77, 84, 85,
   86; Magistrates' Association, 77, 78, 78–
   79, 86; police cautioning, 79–80; reform
   of, 76–77, 77–78
Greenberg, David F., 29, 40
Greenberger, Martin, 208
Greenholtz v. Inmates of Nebraska Penal
   and Correctional Complex, 185, 191
Grunhut, Max, 86, 89
Gunther v. Iowa State Men's Reformatory,
   122

Haas, Kenneth C., 29
Haitovsky, Y., 50
Half-way house, 18, 20
Hamilton, Alexander, 183
Hamilton v. Schiro, 167
Harris, M. Kay, 164, 165, 176, 178
Harris County jail, 167, 168–176
Harvard Law Review, 161–163, 165, 190,
   192
Hawkins, Gordon, 9, 28, 39
Heard, Jack, 168, 172, 177
Heclo, Hugh, 138
Heise, D.R., 50
Henley, Judge J. Smith, 157, 159, 160,
   165
Hepburn, John, 2, 5, 139, 149, 150
Hickey, William L., 65, 70
Holland v. Donelson, 167
Holt v. Hutto, 163
Holt v. Sarver, 156, 157–159, 160, 161,
   163, 164, 188, 190
Hooley, F., 88
Horowitz, Donald L., 190, 191
Hosie, K., 85, 90
Houston Post, 171, 177
Hromas, C.S., 49, 51
Hudson, Joe, 211, 216, 217, 218
Hutto v. Finney, 163, 188, 192
Hyman, Drew, 59, 70

Illinois, 10, 32, 34, 37, 40, 64, 96
Incapacitation, 6, 7, 32, 33, 36–37, 114–
   115, 203, 210–211
Indiana, 9, 10, 32, 34, 37, 40
Ingleby, Viscount, 89
Ingleby Report (Great Britain), 73, 84
Inmates. *See* Prisoners

Inter-University Consortium for Political
  and Social Research, 97
Iowa, 10, 142
Isaacsson, John, 137, 138

Jackson, John, 43
Jacobs, James B., 30, 137, 138, 149, 150
Jails: conditions in, 5, 96, 97, 169–170;
  crowding, 98, 170; definition, 96; and
  elected officials, 167, 188; federal
  action, 170–171; health standards, 99–
  100, 107–108; and judicial interven-
  tion, 167–176; politics of, 100–101,
  102; population of, 95; pretrial detain-
  ment, 170, 171, 185; programs in, 96–
  98; reform of, 102, 150–151, 167–176;
  state standards, 95, 98–99
James, Howard, 60, 70, 85, 90
Jay, P., 78, 84, 89, 90
Johnson, Carolyn, 96, 104
Johnson, Frank M. Jr., 159, 164, 165
Jones, Charles O., 177
Jones v. Metzger, 164
Jones v. Wittenberg, 159
Joper, J., 28
Judges, 182–183, 184, 186. See also Bue,
  Judge Carl O.
Juvenile courts, 60, 62–63, 65, 68–69. See
  also Great Britain
Juvenile justice systems: diversion and
  deinstitutionalization, 60–63, 63–64,
  65–67, 69; failure of, 59–60, 62; history
  of, 59–61, 62–63; reform of, 59–63,
  64–69; status offenders, 60–61, 63, 65–
  66, 69, 75. See also Great Britain; Bayh
  Act; Corrections; Juvenile courts
Juvenile facilities, 8, 63, 76. See also Great
  Britain; juvenile justice system
Juvenile Justice and Delinquency Act of
  1974, 76, 85, 88

Katkin, Daniel, 59, 70
Katz, Michael B., 59, 70
Keating, J. Michael, 150
Keely, Sara F., 120
Kelly, Clarence M., 28
Kent v. United States, 60, 71
Kentucky, 10, 112, 122, 144
Keve, Paul, 24, 30
Kilbrandon, 74, 90
Kirkland Correctional Institution, 150
Kitchener, Howard, 207
Kittrie, Nicholas, 69, 71
Klein, L.R., 50, 51, 210, 218
Klein, Malcolm V., 67, 71, 90
Kobrin, S., 90
Kotter, John P., 132–133, 138
Kramer, John, 70
Kravitz, Marjorie, 96, 104

Land, Hilary, 86, 90
Landes, William, 207
Landry, Edward, 168, 177
Laue, James H., 149, 150
Law Enforcement Assistance Administra-
  tion (LEAA), 18, 63, 64, 71, 95, 96, 97,
  99, 104, 177
Leavenworth prison, 110
Lee v. Washington, 122
Legislators: view of corrections, 31–32, 34–
  39
Lehmann, Michael P., 192
Levine, Mark, 104
Levinson, Harry, 128, 138
Lewis, Roy, 71
Lewisburg prison, 119
Lexington prison, 112
Lieber, F., 10
Lindblom, Charles, 156, 208
Lindsay, Jon, 170–171
Linnerooth, Joanne, 216, 218
Logan, Charles H., 39
Longford, 84, 90
Longford Report (Great Britain), 73–74
Louis, Meryl Reis, 127, 129, 138
Louisiana, 10
Lowell, Harvey D., 63, 64, 71
Lowi, Theodore, 5, 10, 40
Luery, David, 43
Lugar, Richard G., 28
Lundman, Robert J., 9
Lyons, E.A., 172

Mabbot, J.D., 40
Mabli, 122
Macauley, S., 61, 70
McCann, Joseph, 2, 5, 125
McCleery, Richard, 137, 138
McCormick, Richard T., 138
McCoy, Candace, 3, 4, 179
McCrea, T.L., 104
McDermott, Robert, 62, 70
McDonald, Douglas, 101, 104
Mack, Judge Julian, 59, 71
McKee, J., 123
McNabb, Margaret, 63, 71
Manhattan Bail Project, 171
Marion prison, 110
Marshall, John, 183
Manson, Tycho, 9
Martell, M., 85, 89
Martinson, Robert, 16, 24, 28, 39, 122,
  211, 216, 218
Maryland, 10, 48
Massachusetts, 64, 69, 76, 81, 82, 86, 87
Massachusetts Advocacy Center, 87, 90
Mattick, Hans, 15, 28, 95, 96, 98–99, 101,
  104
Mattingly, John, 64, 71

Menninger, Karl, 30, 40
Mental hospitals, 185. *See also* Jails
Messinger, Sheldon, 148
Michael M. v. Supreme Court, 121
Michigan, 10, 48, 111, 117
Mikesell, John, 101, 104
Milin, Richard, 96, 104
Miller, Alden D., 64, 71, 85, 90
Millham, S., 85, 90
Milliken v. Bradley, 191
Minnesota, 32, 34, 37, 40, 142, 144
Minor, J., 121
Mishan, E.J., 216, 218
Mississippi, 10
Missouri, 10
Monell v. Department of Social Serv-
    ices, 188, 190, 191, 192
Monroe v. Pape, 155, 187, 192
Morales v. Turman, 85
Moran, B., 122
Morris, A., 84, 90
Morris, Norval, 61, 71
Muniz v. U.S., 190

Nachmias, David, 39
Nagel, Jack, 3, 43
Nagel, Stuart, 3, 5, 195, 206, 207
Nagel, William G., 43–47, 49, 51
Nagin, Daniel, 49, 50, 51, 122, 210, 217,
    218
Nakamura, Robert T., 9, 40
Nakell, Barry, 218
National Advisory Commission on Criminal
    Justice Standards and Goals, 15, 28, 59,
    60, 69, 71, 76
National Broadcasting Corporation, 59
National Center for Juvenile Justice, 63
National Clearinghouse for Legal Services,
    10
National Clearinghouse on Criminal Justice
    Planning and Architecture, 53, 169, 170,
    171, 177
National Commission on Law Observance
    and Enforcement (1931), 15
National Institute of Corrections, 123
National Institute of Justice, 8, 207,
    209
National Prison Project, 156, 163
Nelson v. Heyne, 85
Nevada, 10
New Hampshire, 10
New Jersey, 96
New Mexico, 10, 125, 138
New Society, 81
New York City, 101, 119
New York State, 99–100, 101, 111, 119,
    143, 144, 149, 149–150
New York City Department of Correction,
    101

New York State Commission of Correction,
    9, 99–100, 104
New York State Comptroller, 105
New York Times, 9
Newman, Edwin, 59
Newman v. Alabama, 163, 164
Nie, Norman, 207
North Carolina, 101
Northern Ireland, 78

O'Connor v. Donaldson, 192
O'Donnell, Pierce, 206
Ohio, 10
Ohlin, Lloyd, 64, 71, 85, 90, 138
Oitzinger, James, 168
Oklahoma, 10
Ombudsmen, 142–143, 145
Oran, Daniel, 164
Oregon, 10
Orr v. Orr, 123
Ostrowski, Thomas, 3, 4, 164,
    167
Owen v. City of Independence, Missouri,
    188, 192

Pabon, Edward, 64, 71
Packer, Herbert L., 218
Palmer, Ted, 64, 71
Palumbo, Dennis, 39
Parham v. J.L. and J.R., 185, 191
Parole, 19, 143, 185
Pauly, Mark V., 216, 218
Pennsylvania, 9, 64, 119
Perry v. Elrod, 192
Peters, Charles, 138
Philadelphia Family Court, 59
Philadelphia Inquirer, 11
Phillips, Douglas E., 9
Pincoffs, Edmund L., 40
Pleasanton prison, 112, 122, 123
Portney, Kent E., 31
Pound, Roscoe, 59, 71
President's Commission on Law Enforce-
    ment and the Administration of
    Justice, 15, 59, 60, 71
Price, Albert C., 31, 41
Priestley, P., 87, 90
Prisoners, 1–2, 7, 8, 15–16; grievance
    system, 139–148; needs of, 118; rights
    of, 23, 110–111, 146, 148–149, 155–
    156, 179–180, 181–182, 183, 185, 187–
    189
Prisons, 8, 139; construction of, 4, 9, 20–
    21, 43; discrimination by race, 181, 191;
    discrimination by sex, 109–118; failure
    of, 15–16, 25–26, 31, 46; integration of
    sexes, 112, 118–120; judicial interven-
    tion, 141–142, 155–156; life in, 23–25,
    110–112; women's, 110–112. *See also*

Attica; Bedford Hills; Alderson; Pleasanton; Leavenworth; Marion; San Quentin; Kirkland; Auburn
Procunier v. Navarette, 192
Puerto Rico, 4
Pugh v. Locke, 156, 157, 159, 159–161, 164
Punishment, 6–7, 17, 113–114

Radzinowicz, Leon, 9
Reagan, Ronald, 7, 9, 11
Reed, Amos E., 7, 8, 11
Rehabilitation, 6, 17, 32, 33, 36–37, 115–116, 210
Reixach, Karen, 5, 95
Resnik, Judith, 2, 99, 105, 109, 120
Restitution Programs: efficiency of, 210–211; models for, 211–214; problems with, 209, 211, 214–216
Retribution, 32, 33–34, 37
Rhode Island, 10
Rhodes, William, 206
Rich, Daniel, 15
Rich, William, 207
Richette, Judge Lisa, 59, 70, 72
Richmond, Samuel, 207
Robbins, Ira P., 160, 164
Robinson v. California, 155
Ross, J., 122
Rostker v. Goldberg, 121, 123
Rothbard, Murray N., 217, 218
Rothman, David, 15, 26, 28, 30, 59, 72
Rottenberg, Simon, 217, 218
Rourke, Francis E., 10
Rumsfeld, Donald, 129, 138
Rutherford, Andrew, 2, 4, 66, 72, 73, 85, 86, 89, 90

Saks, Michael, 207
San Quentin prison, 110
Schaller, Jack, 43
Schattschneider, E.E., 170, 177, 178
Schein, Edgar, 125, 127, 138
Scheuer v. Rhodes, 191
Schmidt, Anne, 207
Schrag, Clarence, 148
Schultze, Charles L., 10
Schuman, David, 29
Schur, Edwin, 69, 72
Scotland, 74, 83, 84
Seidman, Harold, 10
Selznick, Philip, 10
Sentencing, 18, 19, 20; averaging approach, 195, 200–206; cost of release, 195–198, 204–205, 207; determinate, 37–38, 195, 200, 202, 205–206, 208, 215; statistical approach, 195–200, 202–204, 205–206, 208

Sharp, Elaine, 39
Shaw, Nancy, 99, 105, 120
Shemaitis v. Froemke, 190
Sherman, Michael, 9
Sherriffs, A., 123
Siedman, Robert B., 29
Silberman, Charles E., 29
Singer, Linda, 149
Singer, Neil M., 105
Singer, Richard, 206
Sjoberg, Gideon, 10
Skoler, Daniel L., 105
Smallwood, Frank, 9, 40
Smith, Daniel D., 63, 68, 72
Smykla, J., 122
South Carolina, 144, 149
Spady, James A., 43
Specter, Arlen, 28
Spiller, Dudley P., 164, 165, 176, 178
Sprowls, James T., 61, 69, 72
Stapleton, W., 61, 69, 72
State v. Chambers, 122
Steele, Eric H., 30
Steele, Fritz, 132, 138
Stender, Fay, 29
Stewart, M., 84, 89
Stokey, Edith, 207
Stone, Christopher, 9
Strum, Philippa, 191
Supreme Court: cases, 85, 120, 121, 122, 123, 155, 156, 163, 164. *See also* Burger Court; Warren Court
Sutton, Paul, 207
Sweet, R., 96, 104
Sykes, Gresham M., 30, 148

Taylor, Stuart, 9
Teitelbaum, Lee E., 61, 69, 72
Teitelbaum, Vaughan, 61, 69, 72
Tennessee, 2, 10
Texas, 9, 10, 176
Thirteenth Amendment, 181
Thomas, Norman C., 10
Thomas, Wayne H., 105
Thorpe, J., 90
Todaro v. Ward, 111
Toledo Law Review, 190
Tucker, Robert C., 11
Turner, William Bennett, 190

Ulen, Thomas S., 101, 103
U.S. Army, 137
U.S. Senate, 90
U.S. Supreme Court, 59, 60
University of Delaware, 15
Utah, 10

van den Haag, Ernest, 28, 40
van Tijn, David, 28

Virginia, 9, 10
von Hirsch, Andrew, 40, 41

Wales, 73, 74, 77, 83
Wallace, George, 159
Ward, Frederick, 65, 72
Warren Court, 179–181, 187, 189, 191
Washington State, 10, 11, 96, 98
Washington v. Lee, 189
Wayson, Billy L., 96, 98, 102, 105
Weber v. Kaiser Aluminum, 191
Weiman, Thomas, 207
Weimer, David, 5, 95
Wellford, Charles, 206
West Virginia, 49, 112
Wheeler, D., 50
White, Michael, 207

Wildavsky, Aaron, 208
Wilkins, Leslie T., 30, 208
Wilmington Evening Journal, 30
Wilson, James Q., 28, 40
Wolfgang, Marvin E., 9
Wooden, Kenneth, 69, 72, 85, 91
Work release, 18, 143
Wright, Erik Olin, 9
Wright, Virginia B., 105
Wyoming, 10

Yanich, Donald, 3, 4, 5, 15, 28
Yin, Robert K., 125, 138
Young, Thomas A., 159, 160, 164

Zander, M., 87, 91
Zeckhauser, Richard, 207
Zimring, Franklin E., 39

About the Contributors

Bruce Bullington received the Ph.D. from the University of California at Los Angeles. He is an associate professor of criminal justice and a senior member of the graduate faculty in the Community Systems Planning and Development Program at The Pennsylvania State University. His writing has focused on the topics of drug use and juvenile delinquency and includes a book, *Heroin Use in the Barrio,* published in 1977 by Lexington Books.

John Byrne is a visiting assistant professor at the Center for the Study of Values, University of Delaware, and a research associate of the College of Urban Affairs and Public Policy. He has conducted and published research in the areas of criminal-justice policy, energy policy, and political economy. He is coauthor of the study, "Correctional Standards for Delaware: A Cost Analysis of Present Operations and Policies of the State's Correctional System," cited in the Third District Court order requiring Delaware to reduce overcrowding in its prison system.

Daryl R. Fair received the Ph.D. from the University of Pennsylvania and is professor of political science at Trenton State College. His research on judicial policymaking has focused most recently on the role of the federal courts in prison reform. He has published articles in journals such as *Wisconsin Law Review, Rutgers-Camden Law Journal, Social Science Quarterly, Western Political Quarterly,* and *American Journal of Criminal Law,* as well as in several books.

Thomas N. Gilmore is the associate director of the Management and Behavioral Science Center, The Wharton School, University of Pennsylvania. He has worked extensively with senior executives in the public sector, especially in corrections. His major research interests include the relationship between politics and management, interorganizational relationships, and management and organizational development.

Charles M. Gray received the Ph.D. from Washington University. He is assistant professor of economics at College of St. Thomas and serves on the affiliate faculty of the Humphrey Institute of Public Affairs at the University of Minnesota. He previously held staff economist positions within the Federal Reserve System and with Minnesota's Crime Control Planning Board. He edited *The Costs of Crime,* and his research in the economics of crime and justice has appeared in numerous journals and compendiums. He has been a consultant to state and local governments throughout the nation.

John R. Hepburn received the Ph.D. from the University of Iowa in 1973. He is associate professor of sociology and Fellow of the Center for Metropolitan

Studies at the University of Missouri at St. Louis. Among his current research activities are an analysis of the exercise of authority among correctional officers and involvement in a study of the institutional impact of determinate sentencing.

Drew Hyman received the Ph.D. from the University of California at Los Angeles. He is an associate professor of community development in the College of Human Development, The Pennsylvania State University. His work is focused on policy and development in human-services systems in the United States and on ombudsman and complaint-handling systems. He has published articles in *Administrative Science Quarterly, Journal of Voluntary Action Research, Social Problems, Criminal Law Bulletin,* and *Citizen Participation* and is the author of chapters in several books.

Daniel Katkin is professor and head of the Program in Administration of Justice at The Pennsylvania State University. He is a graduate of The City College of New York, Columbia Law School, and The Institute of Criminology at Cambridge University. He is the author of two books and many articles on juvenile delinquency, criminal law, and social policy.

Joseph E. McCann III received the Ph.D. from the University of Pennsylvania. He is assistant professor of business policy at the University of Florida, Gainsville, and a research associate of the Management and Behavioral Science Center at The Wharton School, University of Pennsylvania. He has done extensive organizational-development work in criminal justice, in particular building effective working relationships among the key agencies involved with community corrections. He coauthored (with Jay Galbraith) the chapter on interdepartmental relations in the *Handbook on Organizational Design* (1981). Current interests include reorganization in the public sector and strategic planning.

Candace McCoy is assistant professor of criminal justice and urban administration at the University of Cincinnati. She is currently on professional leave, studying in the Program in Jurisprudence and Social Policy at the University of California, Berkeley. Ms. McCoy, an attorney, has litigated cases concerning corrections and civil rights.

Jack H. Nagel is currently acting dean of the School of Public and Urban Policy and associate professor of political science, public policy, and public management at the University of Pennsylvania. He received the B.A. in political science from Swarthmore College and the Ph.D. in administrative sciences from Yale University. He is the author of *The Descriptive Analysis of Power* and is now working on a book about political participation.

Stuart S. Nagel is professor of political science at the University of Illinois, coordinator of the Policy Studies Organization, and a member of the Illinois bar. He has been a visiting Fellow at the Law Enforcement Assistance Administration and assistant counsel to the U.S. Senate Judiciary Committee. He is author or coauthor of several books, including *Decision Theory and the Legal Process* (Lexington Books, 1979) and *Legal Policy Analysis: Finding an Optimum Level or Mix* (Lexington Books, 1977) and editor of *Political Science of Criminal Justice* (1982), *Modeling the Criminal Justice System* (1977), and *The Rights of the Accused: In Law and Action* (1972).

Thomas S. Ostrowski is an associate professor of political science at Gannon University. He received the Ph.D. from the University of Houston in 1978. As a research associate of Gannon's Institute for Community Development, he has directed several studies of urban government. Currently, he is directing a study of urban revitalization through public-private partnerships.

Kent E. Portney is an assistant professor of political science at Tufts University. He received the Ph.D. in government from Florida State University and has published articles on comparative state policymaking and citizen participation.

Albert C. Price is an assistant professor of political science and a member of the graduate faculty of public administration at the University of Michigan, Flint. He received the Ph.D. from the University of Connecticut in 1980, and his research interests include criminal justice and public policy.

Karen A. Reixach is a graduate student in public policy analysis at the University of Rochester. She received the M.A. in English from the University of Chicago and has edited a number of social-science texts. Before returning to graduate school, she chaired the Judicial Process Commission, a Rochester-based criminal-justice action group with an emphasis on alternatives to incarceration.

Judith Resnik is an associate professor of law at the University of Southern California Law Center, where she teaches courses on prisoners' rights, civil procedure, and federal courts. She received the A.B. from Bryn Mawr College and the J.D. from New York University School of Law. Before coming to USC, Ms. Resnik was a clinical lecturer at Yale Law School and supervised the provision of legal services to prisoners at the Federal Correctional Institution in Danbury, Connecticut.

Andrew Rutherford is a senior lecturer in the Law Faculty at the University of Southampton, England. He worked for several years in borstals in England and has taught and undertaken criminal-justice research in England and in the United States. He is author of *The Dissolution of the Training Schools in*

Massachusetts (1974), and coauthor of *Community-Based Alternatives to Juvenile Incarceration* (1976), *Juvenile Diversion* (1976), and *Prison Population and Policy Choices* (1977).

David L. Weimer is an assistant professor of political science and public policy analysis at the University of Rochester. He is the author of *Improving Prosecution?* (1980) and a number of articles dealing with prosecution and corrections. His other research interests include the politics of regulation and natural-resource policy. He is currently on leave with the Office of Oil Policy, U.S. Department of Energy.

Donald Yanich is a research associate at the College of Urban Affairs and Public Policy, University of Delaware. His research and teaching interests include criminal-justice policy and social-welfare policy. He is coauthor of the study, "Correctional Standards for Delaware: A Cost Analysis of Present Operations and Policies of the State's Correctional System," cited in the Third District Court order requiring Delaware to reduce overcrowding in its prison system.

About the Editor

Jameson W. Doig is professor of politics and public affairs at Princeton University, where he is director of the Research Program in Criminal Justice, Woodrow Wilson School. He is currently a member of the New Jersey Supreme Court's Probation Planning Committee and consultant to The Daniel and Florence Guggenheim Foundation on criminal-justice projects. He has served as vice-chair of the New Jersey Advisory Council on Corrections and as chair of the American Society for Public Administration's criminal-justice section. His writings include chapters in two earlier Lexington Books, *Crime and Criminal Justice* (1975) and *Determinants of Law-Enforcement Policies* (1979), and he is co-author of *New York: The Politics of Urban Regional Development* (1982).